Mindele's Journey

Memoir of a Hidden Child of the Holocaust

MARIETTE BERMOWITZ
EDITED BY NANCY WAIT

Some of the names have been changed to protect
the privacy of the individuals involved.

Copyright © 2012 Mariette Bermowitz
All rights reserved.

ISBN: 1468001051
ISBN-13: 9781468001051

I dedicate this memoir
to my father, Abe Birencwajg,
and my mother, Zysla Cyngler.
To my sisters Esther, Rebecca and Frieda,
and my brother Zelik.
May their voices be heard throughout time.

And to "les Tantes,"
Marie, Marthe and Marie-Thérèse Leloup,
and Sister Cécilia, whose courage, love and devotion
have sustained me.

Ô ma mémoire
Mon beau navire
Ô ma mémoire
Avons-nous
Assez navigué ?

Guillaume Apollinaire

O memory,
My beautiful ship
O memory
Haven't we
Sailed long enough?

Germany 2005

Annaliesa stands like a lioness, tall and forbidding as she surveys the guests who have come to celebrate her eightieth birthday. She must have been a beauty at one time and age has chiseled her bones and defined her features in such a way that she could still be called a handsome woman. Only her hands, clasped against her sapphire-colored Indian sari, betray the years of infinite use. She is a doctor; her accomplishments featured in the honorary pamphlets prepared for the occasion by her son, the caterer. They record her current mission, helping the children of Turkish immigrants. Ah, she appears to have noticed us. In a sweep of blue silk, she makes her way through the crowd to greet us. Her height is such that I find myself stretching to meet the intensity of her steel gray eyes.

On m'a dit que vous parlez français, she says, uncurling a hand toward me. I am surprised to hear her addressing me in my native language and flattered by her attention. I think she is pleased her cousin Wilhelm has brought me. They are meeting now for the first time since he left Germany some thirty years ago. Wilhelm thought this gathering of the clan was a good time for me to meet the family he was reuniting with after so many years.

"And you, my dear cousin," she continues in English to Wilhelm. "What has become of you since you left Germany? Such a handsome young man you were. Of course you still are, in a graying sort of way."

Wilhelm arches his brow and I smile, knowing how he frets that his hair seems to be thinning so quickly. As she speaks, I notice the imperfection of her teeth, the overbite that suddenly tames her overwhelming presence. She continues in German without pausing for his reply. Then, noticing another group eager for her attention, she gathers her scarf around her robust shoulders, waves her fingers in the air like a wand, and takes off saying, "I will see you tomorrow in my house, when the party continues."

The party will continue. It is a chilling thought. Out of nowhere my ghosts appear. My father and mother, baby Frieda, my half-sisters Esther and Rebecca, and my half-brother Zelik. I feel them with me in this room, looking down at the Germans drinking champagne. They are looking at the satin curtains, the tables brimming with elaborate platters of venison, cured ham, and *pâté en croute*. They are looking at the vegetables soaking in every sauce imaginable and cheeses in every size and shape. Now the ghosts are looking at me. The wandering shadows leave me spellbound. What am I doing in Germany where everything I hear and see evokes a memory?

Poppa's ghost stares at me from behind a platter of smoked ham. He looks emaciated from the years of starvation during the war. He never regained his appetite, eating only chicken soup and sometimes chicken wings. What must Poppa think of me with a German lover? I remember his reaction to my Italian Catholic

Mindele's Journey

boyfriend when I was twenty, saying in Yiddish, *Ich chub faloirin alleh meine kindeh un az dee vest eem faheireten vil ich zitzen shiva far dir oychet.* I have lost them all. And if you marry this man, I will sit Shiva for you too.

Wilhelm squeezes my hand, asks if everything is all right. "Oh, yes," I say, holding his hand tighter. The elegant French doors are thrown open and the procession of family and friends weaves into the dining room where thirty or more tables are set to dazzle the eye. Centerpieces of exotic bouquets, sparkling crystal glasses, and gold-rimmed plates framed with exquisitely detailed silverware. The seating card with our names is lavishly printed in calligraphy. The man on my right introduces himself as Kurt, the son of Wilhelm's Uncle Stephan, and holds out two fingers for me to shake. Then he abruptly gets up, saying he needs to talk to his wife at the next table. I turn around to find Wilhelm, but see him engaged with a group on the other side of the room.

I silently watch the guests. I can't help noticing how simply the older women are dressed, and yet how elegant they look. I pick up the menu with a sigh. The dishes are so complex and numerous, I can't help thinking they must have been adapted from those ancient feasts linked to festivals that were meant to endure. Three appetizers, two main courses—one fish, one meat—followed by sorbet to clear the palate. Then a *Suprême de Pintade en croute de Noisettes au Jus bleu d'Auvergne avec sa déclinaison de légumes.* This would be an almond crusted hen in blue cheese sauce accompanied by assorted vegetables, but I like the sound of it better in French. Then the desserts addressed in the menu as *Farandole de Desserts. Farandole* means dance, an endless array of desserts on the buffet

3

table where the guests are mesmerized by the panoply of sweets set out on the starched linen cloth.

This sublime feast is only the beginning. After the meal we are treated to a slide-show tribute prepared by Annaliesa's other son, a doctor like herself. She is sitting at the front of the room. Her grandchildren pull on the panels of her sparkling gown as they vie for attention. Several of her friends have prepared speeches. I try in vain to understand their German. But even though I can barely make out what they are saying, I'm impressed by the emphatic punctuation as they recall the long and prolific life of Annaliesa. Then the music begins—songs and melodies chosen to correlate with the different periods of her life as she appears in the slide show. First the soft sweet chords for the baby Annaliesa lying naked on a bearskin rug. Everyone laughs. More pictures follow with family, and it all seems so innocent until the next slide clicks into place. Here we see a fourteen-year-old Annaliesa smiling and flirting with the camera as if it were a suitor. The music changes to a march and Annaliesa stands proudly in her *Bundes Deutche Madchen* uniform, the Nazi Youth group, a swastika fastened to her left arm. I can't believe my eyes. My stomach is churning. I want to escape somewhere, anywhere, but I am frozen in my seat. I close my eyes and my mind is suddenly flooded with pictures—this time from my own past.

∽

I am four years old, huddling against my father. We have been hiding for days, waiting for the rumbling down the street to stop. My stomach hurts. I need to go to the bathroom. I start to cry. A woman tells me to stop crying or she will give me to *them*. I don't know what she means, but Poppa does. He shakes his head and tells me this will not happen. Then he picks me up and carries me in his arms to the outhouse out back. He stumbles in the dark as I continue sobbing. Through the gate I hear the stomping of soldiers marching up the street. Then I see boots lift in unison, arms swinging from left to right. I see the symbol that is now on Annaliesa's arm. It is black and white with lots of red.

The lights come on. The guests retreat to the *farandole de desserts*. I say to Wilhelm, "The show is over, let's go back to the hotel." Annaliesa's daughter-in-law regrets that we cannot stay longer, and reminds us to come to the house tomorrow for more festivities.

We walk out into the gentle glow of streetlamps and a fountain gurgling in the square. The night air feels good on my face. I put out my hand and Wilhelm takes my arm. We make our way slowly through the darkened streets back to the hotel.

That night we make love but it isn't the same. As our bodies separate I feel something in me has died. I watch him drift off to sleep, his hand resting on the feather quilt. Moonlight casts a faint glow against the ceiling. Movie scenes flash through my mind. *Hiroshima, Mon Amour*, where members of the Resistance shave a French woman's head, and a Japanese man whispers about the atom bomb as he lies with his lover. Then I see Charlotte Rampling lowering her eyelids in *The Night Porter*. Now I see my father in the corner, rocking and chanting Kaddish, the prayer for the dead.

Morning comes. We have promised to go to Annaliesa's house, an impressive mansion framed by towering trees. Springtime leaves gently fan the Art Nouveau entrance. I feel anxious. The house, the stones, the ground have all witnessed history. The commanding Annaliesa greets her guests in a loose-fitting sarong glistening with gold lamé. Wilhelm is swept away in the crowd. I find myself alone, surrounded by strangers. The need to escape to somewhere safe overwhelms me, and I flee to the kitchen. Here I can hide in the warmth of a corner that looks familiar. A wooden table and chairs seem to extend a welcome by the curve of their backs. I sit and admire the immense stove where I can imagine Annaliesa's son, the caterer, preparing platters of delicacies. Then I notice the memorabilia hanging on the maize-colored walls. Wooden showcases filled with little spoons lined up like sentinels. Hundreds of thimbles glued to frames. Shelves of regional pottery, picture postcards neatly pasted behind glass remind me of my own travels abroad. I feel warm and safe with the familiar smells and objects in this kitchen. Some of the other guests pass in and out on their way to somewhere else, and don't appear to notice me. No one seems to wonder why I am sitting alone.

Wilhelm suddenly appears in the doorway, an anguished look on his face. He lifts me off the chair saying, "I thought I'd never find you!"

Mindele's Journey

"I was hoping you would come back sooner. Where have you been the last hour?"

He hesitates before answering. "Annaliesa's son, the one who made the slide show, wanted to show me his office."

"Was it interesting?"

"I'll tell you later," he says, grabbing my hand and leading me to the door.

We are silent during the drive back to the hotel. I stare out the window at the city streets so clean and orderly. It's hard to believe that this was once a war zone. It's a relief to be in the car, out of Annaliesa's house. I try to imagine the conversation with his cousin. I want to know what they talked about, yet I am afraid to know. Finally I can't bear it any longer. "So, what did you and your cousin talk about for such a long time?"

"His collection of Nazi memorabilia," Wilhelm says, staring straight ahead at the road.

"He's a Nazi? What did you say to him?"

"I mostly listened. And it's not what I said to him, it's more what he said to me. That Hitler gave hope to the German people. They felt betrayed by the Treaty of Versailles, that's why so many of them joined the Rhineland Party. He promised them a glorious destiny."

I don't know how to respond. As if reading my thoughts, he says, "Well, there wasn't much I could say. After all, we were guests in his house."

Why couldn't he explain to his cousin the cost of that glorious destiny? Mention the millions murdered because of this *leader*? Why couldn't he have mentioned me? My loved ones who had been slaughtered for the glorification of the Fatherland? But I am silent, the words shattering somewhere inside my head.

My thoughts feel all tangled. I recall a phrase I heard throughout my childhood. An innocent phrase that has stuck in my head like a wicked mantra. *Comme il faut.* As you should. *Assieds-toi, comme il faut. Tiens-toi, comme il faut. Réponds, comme il faut.* Sit, as you should. Stand, as you should. Answer, as you should. It was the same as "children should be seen and not heard," but far worse. An insidious molding of a child's mind into behavior that met with adult acceptance, aligning a society into rote thinking. A society that would perform *comme il faut.* A world that could be led into mindless and cruel acts because it had been decided *comme il faut.* "We were guests in his house," was just so *comme il faut.*

I burst out, "I can't accept this. I will write Annaliesa and tell her how disturbing it was to see her in a Nazi uniform. It wasn't so much that she had been a *Deutsche Bundes Madchen,* but why did they have to show it at the party?"

"Yes, we'll write a letter," he says, pulling me closer to him in the car.

I tell him about *comme il faut.*

"Yes, we have that in German as well. We say *Wie es sich gehört.* How it is expected. Yes, The Germans did as they were told, trained from childhood on."

My eyes fill with tears. Wilhelm's perception of the war is so different from mine.

We continue our trip north to Berlin, stopping in his hometown. He points out the places he knew as a child. The house where his parents lived after the war is still there, surrounded by the garden where his mother tended her flowers. I think I would have liked her. In the photograph he showed me she had a forlorn look, despite her fashionable dress. I study the road map, finding it a challenge to connect the lines of our route in a country I have been reluctant to visit. But it is spring. The countryside is splashed with colors glistening in the rain. Musty earth smells seep through the car window as the ever-changing landscape disappears into the distance. Then, unaccountably, I make an absent-minded miscalculation that takes us on a road going east toward Poland. Neither of us is aware of the mistake until we arrive at the crossroad between Germany and Poland. A Polish sign points to *Oswiecim*, better known as Auschwitz.

Wilhelm says, "We're so close, why don't we go visit the museum?"

I am horrified at the thought. Auschwitz was the end of the road for my family. They traveled in cattle cars. Their bodies hurled into each other as the trains sped toward the slaughterhouses of the Third Reich. But I will not cross the border. I will not visit *Oswiecim*. For me, there is no need to visit a museum of horrors. No need to roam through the decayed prisons of a nation's guilt.

Spring in Berlin, the air fragrant with renewal, is like any northern city waking out of its winter dreariness. As in so many European cities, young people sit in cafes and smoke with their friends. They fill the shops and the bookstores near our hotel not far from the fabled *Unter Den Linden Boulevard*. Then, first in a kiosk, then in bookstores, postcards of the Second World War seem to appear out of nowhere. How did they become tourist mementos? Berlin devastated, a heap of smoldering rubble. Soviet soldiers brandishing flags, moving steadily forward in massive chains of tanks, crushing everything beneath them. Then, as if to ease the collective memory, the postcards are interspersed with pictures of the blond goddess who left Hitler's Germany, Marlene Dietrich. It is April 2005. Berlin is commemorating the sixtieth anniversary of the Soviet invasion, that final, unimaginably brutal battle of 1945.

We have no need to talk as we stroll down Unter Den Linden Boulevard. The stones and buildings speak a language of their own. At the Brandenburg Gate a triumphant leader perches under the statue of a chariot drawn by the winged goddess of victory. As I look up, I can almost hear the echo of shouting crowds. We come to the northern wing of the gate, the *Raum der Stille*, Room of Silence. The place where one can sit and contemplate peace. And farther to the left, a gargantuan stone cemetery dedicated to victims of the Holocaust. Here, under an implacable sky, one can meander into a maze of concrete slabs and reflect upon man's inhumanity to man. Farther down the boulevard an enlarged version of the Käthe Kollwitz sculpture, "Mother and Her Dead Son," slumbers under a cold cement cupola in the *Neue Wache*, formerly a Prussian guardhouse. It is now a memorial to the "victims of war and tyranny." I think of my mother

Mindele's Journey

at the camp. Was she pushed to the ground even as she held baby Frieda in her arms?

✵ ✵ ✵

That night at the hotel Wilhelm feels a headache coming on and goes to bed early. "It feels so good under this quilt," he says, closing his eyes. "It's just like the one my mother had on my bed when I was a child."

My mother had a quilt too. It was part of the trousseau she brought from Poland. It is the only thing I have that once was hers. A quilt made from random cloth connecting all the members of the family. Home, warmth, love, tradition, all magically stitched together. This sacred gift from the past is a reminder that my family once lived and laughed and loved in homes they cherished in Poland, France and Belgium. In 1942 and 1943 they were eradicated from the face of the earth. But my randomly stitched quilt survived Hitler's order and logic. It survived. Scraps of material bonded through time, resisting destruction, just like my memories.

Lodz, Poland 1938

My mother, Zysla, which means sweetness in Yiddish, was a mail-order bride. At thirty-five she was still single. Life was not easy in Lodz. Zysla Cyngler earned her living as a cook for a Polish family. So when her cousin Yankel who lived in Belgium wrote to her about the widower in Brussels with three children, she did not hesitate. This was her chance.

She placed her trousseau of hand-embroidered sheets and pillowcases in her feather quilt that she rolled up and tied with cords. The practice was as ancient as the nomadic travelers who placed their meager possessions inside the bedding and quilts they took on long journeys. It was a fine quilt, sewn for the occasion by the female members of her family. It was customary then for the family of the bride to sew a quilt as part of her dowry. They sat in a circle, symbolizing the continuity of life and hope, and sorted scraps of material retrieved from the old sewing basket. Nothing was ever thrown out. The scraps came from the hem of a dress, or the sleeve of an old blouse, the remnant of a babushka, or maybe a tired old nightgown. They sorted and stitched, the rhythm of needles ticking against so many thimbles. The women's skilled hands danced among the patches. And as they designed and combined the random pieces into so many patterns of beauty, it was like they were picking flowers for one final bouquet, holding a piece of everyone in the family. They laughed and told stories, recollecting how Yossele's trousers acquired a patch in that unmentionable place, and how many times Gittel burned her apron, or how many babushkas Rifcha had lost.

On a cold dreary day in February 1938, Zysla said good-bye to her beloved family and her homeland. She traveled alone on the train, huddled against her quilt bundled with hand-embroidered cotton sheets and pillows, napkins, and tablecloths that she had lovingly decorated with flowers and her initials. Turning away

Mindele's Journey

from the winter landscape speeding by, she took out the photograph of her husband-to-be and his children. The girls, Esther and Rebecca, at fifteen and fourteen, were beautiful. Zelik was younger, and looked frail and sad. They seemed old enough to take care of themselves. It was a reassuring thought. She looked more deeply into the picture to study the features of her Abraham. He was forty-two and kind looking.

His wife had been killed crossing the street. A driver had lost control of his car, slamming into her before she was able to reach the sidewalk. After the period of mourning was over, his friend Yankel, a tailor in Liège, Belgium, convinced him to meet his cousin Zysla. Yankel thought they would make a good match. Of course it was up to the rabbi to decide but Yankel would write a letter of introduction. A *shiddach* was arranged. Letters and photographs passed back and forth. Within a year it was all settled. Zysla Cyngler would be his wife. He was a tailor, and quite a gifted one, according to the letters Yankel sent to the rabbi. Yankel also said he was eagerly awaiting his new bride. There were rumblings of war and life was getting more difficult every day, but he assured her she would lack for nothing.

I wonder what Mamma's thoughts were as she left everything behind to go to a country that must have seemed as distant as the moon. How did she imagine this man she had never met who was to become her husband? Did she worry that her new husband might not find her attractive? Or that Yankel had not told the rabbi everything there was to know? Were there secret fears in her heart as she held on to the quilt with songs and loving words sewn into the seams?

Mariette Bermowitz

Still, I imagine my mother humming as she traveled those long hours on the train, songs the women sang when they sat together in the evening to sew her wedding quilt. They might have joked and chided her about her wedding night. I can almost see the blush I imagine might have transformed her alabaster pallor into the color of rosebuds.

I wondered if she saw soldiers on that train ride from Poland through Germany. Armies with their hypnotic display of grandiose pageantry. Did she hear crowds thundering their allegiance to the man claiming his right to be the leader of a master race? Or did Zysla, sweet Zysla, have other thoughts? She must have wondered if she would ever see her brothers and sisters and cousins again. No doubt she was comforted that her cousin Yankel from Liège would be meeting her train. Liège was not far from Brussels, after all. Yankel knew Abraham and spoke highly of him. That must have been a comfort too. Did she play a tune in her head about her future children? *Oy Zyssele, oy Zyssele heer kimt Moishele.* As she wove her dreams, smiling at an imaginary little Moishele on her knees, she could not possibly have imagined the tragedy that was lurking in the shadows.

My father told me later how much she hoped for a child, especially a boy. Sweet Zysla dreaming about a baby as she sat listening to the rhythm of the train rocking against the rails did have one, but it was a girl. I was born in December, nine months after their wedding in March, 1938.

Liège, Belgium 1920s

Yankel Cyngler married Wilhemina in 1920 when he arrived in Belgium. He left Poland and its pogroms in hope of finding a new life in a country where some of his childhood friends had found work. He quickly understood that survival depended on adapting to the customs of his new country and learning the language. Mina, as Wilhemina preferred to be called, was tall, blond, and Dutch, and was adamant that he convert to Catholicism and raise their children as Catholics. Yankel, young and impressionable, was smitten by the blond goddess and did not need much prompting. He was eager to leave his past behind. Hadn't he run away from a place where he no longer felt safe? Wasn't it much easier not to be a Jew in the world he lived in? After all, he was not that convinced of the existence of a superior being or the teachings and laws attributed to Him.

So Yankel Cyngler became Jacques Cyngler, and learned to speak French. His only resistance to Mina was his refusal to accompany her to church on Sundays. They had three sons. Joseph was named after Yankel's father, which Mina accepted because Joseph was also a French name. Then Jean and Max were born. Yankel/Jacques did not tell his children about their heritage. Occasionally he felt guilty.

Mina forbade him to speak Yiddish at home, so he no longer spoke Yiddish except with his Jewish friends, Abraham in particular. At home he spoke French and German. Mina preferred German because it connected her to her childhood home near the German border.

Jean, the second son, often asked his father to tell him stories about Poland. He was curious about his father's accent and the country he came from. Yankel/Jacques felt a rekindling of his roots as he spoke about the joy and sadness of life in Poland, yet it made him anxious to think about his parents and the family he had left behind. He preferred not to think about it too much until his cousin Zysla came to live in Belgium.

At the time Zysla arrived in 1938, Jacques was the proud owner of an upscale clothing shop in Liège. He looked forward to seeing his newly married cousin and her husband Abraham when they came on their monthly visit, reconnecting him to the world he thought he had given up. He knew Mina did not approve of the intimacy he was developing with his Jewish cousin. Tensions were building up all over. There were reports from Germany of hoodlums destroying Jewish property, and indiscriminate attacks on Jews. It was more alarming by the day.

Brussels 1938

I was born on the Rue Haute in the Hôpital St.Pierre during an unusually frigid December. I don't know the details of my birth, but Poppa once

Mindele's Journey

told me in a very rare and special talk on the subject, why I had a slight bump on both sides of my face. "You didn't want to come out so the doctor took these tools and pulled you out. Always stubborn you were."

My birth certificate seems to have been a very complicated affair. My father wanted to call me Mindele, a Yiddish name, but according to Belgian law only Christian names were legal, so I became Mariette. Yet Poppa hardly ever called me Mariette, reserving it for a warning whenever I did anything that displeased him. Instead of raising his voice, he would roll the "r" in Mariette, a guttural warning that needed no repetition. Zysla loved her newfound family, especially Esther, who at eighteen was more a sister than a daughter. Esther not only helped with the chores and the new baby, she introduced her to the city. On their excursions through the old neighborhoods of Brussels, Esther pointed out the historical landmarks she loved. She took Mamma around to the shopkeepers, the laundry at the end of the street, and the parks the family enjoyed on the weekend. Zysla and Esther often lingered in the flea market off the Rue Haute, a glittering paradise of trinkets and cheap glamour where they bought inexpensive jewelry, vintage clothing, and whatever else caught their fancy.

Zysla was thrilled with her new baby daughter, and was excited to visit Yankel to show him what she considered her "blessed gift from the Almighty." She refused to call Yankel Jacques. She always asked Esther to accompany her, as she was afraid of traveling alone.

17

Mariette Bermowitz

Brussels 1942

Poppa sat silently before his sewing machine in the tailoring workshop he set up in the attic above the apartment where our family lived on the sixth floor, 33 Rue du Lavoir. Esther was engaged to Jean, a dark Valentino look-alike who brought me chocolates and made me laugh when I sat on his lap. Esther was studying voice at the conservatory and planned to be an opera singer. My other sister Rebecca worked in a clothing shop not far from the house on the Rue Haute where Poppa delivered the custom-made suits endlessly created on his sewing machine. My brother Zelik helped him when he came home from school.

My sister Frieda was born when I was three. Mamma was in poor health afterward, so Esther took care of me. Frieda cried a lot. Even when Mamma recovered, she didn't have time to pick me up anymore, as she was so busy with the cooking and washing. But sometimes she left Frieda home with Poppa and took me out with her alone. I was so happy holding her hand tightly as I skipped along the cobblestones. When we got to the *lavoir* where she brought the laundry, I entered a magical land of scents and the sound of women's laughter echoing against the damp tiled walls. Jars and buckets and bottles were strewn everywhere. I watched Mamma by the steaming kettles, her head enveloped by clouds of humidity. Then the noise and clatter shifted to a lullaby as I was rocked asleep in the stroller. On the way home we stopped at the corner *épicerie* to buy groceries from Monsieur Greenberg. He loved to talk to her in Polish because he came from a shtetl not

18

Mindele's Journey

far from Mamma's in Poland. They always seemed to have a lot of things to discuss. When I began to cry, Monsieur Greenberg stroked my hair with his enormous hand that smelled like the pickles marinating in the huge barrel outside the store. He let me hold the jar as he selected the ripest one he could find because he knew that it made me feel important. Ever since then I have loved pickles.

Mamma climbed the six flights of stairs to the apartment loaded down with laundry, groceries, and the extra jar of pickles, a present from Monsieur Greenberg. I cried when I saw my little sister Frieda, knowing my idyll with Mamma had come to an end. Then my beautiful sister Esther came in and lifted me from my mother's arms. I buried my head in Esther's scarf, sniffing the sweet combination of violets and roses, her favorite fragrance. As she held my cheek gently against hers, I felt I was part of her. On Friday night just before sunset Mamma placed the candles on the table in preparation for the Sabbath. Despite the scarcity of food and supplies she always seemed to create a feast. Esther helped with the table setting. When Jean, Esther's fiancé, was invited, there were seven places set for dinner. Esther had met Jean, Yankel's son, on one of her excursions to Liège, and they had fallen in love. When Esther was accepted at the Brussels Conservatory of Music, Jean found a job in Brussels just to be near her. Now every Friday she rushed home from the conservatory to change into a dress and a pair of high heels to match her outfit. Then she slid amber combs into her long curly black hair, and dabbed perfume behind her ears. I didn't understand why Esther blushed every time

Jean whispered in her ear, or why they laughed so much. Then Jean gave me the box of chocolates he was hiding behind his back, as he knew I would carry it off, leaving him to be alone with his sweetheart.

On Sundays when the weather was fine, Jean and Esther took me to the *Parc Des Buttes Chaumont*, one of the many quaint little parks in Brussels. Rebecca and Zelik sometimes came too, and took pictures of the young couple holding hands. Jean looked dashing in a double-breasted suit. Esther smiled and tilted her head toward the fountain. They planned to marry and start a family as soon as Esther graduated from the conservatory. In the meantime I was their practice baby. Jean took my picture in a pale blue coat with a matching bonnet as I stood before an equestrian statue. The photograph survived the war and became one of the few items retrieved from our apartment by a kind neighbor. Belgium was an occupied country then, but it was impossible to tell by looking at the faces in the pictures. Rebecca with her fox fur collar smiled as the sun glinted off the combs in her hair. We were all smiling into the camera. A moment frozen in time. A testament to the existence of my family. There are no pictures of Frieda. Frieda remains a name without a face. A face I have invented when I've looked at my own in the mirror, wondering if we would have looked alike.

The turmoil of the Nazi occupation must have caused tremendous anguish for my mother, a stranger in a strange land who did not speak the language. At home she sang gentle Polish lullabies to rock me to sleep. *Ah, ah, kotki dva..charebure obidva.*

I can still hear my mother's crystalline voice as she held me tenderly in her arms, the odor of milk mixing with her perfume. I remember how tightly she held me as she stood at the window. We looked at the rain splattering the rooftops, striking ominous sounds against the windowpane. I looked up at the immense gray sheet hanging over the city and said, "Mamma, what's above the sky?"

"More sky," she said.

"But Mamma, where is the end?"

"There is no end," she whispered, holding me against her breast.

It was November. In a few weeks, I would be four years old. It was very still in the house. Frieda seemed to be crying more than usual, and when Mamma held me in her arms, she cried too. I didn't know why Poppa and Mamma spoke in such hushed voices. I wondered where Esther and Rebecca had gone. I never saw Zelik anymore either. They always used to come home from school or work, and then we would eat dinner together. I was beginning to feel hungry up in the attic with Poppa. He was finishing up some work to bring to the store on the Rue Haute before the Sabbath. The sky above the Rue du Lavoir was bloated with snow. There was no heat in the apartment and we wore heavy sweaters. At night we all slept together in the big bed under the quilt Mamma brought from Poland. It kept us warm even though my breath turned into a fine haze if I stuck my head above the edges.

I was with Poppa in the attic so that Mamma could do her work downstairs in the kitchen where Frieda was sleeping. The roof was slanted, and sometimes I climbed up the ladder to the skylight to look out over the rooftops and the church spire. The world out there looked vast and infinite. It was so much warmer in the attic with the heat rising up from the other apartments below. As I sat and played with the scraps of material Poppa gave me, I heard little Frieda crying and Mamma trying to quiet her.

Suddenly I heard loud voices coming up the stairs. There were shouts, and people running. Poppa hurried to remove the ladder that led down to our apartment. He pulled it up and closed the trap door, locking it. Locking us out from the world below. He took the ladder to the skylight and opened the window. Cold and snow came rushing in. Poppa held me tightly and pulled me up to the roof. Then he removed the ladder and closed the skylight behind him. We stood alone on the rooftop looking out at the city. Brussels was covered in a veil of white. Poppa grabbed my hand and whispered, "Hold on very tight because we are going to run!" As we took off he muttered under his breath, *Juden Raus*. Out with the Jews.

Not until years later did I understand the meaning of "Out with the Jews." But it would take a lifetime to fully comprehend the agony of my father's decision that day to close the trap door. A decision that destroyed everything he had lived for and loved, except for the one child he dragged with him into the future.

We made it to the end of the street where the trains disappeared under an overpass before head-

Mindele's Journey

ing into the Gare du Midi. We had often been to the station, boarding a train to Liège to visit Mamma's cousin Yankel. A train was now pulling in and we managed somehow to climb into a car at the end as the train slowly pulled away, leaving Brussels behind. Mamma, Frieda, Esther, Jean, Rebecca, Zelik. I would never see them again.

Liège, Winter 1942

As night closed in the temperature dropped. Streetlights cast quivering halos on snow-covered sidewalks. Poppa shivered and quickened his pace, squeezing my hand so as not to lose me in the crowd. He draped his sweater around me and it hung down like a cape, the arms tied around my neck to keep me from losing it. We ran down side streets where it was darker and less crowded. Poppa coughed and stopped to catch his breath. We finally reached the front steps of cousin Yankel's house. Poppa looked around furtively and rang the doorbell, stooping as if he could make himself disappear. No one answered so he rang again, and this time a voice called out from behind the door, "Who is it?"

Mina opened the door. She looked angry but she let us in. Poppa pushed me in front of him and we followed Mina up the stairs to the top floor. The room was packed with people. They were all staring at us. Suddenly a baby started screaming. It was Mina's granddaughter Andrée. Her mother, Sarah, was rocking her cradle. "I knew this would happen!" Mina shouted angrily.

Sarah's ten-year-old twin sisters were there too, and her younger brother Jean who was retarded. Mina had never wanted her son to marry a Jewish girl, much less one who had a retarded brother. But with her long blond hair, blue eyes, and dainty features, Sarah looked more Christian than Jewish. Her good looks had undoubtedly so bewitched her son that he was prepared to hide the whole family of his in-laws in the attic of her house. And now Yankel/Jacques' family was showing up. What a fool she'd been to marry a Jew, even if he allowed their children to be raised as Christians. It was only bringing them bad luck.

One night when we were hiding in Mina's house, I was hungry but dared not ask for seconds, as there wasn't enough for everyone. Poppa consoled me by giving me some of his food. But I was still hungry, and my stomach was growling so much I couldn't sleep. So later, when everyone else was asleep, I slipped out the door and went downstairs. There was a light in the kitchen. Mina sat at the table with her head in her hands and looked startled when she saw me. I pointed to the food beside her on the table and asked if I could have some. "No," she said. But I kept begging for something to eat, and maybe I was crying, because suddenly she grabbed me by the collar and pushed me out the front door onto the icy cobblestones and slammed the door.

I huddled in the doorway sobbing. It was raining. I was afraid of the dark. I was afraid of the sound of boots striking the cobblestoned streets. When the soldiers appeared, they carried a red flag with a white circle in the middle, and a black cross with all

Mindele's Journey

of its ends bent. The soldiers had the same emblem on their arms, and the emblem moved every time they raised their arms. I was so scared, I began to see strange things. I saw the red in the flag turn into blood dripping onto the white snow. The crosses on their arms seemed to fly into the air, twisted and splattered with blood. I thought they were coming for me. At that moment, all faded into darkness. What happened in the following days saved my life.

Banneux 1942 - 1943

I woke to the sound of chanting voices. It was so dark I couldn't see a thing. I reached out and touched the edge of the metal bed with one hand and a cold wall with the other. Then I began to shriek in despair. The door opened, letting in a beam of flickering light, and shadows began floating into the room. There was music too, and strange sounds, *Kyrie Eleison, Christe Eleison, Kyrie Eleison*. Faces surrounded my bed, disembodied faces framed in white cardboard boxes with long black veils. It was as if moons were fluttering around me. When the light came on I realized the ghostly creatures were really women dressed in black, wearing what appeared to be white helmets around their heads. The moon ladies were chattering excitedly in a language I didn't understand, but their voices were like music. Their robes had a strange sweet smell. When the one nearest to me opened her arms and smiled, I stopped crying.

I had been placed in the convent of Mater Dei in Banneux Notre Dame. Years later I learned that it

Mariette Bermowitz

was Sarah who brought me to the convent. She had taken her twin sisters to another convent nearby.

"Soeur Cécilia, Soeur Cécilia," whispered the nun as she took me in her arms. Sister Cécilia, the Mother Superior, exclaimed, *Mais c'est un cadeau de la Vierge cette petite. Nous allons bien nous en occuper.* They thought I was a gift from the Blessed Mother. In 1938, the year I was born, a miraculous event took place on the outskirts of Banneux, a rural village near Liège. The Virgin Mary had appeared to a young girl named Mariette, and ever since, throngs of tourists had visited the little chapel among the fragrant pine trees, built to commemorate the apparition. Sister Cécilia seemed to know that I was born around that time and also that the name on my birth certificate was Mariette, a fortuitous combination.

One after another, the nuns swept me into their billowing arms and whispered their names in my ear. Clotilde, Reine-Marie, Chantale, Lucie, Marguerite. I was now Mariette. At home everyone called me Mindele, but from now on my name would be Mariette de Jésus, a name Sister Cécilia chose for me. She dared not explain my origin to the other children who attended the convent school. I quickly adapted to this new-sounding name. All the sounds around me were new and strange.

Sister Cécilia seemed very uneasy that I couldn't speak French. She was not at all familiar with the Yiddish I answered her with. She tried her limited Flemish on me, but that didn't seem to get a response either. When she realized I was speaking to her in Yiddish, she became even more concerned and said, *Il faut lui apprendre le français, à cette petite, aussitôt que*

Mindele's Journey

possible. "We have to teach French to this little one, as soon as possible."

The convent of Banneux Notre Dame was also a private Catholic boarding school for grades one through six. Though I was not yet old enough for the first grade, Sister Cécilia introduced me to a few of the older students she assigned to be my special mentors. They were told that I was an orphan and would be staying in the convent until a family was found to adopt me. To them I was just another casualty of the time. She did not tell them how I arrived one afternoon with Monsieur M., the convent's gate-keeper. Only Sister Cécilia knew how important he was in the Underground, whose headquarters were in the basement of his house. He was in direct contact with l'Abbé Jamin, the priest determined to save as many Jewish children as possible from discovery and deportation. Some were placed in convents or with families, while others were transported north where they could be sent to safety in England.

The nuns quickly put an end to all the whisperings in the dormitories that I was found wandering the streets, and in the next few months I found many new playmates. No doubt following their budding maternal instincts, the girls took turns playing with me in the large courtyard behind the classrooms. One in particular, Julie, was especially protective. She knew how concerned Sister Cécilia was, always inquiring as to my whereabouts, often spiriting me away from the group without reason. Julie was told to bring me immediately into the main parlor if soldiers in cars or on motorcycles were heard coming down the gravel road leading to the convent. These tactics became a game called *cache-cache*. Hide and seek.

We practiced on several occasions. Sister Cécilia led me into the nuns' bedroom. There was a very large basket near her bed and she told me to climb into it. I was not to speak or Julie would discover where I was hiding. I was told to remain there for long periods of time. But I knew that when Sister Cécilia removed the lid, there would be a delicious piece of chocolate in her hand, and Julie peeking in from the door.

I loved playing in the courtyard with the other students who taught me their favorite games and the French words associated with them. One afternoon Sister Cécilia was looking at our little group in the distance, her small frame firmly planted under the carved cement archway leading into the convent. Her steel-gray eyes swept the courtyard. Then she bounced down the steps and ran toward us. The students tried not to laugh as she waved the billowing black sleeves of her robe into the air and nearly tripped, shouting, *Ma petite Mariette, viens vite. J'ai quelque chose à te montrer.* "Quickly, my little Mariette, I have something to show you!" I beamed with pleasure to be so singled out as she hurried me off to the convent halls, leaving my playmates to wonder what could possibly be happening this time.

Sister Cécilia decided that even though I was only four, I should be placed in Sister Marguerite's first grade class. But first she had to teach me French. She had a no-nonsense look in her eyes as she said in a deep, resonant voice, *Voilà, ma petite, on commence la leçon dès maintenant.* "Well, little one, the lesson

Mindele's Journey

begins right now." I felt safe in her presence, holding her hand as we walked down the long convent corridors. As she pointed to various things she wanted me to notice, I thought how she smelled like incense in the chapel. Her skin was as white as the alabaster statues, though when I touched her hand the skin felt as soft as the satin ribbons she tied in my hair. When I couldn't walk fast enough to keep up with her, she lifted me into her arms. I loved putting my face against her cheek.

Now, every day after *le petit déjeuner*, Sister Cécilia appeared in the refectory and we set off somewhere. If the weather was warm we went to the garden. I loved going to the garden where Sister Marguerite talked to her plants and flowers as she bent down to remove intruding weeds. It was her favorite pastime, away from her duties as teacher and supervisor of the household staff. Sister Marguerite had the same name as the flowers she nurtured, the white daisies called *marguerite*. She fussed over them, showering them delicately with her watering can, patting their moistened leaves and whispering prayers as she cut them to create the breathtaking bouquets that graced the altar in the chapel. I watched and listened, and developed a love for words.

Learning French became so much fun. Sister Cécilia pointed to objects and sang the words as I repeated them. Her voice was like the little bells I heard in chapel. She giggled almost the same way I did when I stumbled on certain sounds. I insisted on naming everything I saw. I learned about cachepots, reserved for the flowering plants that survived cold Belgian winters. Ferns, ivy, the blooming begonias

29

and petunias in brown earthenware pots, flaming geraniums spreading their green leaves against the window, and lots of sparkling violets in every corner, their color exploding against the mournful convent walls.

Sister Cécilia made me understand all this as I skipped down the corridors looking in wonder at the strange round windows high above the doors. *Ça, c'est un oeil de boeuf, un oeil de boeuf.* "That's a bull's-eye, a bull's-eye." I thought she was being silly. Julie had shown me the enormous *boeuf* grazing in the pasture behind the schoolyard. Why was Sister calling this window *un oeil de boeuf?* But Sister said it was the name of that particular window. I learned that names were given to objects because they resembled other things, and made for interesting stories. Such as the name for the small window called a *vasistas* high above the kitchen door that swung out to let the air circulate. Sister Marguerite explained during a show-and-tell class that *vasistas* was a German word adopted during the first big war when the Germans came to France. Never having seen such a strange window, a German soldier looked up and said, *Vas ist das?*

It reminded me of the time Mamma brought home all those pickles from the grocery store, and Poppa said, Voos *is doos?* Mamma answered, *Greenberg, voo den.* "Greenberg, of course." Monsieur Greenberg, knowing how much I liked pickles, always gave Mamma an extra jar for her Mindele. I didn't tell my *voos is doos* story to Sister Marguerite.

Another time when I was in the chapel, blissfully in awe of the light coming through the stained-glass

Mindele's Journey

windows, Sister Cécilia ran her fingers against the panels of the entrance door and exclaimed, *Mais comme c'est sale!* "How dirty this is!" I kept repeating *sale, sale, oeil de boeuf, oeil de boeuf,* proud that I could finally say these complicated words with the smiling approval of Sister Cécilia. She rewarded me by taking me up the newly-installed elevator. I jumped for joy in the *ascenseur* with its fresh smells of polished wood. Mentally I was repeating *ascenseur, sale, oeil de boeuf* so many times that when Sister asked me to repeat what I was learning I shouted, *sale soeur!* She paused for a moment at my answer, seemingly in shock, then burst into laughter. Seeing that I pleased the Sister so much, I kept repeating *sale soeur, sale soeur.* Prompted by Sister Cécilia, I said it to each nun we met in the hallway. They looked at me with raised eyebrows. But holding onto Sister Cécilia's hand made me suddenly brave and I added *bonjour sale soeur!*

We finally reached the kitchen where Sister Clotilde was barely visible behind the large steaming kettles on the oak table. *Ah, tiens, voilà sale Soeur Clotilde.* "Ah, there's dirty Sister Clotilde," chuckled Sister Cécilia, and the two sisters burst into uncontrollable laughter.

I loved Sister Clotilde. Being able to pronounce her name was a reward in itself since it took me quite a few attempts. When I pronounced it just the way she did with her Flemish accent, she scooped me off the floor and swirled me around the kitchen. She stopped in front of the cupboards where she aligned all the cooking utensils and pulled out the drawer where she hid her delicacies. Then she handed me a bar of Côte d'Or chocolate. It had the most beautiful wrapping I had ever seen. I tried not to tear the picture of the gold elephant resting on the brown paper. When some of the chocolate melted and smeared my fingers, Sister exclaimed in delight, *Oh, les sales petits doigts!* She watched me lick the chocolate off my *sales petits doigts,* my dirty little fingers, then, in her Flemish accent as if she was starting a motor, she said, "OK, Mariette, don't tell anybody!" Only it came out sounding like, *D'acorrrd, Marrriette, ne dis rrrien a perrrsonne!* I glowed with pride as I leaned against her white starched headdress and gave her a kiss, leaving a dark chocolaty stain on that purest of white.

Life in the convent was filled with mysteries. I felt as if I had entered the pages of a fairy tale book. I learned to sing some of the Latin chants when Sister Lucie took me to the chapel. She held me close as she helped me repeat, *Kyrie Eleison-Christe Eleison Kyrie Eleison.* I listened carefully, knowing how important it was to learn about my new surroundings. Sister Chantal at the organ, sitting on her worn needle-point pillow, her eyes glued to the sheet music as her long white fingers danced upon the keys. Monsieur l'Abbé held a strange burning object attached to chains. When he began to swing it gently back and forth, veils of fragrant smoke made their way toward the stained-glass windows, framing the biblical scenes in clouds. But when the sun came through the stained glass, the angels glowed with color, and all the saints and apostles disappeared into the light. The windows were my picture books, read through the changing light of a bleak Belgian winter. Sister

Mindele's Journey

Lucie pointed out Jesus and Mary along with all the angels and saints, and discouraged me from asking too many questions.

One night during my bedtime story, Sister Reine-Marie said that soon I would have my own room. She assured me that it was right next to the sisters' dormitory so I shouldn't cry, but I cried anyway, a stream of terrible sobs, because I was afraid they wanted me to go away. Then the sister gave me the name of my angel, the one whom she said watched over me. I stopped crying and asked, "But why can't I see him?"

"Special things can't often be seen, but they can be felt."

I thought about that for a moment. "Well then, Poppa and Mamma are here, aren't they?"

She turned her head away from my pillow with a muffled "Yes," as she glided away to get another storybook.

Christmas was coming, and the start of my second year at Banneux. The *pensionnaires* were excited about going home for the holidays, which made me think Christmas must be very special. Sister Cécilia told me it was the celebration of the birth of a very important king. His name was Jesus, and since my name was now Mariette de Jesus, I asked the sister if we were related.

"Yes," she said. "Jesus is indeed an ancestor of yours, and you should be very proud. But it's a secret. You mustn't tell anyone." Sister Cécilia knew how to make me feel so special.

During the very cold winter of 1943 the sisters worried about the German troops moving closer. There were rumors that very soon they would be

Mariette Bermowitz

coming to the convents for food and provisions. Questions would be asked about the children and the school. Sister Cécilia paced the long marble halls holding her rosary. She recited her prayers out loud, then stopped and looked around, as if someone had tapped her shoulder. Even the chimes of the big oak clock in the entrance hall seemed to startle her. She forgot I was walking beside her. When I pulled on her long black dress to get her attention, she looked at me with a smile and said, *Ah, my petite Mariette, si tu savais, si tu savais.* "If you only knew."

The pine trees surrounding the convent looked like giant people waving green cloaks laden with snow. A fresh layer of snow sparkled in the faint afternoon sunlight. Little birds fluttered about from branch to branch, fanning snow dust into the air. Sister Lucie and I watched them from behind the large parlor windows. We were waiting for the big event that afternoon. Most of the other children were gathered near the entrance. Suddenly we heard cheers and clapping, and we ran into the hallway. An enormous pine tree was being hauled into the building. It smelled like wet earth, like the forest. It bled sap onto the marble floor. Sister Clotilde shouted, "Attention, attention!" as the tree was carried up the stairs to the refectory, there to be lifted up to its original position, tall and dignified once again.

The students had boxes full of decorations they prepared in class. I was assigned to the group placing candles in holders and clipping them onto the branches. The glittering ornaments fascinated me. There were angels hanging from silver threads, little toy animals, miniature houses speckled with glitter,

Mindele's Journey

clowns and soldiers, trumpets and drums, strands of paper lace and cottony clouds. Underneath the lowest branch was a humble shed made of twigs. Little clay figures and clay animals that were made in class surrounded a tiny creature. The sisters brought in brilliantly wrapped boxes and placed them around the tree trunk, each bearing the name of a student on labels outlined in gold.

When Sister Cécilia showed me the pink-ribboned box with my name, I hopped and skipped and danced around the tree, beside myself with joy. I was dying to open my beautifully wrapped box, but Sister Cécilia said there was another gift for me under the tree. I found it by reading my name from among all the other glistening boxes heaped under the sparkling garlands. It didn't take me long to recognize the bold M followed by the other letters of my name. The children were to take their gifts home when they left for winter recess. I was afraid I wouldn't be able to open my gifts because I didn't know where my home was anymore. Then Sister Cécilia said that I was to spend the holidays with Sister Reine-Marie and her family in a town called Theux.

Sister Clotilde, known as *bonne fourchette* (someone who appreciates good food) turned her kitchen upside down preparing the last meal before the holiday. The local farmers had generously contributed bread and eggs, chickens and flour. She had transformed these riches into an unforgettable aroma filling the halls since dawn, spilling into the chapel, teasing the mind away from prayers.

Holiday fever reached a peak when the students dressed in their starched blouses and plaid uniforms filed into the dining room. There was a somber mood as we all sat down to recite prayers, but when sumptuous platters of food were placed on the tables, everyone dissolved into laughter and giggles. Sister Clotilde, rosy cheeked and beaming, exclaimed, *On mange les enfants!* We all turned around for Sister Cécilia's approval, but she was nowhere to be seen. She had been summoned to the parlor. Monsieur M., the gatekeeper, had come to warn her that the German High Command would be visiting the convent that afternoon.

I was quickly dispatched to Theux, where Sister Reine-Marie's family lived. The wheels of the old car made cracking sounds on the new snow covering the icy roads as her brother Henri drove through the pine forests. Henri knew the pass well, but now he felt uneasy about the German occupation and the recent arrests in a neighboring village. When we finally arrived at the cozy little house on the outskirts of town, Henri let out a cry of relief. The family was waiting outside, and as he lifted me out of the car he said, *La voilà, la voilà!* "Here she is!"

Sister Reine-Marie's brother and his wife had two children. Yvette was eleven and Yvon was nine. They had been told I was an orphan, and wanting to make me feel welcome they whisked me off to the playroom. Right away, I felt like part of the family. My room was right next to theirs. It smelled like pine needles. A lovely flannel nightgown patterned with bouquets of roses and forget-me-nots had been placed on the pillow as a gift from the children. Then Sister Reine-Marie's sister-in-law gave me a gift wrapped in a box with so many layers of tissue paper

Mindele's Journey

that at first I thought the box was empty. But then I discovered *her* at the bottom, a beautiful doll resting on a tiny lace pillow. She was dressed in one of the many splendid outfits that accompanied her in a miniature suitcase, and seemed nothing less than an apparition, unlike anything I had ever seen. Her cheeks were pink, her eyes a piercing blue, her hair a sleek swirl forming an aureole around her delicate face. The daintiness of her features imbued her with a quality above anything human. I couldn't stop looking at her, and I couldn't put her down. I named her Yvette, after Sister Reine-Marie's niece, and that night I placed her under the sheets and fell asleep holding onto one of her little arms. From then on Yvette was my prize possession. Throughout the remaining years of the war, I held her so close it was like she had become an appendage to my body.

I was happy at Theux. At the end of the holiday when Sister Reine-Marie said it was time to return to Banneux, I didn't want to leave my new family. Sister promised I would come back.

Fraiture 1944

The town of Banneux was blanketed in snow that February of 1944 when the Leloup sisters came to collect me. Sister Cécilia and I were waiting in the parlor when two passers-by paused to delight at the delicate stalactites hanging from the branches of the tree down by the gate. Sister Cécilia pointed to them and said, "See those two ladies looking at the trees? They are my sisters. I think we should run outside

37

and meet them, you and I." She quickly bundled me in my coat and boots and flew down the hall, dragging me behind like a rag doll. When the janitor saw us coming he threw open the door and we dashed into the biting cold. The snow was slippery under our feet. Sister waved and shouted, "Marie, Marthe, here we are!" as her sleeve billowed like a flag in the wind.

I could barely see the faces of the two women hidden inside long winter coats and fur hats who were laughing as they came toward us. One of them said, "You haven't changed at all, Jeanne, running as if you were still a child! You are not even properly dressed for the outdoors. You'll catch your death and then we won't be able to come visit you! Oh, but it is so good to see you looking so well!" Then they noticed me, a tiny figure made even smaller surrounded by all that snow. I stared up at them with wide eyes. The one in the pretty coat stroked my cheek and said softly, *Oh, mais elle est si petite et si jolie.* We smiled at each other and they whisked me up from the snow into their arms, passing me back and forth between their long winter coats. As we rushed back to the warmth of the parlor, the three of them laughing in the same joyous way that sounded like chiming bells, I was unaware that Sister Cécilia had asked them to take me back with them to their small village. The Germans had become inquisitive and it was no longer safe for me at the convent. The lives of the nuns and the other children were at risk.

The nuns were waiting for us inside, and the aroma of freshly brewed coffee and warmed milk filled the room. An embroidered tablecloth was

Mindele's Journey

laid with Sister Clotilde's jams, a basket of rolls, the good china and the silver coffee service. After we ate, Sister Cécilia said she had something very important to tell me, and sat me down on the small divan. She looked at me with tears in her eyes and said, *Ma petite Mariette, il va falloir que tu nous quittes bientôt.* "My little Mariette, you will have to leave us soon."

Within the hour I left with Marthe and Marie. Sister Cécilia assured me that I would be coming back to Mater Dei, but I wasn't quite sure that was true since the nuns were crying as they lined up on the wide slate stairs at the entrance and waved their good-byes. The memory of their black figures topped with white bonnets remained frozen in my mind like black exclamation points.

And so we left for the Ardennes Mountains in southeastern Belgium. Marthe held my hand, Marie held my little suitcase. Thérèse, the youngest, would be at home to greet us. The Leloup women were unmarried and in their thirties. Their father had not only been the schoolmaster of the town of Fraiture, but its archivist and resident scholar, and their home was a focal point of music and culture. The eldest, Marie, had been something of a child prodigy on the piano and organ. But when they were sent to boarding school, which was the custom, they found themselves in a very confined and rigid atmosphere. They were never allowed to go alone to visit friends in other towns, or go to dances, or participate in any social activities. If they had any dreams of love and marriage, they were snuffed out by a boarding school and college run by nuns. After such deep religious training, Jeanne decided to enter a religious order and became Sister Cécilia. The other girls became elementary school teachers like their father. When he passed away not long after they completed their degrees, Marie took over her father's position in the schoolhouse, which was connected to their living quarters.

It was customary in those days for the schoolmaster to live in the house where he taught, which in this case was a large room with a black potbellied stove and a floor of wooden planks. The wooden desks had round inkwells and a hollowed space for pens that would diligently be dipped in and out of the container without spilling a drop. Yet large colored blotters near the notebooks attested to many mistrials. The classroom was divided into six grades, all taught by Marie with strict discipline, so that when one group was being taught, the other students could silently go about their own assigned tasks. Monsieur Leloup had been a master teacher, and it seemed that he had handed down his expertise to Marie, who was now headmistress of the school. Marthe had found a teaching position in a town about an hour away and now rented a room with a family near the school where she taught. Thérèse, on the other hand, opted for the domestic life that was closest to her heart, tending house and garden, and cooking the wonderful dishes that over the years made her one of the finest culinary experts in the region.

Our journey to the Ardennes was long and hazardous that winter. During the train ride there were frequent blackouts. It seemed that every time a siren went off, the lights were dimmed and we screeched to a halt. Luckily nothing happened. There wasn't

Mindele's Journey

a direct train to Fraiture, the little town nestled deep in a valley no more than a two-hour drive from Germany. Marie and Marthe took turns carrying me until we reached a house where friends waited with a car. But then it seemed the head of the household, Oscar, had just received an urgent call and could not take us by car. There was much whispering and furtive glances cast in my direction.

Marthe said, her voice soft as a feather brushing against my ear, "Don't worry, Mariette. Tante Marthe and Tante Marie will find a way home." This, and the fact she called herself tante, made me trust her. She wiped away my tears, and I fell asleep cradled in her arms.

Oscar returned later and said he would take us to Fraiture that night. Many years later I learned that he was a saboteur in the Underground. They set up roadblocks and dynamited trains and bridges to stop the Germans from advancing. Oscar was killed later that year on just such a mission.

Fraiture was buried in snow. I can still see Thérèse standing on the doorstep in the freezing cold, holding her black and white cat Lulu in her arms, anxiously awaiting her sisters' return. It was a tearful reunion. Thérèse had been worried that we were delayed because of an accident, or that we might have been delayed by soldiers, or mines, or bombs. There could have been attackers, or looters, or strangers, or simply mean-spirited people who could do harm just by the way they looked at you. Unlike her slender sisters, Thérèse was round and full in her starched apron, and smelled of freshly cut vegetables and spices. She picked me up and planted two

Mariette Bermowitz

generous kisses on my cold cheeks. As the sisters stood talking, not even taking the time to sit, so eager were they to reassure each other of their safety, I began my exploration of the living room. Soon I was lost in the labyrinth of wooden chairs and table legs, and climbed onto a sofa covered with white lace doilies. Comforted by candlelight and muffled voices, I fell asleep.

The following days were filled with so many surprises I hadn't a moment to miss Banneux or even think of what I'd left behind. To my young eyes, the old stone house looked like a castle I had seen in one of the storybooks Sister Cécilia read to me. I used to fall asleep listening to her describe where she grew up, and how she ran up and down the stone steps of the centuries-old schoolhouse as a child. I thought only a castle could have been that old. The front of the house faced a cobblestone courtyard outlined by a rambling stone wall covered with remnants of climbing plants. There were other houses nearby, but all that could be seen were the chimneys in the distance, and smoke trailing up to a steel-gray sky.

The windows were quite large, outlined with cement blocks in a geometric pattern. To me they looked like happy faces framed by the dainty lace curtains held back with long white tassels. On either side of the entrance door grew a barren tree so close to the wall I thought they must have been nailed there. I would not have believed that come summer I would see pears hanging from those scrawny arms, or indeed that the entire courtyard would be filled with flowers in every shade of the rainbow.

42

Mindele's Journey

I thought I lived in an enchanted castle. I would get lost going from room to room, investigating the possibilities of the long corridor connecting the living quarters to the kitchen in the back, Thérèse's domain. The arched brick oven practically filled the entire rear wall. It was here, using the last precious bit of flour available in Fraiture, that I learned how bread was made. I watched how the dusty powder was transformed into a soft spongy ball, then kneaded and allowed to rest under a cloth. When the time was right it was cut into equal parts and placed in the hot oven to be transformed into crusty round loaves ready for eating. Thérèse gave me a small pan and told me to do exactly as she did. Before long I had a series of tiny little loaves lined up in the oven next to the big ones. "Oh, Maman, look at my little children baking," I said, taking her hand and pulling her close to the oven so she could see my miniature creations. I had called Thérèse Maman, and from that moment on, Thérèse felt like my Maman. There was an unspoken bond between us when she said, "Yes, Maman is very proud of her little girl."

The smell of baking bread drew Marie and Marthe into the kitchen. Thérèse pointed to my accomplishments. "Show Tante Marthe and Tante Marie what you made."

I said happily, "My other maman and little sister Frieda would be proud of me too! And there is also bread for Poppa and Esther and Rebecca and Zelik." I did not yet know that my mother and little sister were probably dead. Or that my older sisters and Zelik were in the camps in Poland, the country that had once been their homeland. But at that moment, in

43

this kitchen filled with the wonderful smell of bread baking, I had imbued them with life and hope. I had recreated my family while preparing crusty loaves of brown bread. I didn't see Marthe wiping her eyes, or Marie turning pale. And when Thérèse, who was now maman, began an exuberant chant summoning everyone to sit down at the kitchen table—*A table mes enfants! Le dîner est prêt. Cette maman a faim*—I stopped thinking about my other family who would not be coming to dinner.

In the days and weeks that followed, I continued to roam about the house and found an attic to investigate, a cellar, and a laundry room. The laundry room was attached to the main house, its low oak door under the stairway leading to the second floor. Unlike everyone else, I didn't have to bend down to enter. I learned to manipulate the rusty metal latch, which made an unusual creaking sound and added to the feeling that I was entering a magical place. The laundry room was a favorite of Lulu the cat, who seemed to disappear for days into the piles of laundry heaped in straw baskets. Lulu seldom ate the food left out for her, and it was a mystery how she survived until one day I saw her strut triumphantly into the house with a mouse between her teeth. I couldn't look at Lulu for days after that. I kept picturing her holding that little mouse with its tiny pink feet dangling, and it made me very sad. I thought Lulu a killer, a hateful monster, and no amount of cajoling could persuade me otherwise. It made no difference when Maman explained that cats hunt mice and find them a delicacy just as people relish lamb or veal. But this was no comfort, because I was

Mindele's Journey

now on a first-name basis with the sheep grazing in the field behind the house and could not imagine eating one of them. Maman said she had the same problem with her chickens. There was one in particular that she named *Pitite*, spelled in the way of old Walloon, the local dialect, and whenever she called *Pitite!* at feeding time, the chicken recognized her name and would come running first. Maman got very attached to her Pitite, and refused to kill her even when food became scarce.

On Mondays, to the dismay of Lulu, who would be displaced from her favorite basket, Maman began the washing, a daunting task that took two days to complete. Large oval tin basins appeared from the recesses of the laundry room to be filled with sudsy water for soaking the dark colors. There was also a special cast iron tub called a *caboleu* used for boiling the whites. I learned later that the term *caboleu* came from medieval French, and remained in the modern vocabulary, because the women still practiced the old method of laundering in the little villages of the Ardennes.

Boiling the whites was a complicated procedure. Pine tree branches were brought in and cut to size, then placed in the wood burning stove for the *caboleu*. When the fire caught and started to wheeze and crackle, it was time to bring in buckets of water to fill the tub. Sweat dripped from Maman's forehead. Her hair came loose from its bun and hung down her neck in curly strings. Maman provided me with a small pail to fill with water that she would then pour into the *caboleu*. There was also a large rubber hose to speed up the process. Her friend Yvonne often came to help with all the cumbersome equipment and they talked and laughed as the water splashed on the ground and the tangy smell of lemon soap wafted through the air.

Did I remember then, that other time, Mamma wheeling me in the stroller, the week's dirty clothes piled around me, barely leaving room for my face? The women were laughing, their voices muffled by clouds of steam, faces disappearing in a moist haze as they kneeled over a communal wash tub and rubbed their clothes on a scrub board.

Meanwhile, Maman was calling for the pail of water in this place where pine branches smoldered, brightly colored flames danced inside the little black stove, and Lulu poked her nose through the door to see if her territory had been vacated yet.

The laundry was sorted into piles as we waited for the water to boil. The whites went in first, then placed in clear basins of water to stay overnight until they were transferred one more time for rinsing. Finally, they were ready to be dried in the attic. The attic was especially useful during the long winter months when clotheslines could be strung from one end to the other. Maman hauled large wicker baskets up the stairs and I followed behind with a basket of clothespins. As she hung up the clothes and sang old traditional songs, I repeated the phrases as best I could, and tried to catch the melodies.

La petite diligence sur les beaux chemins de France
S'en allait en cahotant voyageurs toujours contents.

As well as drying out the wash in winter, the attic was used for storing seeds and drying flowers.

Mindele's Journey

Newspapers laid out on the old wooden floor were covered with garden seeds. Scores of dried flowers tied in bouquets hung on nails along the stone wall. I could hardly wait to help Maman plant the seeds and gather the flowers. By the time spring announced itself in a burgeoning green beard around the bald spots in the garden, I was in a frenzy of anticipation. I followed Maman everywhere, and to her great amusement, I seemed to be underfoot every place she turned.

Marthe had gone back to teach in a neighboring town, and Marie was fully occupied with lesson plans or practicing the piano. She was also in charge of the church chorale, which she accompanied on the organ at Sunday church services. Marie would sit at the old piano every day. With her eyes half-closed, she appeared transformed as she played, as if savoring a divine memory. Thérèse was left to her own world, her young acolyte trailing behind.

With all the affection Thérèse lavished upon me, I no longer thought about my family. Sometimes Marie would gently reprimand her for spoiling me, saying that it was time for me to learn how to read and write along with the other children in school. Thérèse argued that I was still too young. But Marie insisted, and soon I joined the other children in the front row of the first grade in the old schoolhouse. For a while I missed not following Thérèse's every step, but now and then, as she checked the progress of her garden or hung the clothes on a line stretching between two flowering hazelnut trees, I would catch sight of her smiling face at the window cheering me on.

47

Mariette Bermowitz

Despite the ravages of the advancing German army, the first crocuses of spring stuck their disheveled pink and lavender petals out of the ground. Sweeping patches of golden daffodils nudged the purple stalks of hyacinths. The vegetable garden, seeded and planted earlier, sprouted lacy carrot tops, new lettuce, and cabbages in delicate shades of green. Row upon row of leafy patterns transformed the earth into a mosaic of color. When the pungent lilacs blossomed, sending their sweet fragrance into the school room, it was hard to concentrate on lessons.

I felt shy and distant from the other children. Sometimes I cried for no reason at all and the other children stared at me. At recreation time, when the children went outside for their half hour of freedom, I sought refuge with Thérèse, and much against my wishes, she always walked me back to the classroom.

One day she introduced me to a girl whose name was also Mariette. This Mariette was a little older than me, and because she was so much taller than the rest of us, she had developed a stoop when she walked. "Do you have any brothers or sisters?" she asked. "My mother has just given birth to a baby girl."

I wanted to tell her about my baby sister Frieda, but I couldn't get a word in as this Mariette went on talking about the farm where she lived and the chores she had to do. Then she took my hand and led me to the middle of the recreation yard to teach me how to jump rope and play hopscotch. Her hand felt so boney and fragile in mine that later I asked Thérèse to invite her to the house for lunch because I thought she wasn't getting enough food at home. Though Mariette and I became close, I was told

Mindele's Journey

never to speak about my family, talking instead about the attic and the cellar in Fraiture. She enjoyed hearing about her teacher's private quarters, and these confidences became our private secrets. Sometimes Mariette brought the teacher fresh eggs from the farm, and there was always a sweet-smelling galette in her bag that she insisted on sharing with me.

In the evening after the supper dishes had been washed and cleared away, Marie gave me a small slate and chalk. Under her careful eye, I practiced the intricate letters of the alphabet, fitting them between the lines. Marie was anxious that I keep up with the other children, so I began copying everything in sight. I copied the names on the containers and tin boxes lining the shelves in Maman's kitchen, learning how to spell until I managed the most complicated series of advertisements. *BANANIA L'EXQUIS DEJEUNER SUCRE A LA FARINE DE BANANE.* I was fascinated by the smiling black-skinned man pictured on the tin and the fact that there were black-skinned people in the world. I had never seen one, but Maman said everyone was black in the Belgian Congo. Thus my first lesson in geography and colonialism took place on Maman's lap as she held a large atlas and showed me all the different peoples of the world and how they lived.

Spring gave way to the bounty of summer. The garden was filled with ripe vegetables and the trees were heavy with burgundy plums, jade plums, ruby red cherries, and blushing red apples. Buckets of string beans were brought in for sorting. There were leaks, fava beans, herbs to flavor the soups, and of course Maman's award-winning strawberries.

Mariette Bermowitz

Potatoes were piled into bins in the cellar, while onions were brought to the attic. They would dry in the attic, and then be twisted into garlands to be used for the weeks and months ahead.

I insisted on helping, sometimes getting underfoot as I clamored for attention, but Maman never lost patience. She gave me old pieces of cloth to sort. The lace and satin had been thrown into hatboxes to be used later in patching a torn apron or a dress, or in the long winter months to be slowly and magically transformed into a quilt. I never quite mastered the art of ordering the piles, choosing instead to crown myself with doilies, and the satiny remnants of cast-off clothing. One time I fell asleep in the attic in a pile of cloth, and woke up to see Marie and Thérèse standing over me, smiling as they pointed to Lulu snuggled up against me. Lulu, finding my hair and the smell of the cloth to her liking, had curled up with me. I think that was what finally redeemed Lulu in my eyes. Of course, I never saw her with a mouse again, which also helped. To further endear herself to me, she would often rub her velvety fur against my leg and purr for me to pick her up.

Maman Thérèse was never busier than at the end of the summer when the garden had to be harvested and preserved for the coming winter. Of all the vegetables she gathered, fava beans were her favorite. I thought the large waxy green pods that opened to jewel-like beans were extraordinary. She was forever inventing new dishes for the fava bean. I would find them swimming in an array of different sauces. She also had a special way with the skinny string beans I helped her pick from climbing vines. She cooked

Mindele's Journey

them in butter, which made them turn brown, but when she sprinkled in some vinegar they magically transformed back to green. Later in life when I understood the full extent of her culinary talents, fava beans became my favorite too.

I also learned that her secret cooking spice was the mighty little nutmeg. She introduced me to this flavorful nut during one of our geography lessons. "You see that little brown thing? It's called *muscade,* and it is a gift from God. But like all wonderful things given to us, you must never abuse it. It must be hidden in the cooking for the palate to discover and wonder at."

Maman would often hum and sing when she picked the jewels from her garden. Sometimes I would sneak up behind her just to hear her talking to the tomatoes and cauliflowers, the potatoes, leeks and onions, commenting on their magnificent color and fragrant skin, and how superb they would taste in her soups and special dinners.

It took days of preparation to transform *ce cadeau de la terre* (a gift of the earth) into sauces, soups, and desserts, which were then poured into glass jars and hermetically sealed. She hid them in a secluded cabinet in the cellar called the *garde-manger.* Little did I know that this *garde-manger* cabinet would save our lives as the war came closer.

✦ ✦ ✦

The first days of September brought a fierce chill. Machine gun fire rumbled throughout the valley. But hope was spreading since we had received news that the Americans had landed in Normandy that June. Yet no one dared speak too loudly, because there were still Germans everywhere. Yvonne came running into the kitchen one afternoon with a package wrapped in soiled paper. Before unwrapping the mysterious bundle, she checked the windows to make sure no one had followed her. When she tore open the paper, a mass of orange folds spilled out. *Regardez, c'est le parachute d'un Américain. Il est caché près de chez nous.* But no sooner did this beautiful orange spray of hope hit the floor than Yvonne and Maman crouched down to gather the material up again.

"Oh, my God, my God! We can't keep this! What if the Germans come here?" cried Maman.

Yvonne said, "I'll take it. Such beautiful silk should be used to make clothing."

They decided Yvonne would hide the parachute, and the beautiful fabric disappeared into Yvonne's barn behind the bales of hay.

On the tenth of September, I was in the classroom with Tante Marie waiting for the rest of her students to arrive when Maman burst in howling with joy, *Ils arrivent, ils arrivent!* We ran outside. The whole village was out to greet them, shouting, *Les Américains sont arrivés! Les Américains sont arrivés!* Maman was crossing herself and clasping her hands saying, *C'est un miracle, c'est un miracle.* She told me that these soldiers were our saviors. That they came from America, a country across the ocean. It was *un miracle, un miracle* how they landed on the beaches in Normandy and fought their way through France, finally to arrive and liberate our village. Maman

Mindele's Journey

began singing, "It's a long way to Tipperary, it's a long way to go!"

Non, non, ce sont les Américains, pas les Anglais, chided Tante Marie.

There was a temporary peace at least. The Americans had set up their convoys above the village, pushing the Germans back toward the border thirty-five kilometers away from Fraiture. As winter approached, fierce winds raged through our valley, followed by a brutal and unrelenting snowfall. The roads were hidden under a massive covering of ice. There were no cars, but there were horses, and the horses dragged their heavy loads through the snow. By the end of November, the village was at a standstill. There was hardly any coal left to throw into the old stove in Tante Marie's classroom. We sat on the cold hard wooden benches dressed in coats and hats. Gloves were removed only when necessary. Maman began dipping into her precious supply of jars hidden in the cellar. Her reserve was dwindling but she still had some of the vegetables and she used them on special occasions to make a tasty bouillon.

One of those special occasions was the day I turned six on December 1, 1944. Other than the chicken Yvonne carried in triumphantly that morning, there were not many presents. Maman immediately set her large kettle on the stove and before long a feast materialized. We were about to sit down when the doorbell rang. Everyone fell silent. Tante Marie went to the door exclaiming, *Mon Dieu, Mon Dieu.*

Oui Monsieur, oui monsieur, entrez, she said, leading a strange man and woman into the kitchen. I stared at the tattered clothes hanging loosely over the man's body. How could those rags have protected him from the cold and snow? He was so emaciated that his eyes seemed no more than large black holes. The woman was deathly pale. Tante Marie invited them to sit at the table. Coffee was a thing of the past, but she brought out cups filled with a hot dark liquid called chicory.

When the man saw me, he covered his eyes with his bony hands and cried. His body shook with sobs. When he finally stopped crying he extended a hand toward me, and in a muffled cry said, *Mindele, mein kind.*

It had been too long since anyone had called me Mindele. I was afraid to go near him. I did not recognize him. I had forgotten my past. I had forgotten my Poppa. He handed me a little package and waited for me to unwrap it. He had managed to bring me a small doll that looked so fragile I almost dared not take it. *Merci monsieur.* I couldn't understand why he started to sob again.

They only remained one night. I was told that he couldn't stop crying for the entire time he was at the house. I cried too. I cried because I was terrified he would take me away. But all he wanted was to see the red birthmark on my left leg. I was howling as I pulled down my knee sock to show him the mark that identified me as his Mindele, the child he saved.

Later, I learned that Sister Cécilia in Banneux had given him my address, and the two of them had walked for days, sometimes hopping on tramways. I cannot imagine the hope that drove him to take such a chance, risking his life to see the only child he had left from a family of five children.

Mindele's Journey

By the middle of December the sound of machine guns reverberated against the pine trees in the forests of the Ardennes Mountains. The German army, which had retreated to the border, had reorganized its troops and was once more advancing into the region. Fraiture and the strategic crossroads above the town known as La Baraque Fraiture would soon turn into a bloody battlefield, while thirty kilometers to the south, the Battle of the Bulge became a killing field where almost ninety thousand Americans were killed, wounded or missing. The total was even greater for the Germans.

Fraiture was taken over by German soldiers to be used as regional headquarters, and they wanted the schoolhouse as well. Everything seemed to happen at once. First the sound of cars and trucks, then the loud voices shouting in a foreign language, then the doorbell ringing, echoing down the length of the marble corridor.

I remember Maman grabbing my hand so tightly it hurt. She took me to the upstairs bedroom and told me to remain there and keep absolutely quiet. She lit a candle and placed it on the mantel to keep me company while she went downstairs to be with Marie. The soldiers had brought in an arsenal of radios, machine guns, and containers that were to be stacked into Tante Marie's classroom. When they demanded food and blankets, Maman showed them the pantry behind the kitchen and told them to help themselves to whatever they needed. There wasn't much left. A week before, M. le Curé had warned les tantes of the imminent danger and prepared a room in the rectory for us.

55

The food from le garde-manger had been transported to the priest's cellar awaiting our arrival. But the soldiers had arrived unexpectedly. I was told they were going to stay and that I was never to be alone with them. The next morning when we went down to the kitchen, several men were sitting at our table smoking cigarettes and waving their arms about as they spoke. I observed them curiously, these men in green uniforms, a color similar to the moss covering the roots of the giant oak tree behind the house. As soon as they saw us they stopped talking. I chewed on the pocket of my apron as I watched them gather up their belts and caps and things. Then they bowed to Maman and left.

Les tantes feared being questioned about me. They were afraid my dark hair, brown eyes, and olive complexion, would arouse suspicion. Tante Marie came in, her arms full of coats, whispered something in Maman's ear, and walked to the front door. Their friend Yvonne was waiting for us outside in her old truck, probably the last one available in the village. As we climbed in, Yvonne said at the top of her voice, loudly enough for everyone to hear, "Hurry up! Tante Zélie is waiting for us!" Tante Marie called out *Bon voyage* as we drove away.

The rain smacking into the windshield made it difficult to see, but Yvonne was unafraid. She was one of the fierce Ardennais women who drove a tractor and had worked the earth alongside her brother since childhood. We arrived at the farm. Zélie, Yvonne's elderly mother, was home, seemingly undisturbed by the sounds of warfare. She was sitting at her spinning wheel making yarn from the wool shorn from Amélie,

Mindele's Journey

her favorite lamb. I had seen her before, feeding the wool into the ancient spinning wheel, then delicately gathering the rippling yarn that came out of the fluffy mass onto the tips of her crippled fingers. I was hoping for the sweater she had promised to knit for me, but we were not staying. The plans had changed. We got back into the truck. Yvonne and Maman were speaking in Walloon, the local dialect of the region. It made me unhappy not being able to understand what they were saying, but I was elated that we were going to visit Louise instead.

Louise was thirteen years old and thought of me as her little sister. Her family ran the café-restaurant above the village. There was always a lot of activity there and my presence would not be noticed when I played in the barn with the other children. They thought I would be safe with Louise for a few days while les tantes packed up their belongings to move into the rectory.

I was told not to run outside because of all the cars and soldiers moving about, but on the second day I was left to play by myself. I loved the hay in the barn and its smell of the earth and the cows with their enormous brown eyes that followed me around. There was also a rooster establishing his turf as he made a dash through the cackling hens. Above all I loved the dog, Bobby, with his shiny black coat and curly tail. When he ran out toward the road I ran after him. Just as I reached the dog, a car filled with Germans came to a halt a few yards away. One of the soldiers got out of the car and called me over. I knew I wasn't supposed to talk to strangers, but it was too late to go back to the barn. Then, just as the soldier

57

in the black uniform began talking I saw Louise running toward me. She put herself between me and the soldier and smacked my face shouting, *Je t'avais dit de ne pas courir sur la route!* "I told you not to run on the road!" She turned to the officer then, and told him that her little sister never listened and one of these days would get herself killed. Without waiting for a reply, she grabbed my shoulder and dragged me back to the house.

I went back to Fraiture the next day. The soldiers were no longer in the house but Maman and Tante Marie had their suitcases ready. It was getting very dangerous to remain in the schoolhouse. The neighbors were moving as well, into the cellars where they might be protected from the danger of being killed from the imminent bombing. Some of the young people had been arrested, questioned about the whereabouts of the *maquis* or underground fighters, and then executed.

We walked down to the rectory with a neighbor pushing a wheelbarrow brimming with our belongings. As we came into the courtyard we saw a black car parked outside the house. Tante Marie thought that very strange because there was so much snow on the roads and danger as well. She had to ring the bell twice before the door opened. The priest's face was as white as the collar around his neck. Behind him stood two German officers. Before Tante Marie had a chance to offer her excuses one of the Germans took her hand and invited us to join him and the others in the kitchen. The priest's father and his aunt stood stiffly against the kitchen table. I tried to hide myself behind a panel of M. le Curé's robe.

C'est qui cette petite? One of the officers came up to me with his eyes riveted on mine. Without hesitating, Tante Marie said, "A little girl we adopted."

"That looks like a Jewish child to me," he replied in perfect French. I started to cry. Then the officer reached into his pocket and held out a piece of candy. Tante Marie nudged me to take the treat. I mumbled, *Merci Monsieur.*

He turned to the other officer and motioned him to the door. Before leaving he turned around and said, "We'll be back."

As soon as he was gone, M. le Curé told us to go down into the cellar because the officers had warned him that the fighting above ground would result in great casualties. It was Christmas Eve. Maman took out a tablecloth from a basket and set out some of the precious jars of preserves she had hidden in a recessed corner of the room. There was some bread but it was sticky and spongy, almost impossible to eat. Maman was not one to complain, but with a deep sigh she talked about the crusty loaves she used to make when she still had flour. Someone lit candles and soon the sound of prayers filled the air. We clasped our hands and prayed in thankfulness for what we had. And somewhere above ground a familiar tune could be heard. The soldiers were singing *Stille Nacht* and *Tannenbaum.*

The bombs fell day and night. We could not even go upstairs to see the light of day. Armed with warm clothing and blankets we lived in the basement, surviving on boiled potatoes and the jars of soup retrieved from their hiding places, and hoped that the bombing wouldn't come any closer. We huddled

Mariette Bermowitz

together in blankets and did not take off our clothes because even with double layers of sweaters the cold cut through to our skin. We remained in the basement until we were forced to evacuate on the second day of the new year.

In the face of advancing allied forces, the Germans were evacuating villages in an effort to hold on to their strategic position. They were especially concerned about getting the people out of their cellars so they could occupy them. The soldiers were in a frenzy to hold the Americans back and threatened those who were too slow leaving their homes. They shouted orders into houses, and then threw grenades through the windows. My friend Mariette's mother was killed when shrapnel struck her as she attempted to retrieve something from the cellar. Marictte was close enough so that she witnessed her mother being struck down, never to get up again.

We were forced to join a long march of people, some in carts, but most of them walking away from the conflict to the town of Baclain, while in Bastogne the fiercest battle of the war was ravaging the battlefield. As our sad procession struggled on the road, the horses barely able to pull the heavy cart through ice and snow, I saw patches of red. It looked like red carnations had been strewn around on the snow, but it was the blood of soldiers. It was also the blood of women and children caught in the crossfire when they ran for cover. It took days to reach Baclain, as we kept having to seek shelter during air attacks. We were directed to barns, or abandoned houses where there was nothing to sleep on but torn mattresses. I refused to lie down so Maman Thérèse made me a

Mindele's Journey

bed with two chairs and some blankets she found in a corner. She told me to wear the rosary around my neck, saying it was magical and if I held it between my fingers at night no harm would ever come.

When we finally reached Baclain we found shelter in an unlit cellar along with several other families. Bombs were falling in the countryside all around us. Some were so close that we were able to count the moment they were going to explode by the eerie wheezing sound before impact. It sounded like fireworks. We never knew when they were going to crash down on us. Maman Thérèse held me under a blanket, and when the plaster started falling I thought we were going to be buried alive.

A wounded German soldier was dragged into our cellar. His arm was twisted out of its socket. I was so close to him I could smell his blood. M. le Curé crawled out of his hiding place long enough to cover the soldier with a blanket and give him the last rites. The soldier died moaning a prayer. Prayers could be heard in the darkness from every corner of the cellar. Voices rose above the falling plaster, joining together in a desperate moment of hope. Meanwhile, not far away, the Germans and Americans were massacring each other on the battlefield of Bastogne, the battle that brought an end to the war in Europe, the battle that will be remembered as the Battle of the Bulge.

✴ ✴ ✴

When we returned to Fraiture we faced a scene of total devastation. Massive piles of stones made it look like a monstrous cemetery. Wood from old

Mariette Bermowitz

beams jutted up through the rubble like twisted arms. Dead animals were strewn over fields of snow. Where the school had once stood was now nothing more than a floor and frames around doors and windows. Windows that were no more than gaping eyes stared into nothingness. Tante Marie and Maman scrambled around searching for anything recognizable they could find. There were cries of joy when one of their treasures was plucked from behind a broken door.

The rescue of precious things would take months. Meanwhile, we all went to stay with M. le Curé in the rectory, which had been only slightly damaged. M. le Curé said mass for his elderly aunt who had not survived the trek to Baclain. Her body had not yet been found, and it was assumed she was killed when her cart exploded during one of the attacks on the road. We sat in the old church as rain fell through holes in the roof, and it sounded like the church itself was crying with grief. The bell had been stolen, the steeple was empty, yet when mass began, everyone looked up hopefully as they invoked a carillon of celebration.

Slowly but surely normal life returned. The Nazis had been defeated. Europe was rising from the ashes once again. There was more rejoicing when the Americans reached Fraiture. They came to the church with boxes of food and supplies for M. le Curé to distribute in the village. I gaped at the astonishing array of canned food and packages stacked in the pantry. A smiling American soldier gave me a Mars bar. Maman chided me for making a face, but I didn't like its smell, and I thought the gooey sweet

Mindele's Journey

stuff inside was going to stick to my teeth forever. Still, I was grateful for the supply of food even if it meant adjusting to new tastes.

By April 1945, the birds were trilling and gentle spring breezes were spreading warmth throughout the house. We stayed at the rectory in the large bedroom upstairs, and Tante Marie prepared her classes at the desk in the library room. It would be awhile before the schoolhouse and adjacent classroom would be functional again. In the meantime, a large pantry had been cleared next to the rectory to be used as a temporary schoolroom. One day I was sitting on the stone steps outside the house, watching the birds and enjoying the soft breeze, when Maman beckoned me into the garden. I skipped along the path beside her, through remnants of dead plants and glass debris not yet swept away, thinking I was going to help her plan a new garden. I was so taken with ideas to share with her that I didn't notice a car had pulled up in front of the rectory, and several people had gone inside the house. Tante Marie came to the garden gate, calling me to come in right away. *C'est le papa qui arrive.* That was when Maman told me that my father had come to take me back with him.

My heart was pounding as I ran toward the rectory, oblivious to all the debris littering the path. I tripped and fell into a pile of broken glass. When I tried to get up I couldn't move my leg. The next thing I remember was the priest's brother, Gilbert, bending over my knee trying to remove the splinters of glass. Blood gushed down my leg, which Gilbert said was good. But all I could think of was how much it hurt. And then I thought of the soldier in Baclain, and his blood, and how he died in the cellar with us. Gilbert tried in vain to make me laugh by imitating a clown. When *mon papa* came in to see me I was all bandaged up. He placed a bony hand on my head as if giving me a blessing, and thanked everyone gathered in the room. I started to cry. Then he started to cry too. Gilbert said he would drive me back to Liège himself, saving *mon papa* the long trip again. It would be easier that way, he said.

My knee healed quickly despite my prayers to delay recovery for as long as possible. I was terrified to leave Fraiture, the only home I had known for the last few years. Yet here I am in a photograph taken in Liège, sitting beside an American soldier and smiling as I held my precious doll Yvette against my chest. We were in Yankel's house where *mon papa* had been in hiding during most of the war.

The American soldier was Ira Rothenberg, a distant cousin who spoke Yiddish with my Poppa. Ira brought news from my aunt Rifcha, Poppa's sister in Brooklyn, New York. Ira had been sent as an emissary to find out what had happened to the family. The news Ira would bring back to America would be sad, but he had arrived in time for the celebration of Passover—the first Passover after the war.

Everyone was gathered around the large table. Poppa's friend Yankel sat beside Sarah, his daughter-in-law, with little Andrée on her lap. Sarah's mother, Mme. Goldman, was there, as well as her brother Jean and her twin sisters.

Yankel stood at the head of the table with Poppa. All eyes were riveted on Poppa as he began the ceremony. His voice faltered as if he had forgotten the

Mindele's Journey

words, but then he eased into it, and before long everyone was joining in the songs from the Haggadah. These songs from my early childhood now sounded foreign to me. I pretended to listen, while silently reciting my Hail Mary's and Our Father Who Art in Heaven, crossing myself like Maman had showed me. When I looked up everyone was staring at me, their eyes aghast, as if I had done something horribly wrong. Poppa said in a low voice, "You are never to do that again."

My eyes filled with tears. From then on my Christian prayers were reserved for solitary moments. Before going to sleep I called on the saints and angels to help me keep the secret from my father. The war was over. Little did I know that for me the war had only just begun.

Rue Ste. Anne, Brussels 1946

The years immediately following the war seemed an absurd attempt to create meaning out of meaninglessness. Many of the survivors were emotionally paralyzed, unable to make decisions. A mindless bureaucracy stepped into the chaos. Makeshift agencies were created to resettle the lost, the aimless, and the grieving hordes of wanderers who had escaped annihilation. There were centers for Jewish orphans who would be sent to Kibbutzim in Israel and organizations for locating missing family members. Millions of people were seeking anyone with clues to the whereabouts of their loved ones. Many of these survivors could hardly bring themselves to face another

Mariette Bermowitz

day. They existed in a state of utter hopelessness and despair. My father was one of them. He had lost a wife, three daughters, and a son in a concentration camp somewhere in Poland.

My father survived the war years hiding in an attic, constantly wondering if I was safe. He worried about what had happened to his other children, little knowing that they had been thrust into unimaginable atrocities. With his restless nature he had gambled with fate on numerous occasions. Aside from the time he came to visit me in Fraiture, guided by Sister Cécilia, the Mother Superior of Banneux, there was the time he went to buy tobacco. A chain smoker who missed his packs of *Boule d'Or*, he left the safety of the attic in search of tobacco with some paper to roll his own. He had been warned that such luxuries were no longer available, yet he went anyway, perhaps to taste forbidden freedom, or maybe no longer caring what might happen to him. He got no farther than the next street when he was stopped and told to show his papers. He pretended not to understand and was taken to headquarters to be questioned further, then thrown into a room filled with other men who had also failed to answer questions.

The following day they were herded onto trains heading for unknown destinations. My father had always been a small man, and now the lack of food and the deprivations of war had made him almost skeletal. Ironically, the fact that he weighed less than a hundred pounds saved his life. Being practically wafer thin allowed him to slip through a broken plank in the floor of the train and let himself down onto the rails. He was shot as he sprinted across a field and left for dead. Though he was bleeding, by strength of will and determination, he miraculously made it back to Yankel's house. Sarah found someone to take care of the wound. He survived.

My father brought Mme. Goldman and her son Jean to live with us in Brussels. We settled at No. 8 Rue Ste. Anne, a shabby cold-water flat. The wooden door was rotting and always wet from the rain, which dripped down its sides like tears and made me imagine the door was crying. The long hall that ran to the rear of the house stank of gas and coal fumes, an odor that seeped through the walls of our apartment so we could never get away from it. In the back was a cobblestone courtyard where we went for water from the large slate sink built into the stone. A rather large brass faucet nosed its way out of the wall. The outhouse was also in the courtyard beside the stacks of coal and the low cellar windows without any glass.

In order to go into the bedroom I shared with Jean, I had to walk out into the smelly hallway. But once I was lying in bed, I could see the brass faucet if I raised my head a little. A bunch of dark green moss had nestled into the open ridges between the stones, making it look as though the faucet was a nose with a green mustache. At night when I couldn't sleep I fantasized a dialogue with this face in the wall. Sometimes I climbed out the window and turned on the faucet just to watch the water run. When the moon was out the water sparkled, and I imagined

Mariette Bermowitz

the water was singing to me, just as Maman Thérèse had once sung to me.

I always shut the water off in the morning before I left for school, but one day I forgot. As a punishment, I had to carry in two enormously heavy pails of water. One pail supplied the water for cooking. The other was only half-filled, and was used as a toilet. The smell in the apartment was unpleasant at first, but I got used to it.

Our apartment with two plate glass windows looking onto the street must have been a storefront at one time. There was nothing to see now in that gruesome street with its long stretch of miserable houses where daylight seemed only a promise. Yet it did have one advantage. Because it was too narrow for cars, I could sit on the sidewalk or write on the wall of the telephone building across the street without worrying about traffic. The walls of the telephone building hovered over the street like a shield, darkening the very air we breathed, separating us from the rest of the world.

Mme. Goldman was in a perpetual state of grief over the loss of her husband and two of her six children. Aside from Sarah who remained in Liège and Jean who was with us, there were the twins, Cécile and Renée. To have them live with us would have been too many mouths to feed, so while they waited to be repatriated to a Kibbutz in Israel, they lived in a home for displaced children. Mme. Goldman didn't seem able to cope with the present, or with Jean, her retarded son, who had ironically survived. She would often burst into tears for no reason at all, or so it seemed to me. Her long gray hair was loosely

68

Mindele's Journey

tied back and constantly came undone, dangling like snakes around her face. She rocked herself endlessly, arms folded across her ample bosom, as she sang sad songs in Polish or Yiddish. *Brent, my shtetele brent,* was a song about the village burning down and having to leave behind everything that one loved and cherished. When she sang it was as if all the grief of the past was with us now, in the Rue Ste. Anne.

Poppa was destitute. Yet somehow he managed to borrow money on the promise of work from some tailors he had known before the war. Life now was referred to as "before the war," and "after the war." Poppa wanted me to call Mme. Goldman *Maman.* I obliged him in this, but the feeling of *maman* was reserved for Maman Thérèse in Fraiture. By now I knew that my own mother had died in a most tragic way. Mme. Goldman could not possibly replace her. Yet my mother seemed nothing more than a phantom, unreal and unmourned. Poppa acted as if she had never existed. He never spoke about her. When I asked him about our family he showed me pictures taken of the concentration camp survivors when the Americans came to liberate them. And then he cried.

The bedroom I shared with Jean was small and damp and sparsely furnished, but it had one beautiful thing, the wardrobe. This wardrobe had two exquisitely paneled doors separated by a large beveled mirror that reflected the general shabbiness of the room. It had been saved by a neighbor on the Rue du Lavoir, where we lived before the war. When we returned to Brussels, Poppa had gone back to our old apartment. He was hoping to find some clue as to what might have happened to his family

69

Mariette Bermowitz

that day he and I escaped on the rooftop. The wife of a former customer who had been fond of him, had taken it upon herself to bring the wardrobe into her apartment and keep it until someone from the family came back to reclaim it. Poppa had made a suit for her husband before the war and she always remembered the Jewish tailor and his family who were taken away. Now she gave Poppa the tragic details, including the part that repulsed her more than anything. Someone in the building, one of our neighbors, had betrayed us.

When the wardrobe arrived in the apartment on the Rue Ste. Anne, Poppa smiled through his tears. It was the first time I remember seeing even the hint of a smile on his face. After the heavy oak piece was carried in and placed safely against the bedroom wall, he unlocked one of the lavishly paneled oak doors. I held my breath as if we were about to enter a forbidden place, and when Poppa turned the key and the lock clicked open, I knew something magical had occurred. First I was struck by the smell of mothballs. But it wasn't just another odor to be added to the medley of smells already permeating the ground floor of the house, this was the smell that had kept our past safe.

I watched my father stare in disbelief at the clothes hanging in disarray, the boxes crushed into each other, the hats bent out of shape, the jumble of mismatched shoes on the bottom shelf, and unknown things bundled into sheets. In the corner undisturbed hung a fur coat. Poppa just stared, not reaching out his hand to touch anything. I think he was too overwhelmed. He just stared straight ahead,

Mindele's Journey

perhaps imagining the ones who had worn these things. But I was entranced. He shut the doors and locked them, saying that we would explore the contents another day. That night as I drifted off to sleep, I thought about all the discoveries I would make, the new treasures I might acquire.

One afternoon not long afterward, I noticed that Poppa had left the key in the door. I was alone in the bedroom. Mme. Goldman and Jean were out and Poppa was down the hall in the other room. Here was an opportunity to enter into the forbidden past, touch with my own hands all those things Poppa didn't want to look at. I opened the wardrobe door as quietly as I could. At first all I saw was a jumble of clothes and shoes, but then my gaze fell on a black patent leather pocketbook. It was partly open, and seemed to beckon me. I pulled it out, marveling at the soft red leather lining and the smell of tobacco, but in my excitement I dropped it and all the precious things tumbled out, making a horrible clatter on the bare wooden floor. I picked them up quickly and stuffed them back in the purse. I was afraid my father had heard the noise. I didn't want him to be angry with me. But I didn't have to worry, because when he came in he wasn't angry, just sad.

We sat down together on the bed and he took out a small book in a zippered pocket of the black patent leather purse. It was a picture album. He pointed out the pictures of my sister Esther. The purse had been Esther's. There I was with her on one of our Sunday outings in the park, wearing the little blue coat and matching hat she had bought me. "I remember this

71

outfit," I cried. "Poppa, I remember the outing, and how I couldn't be separated from my new outfit."

Poppa went to the wardrobe and dragged out what looked like a rolled up mattress. His hands were shaking as he gently touched the fabric. "This is your mother's quilt. She brought it with her from Poland with her trousseau when we married right before the war. It was her pride and joy. I will tell you the story another time." His eyes glazed over with tears and he stared into the distance. "Well, it is yours now. We will put it on your bed because it's always so cold in this room."

It would be a long time before I understood the magic of this gift resurrected from the past. I almost didn't want to put it on top of the torn sheets that covered the old horsehair mattress. But of course I did, and the warmth under the precious feather quilt made my body tingle. It became my refuge, a secret tent where I read my favorite stories with a flashlight when everyone was asleep. The quilt became the keeper of my dreams. I lived in a world of make-believe most of the time anyway. The present was a dingy apartment with Poppa, Mme. Goldman, and Jean. No matter how oppressive the war years had been, I had known only love and protection in Fraiture. I thought of les tantes as my family. It was a shock being wrenched away from the safety and warmth I had known with them. Sometimes I thought les tantes had abandoned me. Other times I hated Poppa for taking me away from them, to this dingy apartment with Mme. Goldman and Jean.

The Brussels I knew as a child was a very gray city. Sadness seemed to permeate everything. It rained

Mindele's Journey

constantly, making the cobblestones on the Rue de Ruysbroek glisten. Little brooks would fill the spaces around the stones, and if I looked at them with half-closed eyes, I could almost imagine myself walking on a lake. Sometimes the rain was only a gentle mist floating down, covering me with dew.

We were located off the Place du Grand Sablon in the heart of Brussels, where just beyond the numerous antique shops was Les Marolles, the teaming slum I got to know very well. I felt so alone in this dreadful place until I met M. Gianini, the sculptor who lived in the house next to ours. M. Gianini fascinated me. His face was always covered with white plaster dust that made him look like the religious statues he made in his atelier. One day he left a window open and I managed to peek in by holding on to the window sill and lifting myself off the sidewalk. He thought that was quite bold for a little girl and invited me in. I told him I had to ask *mon papa* for permission.

Visiting M. Gianini was the first of many escapes from the apartment. I loved to sit and watch him bring statues to life by adding delicate colored highlights to the faces he chiseled. As he worked we shared stories. I told him about my other life in Fraiture and he told me about when he was a young boy in Italy and how he missed the blue skies of his native country. He said that was why he made sure to use lots of blue when painting his statues. I told him that I didn't mind the gray skies of Brussels, and I didn't mind the rain either. There was so much rain, yet each rain was different, and different in the way that it changed the face of the city. M. Gianini said

Mariette Bermowitz

that I would change my mind someday when I visited his country.

I also made friends with Mme. Marie, who had a small candy shop at the end of the Rue Ste. Anne. Whenever I passed by I always stopped to look at the displays in the window of candies, toys, pencils, and games. The shop window was so clean it almost seemed as if I could reach in and touch those wonderful things. One day I pressed my nose against the glass and smudged it. While I was trying to erase the smudge, Mme. Marie came out. Her hair was pulled back into a tight chignon and a big white apron was stretched around her bulky frame. "Who are you? Where do you live?" I was afraid she was angry with me, but then she said she had heard a Jewish family had moved in a few houses up, and invited me in to choose a candy from the counter.

Inside was a candy paradise. When I saw the Côte d'Or chocolates individually wrapped in gold paper, I was beside myself with happiness, and told her about Sister Clotilde in Banneux who used to give me chocolate. Mme. Marie told me to stop by as often as I wanted and say *bonjour*. We became good friends, as I often stopped by on my way home from school. When I got older, I insisted on paying for the candy, but even so I would always find something extra in the bag she had given me as a gift.

Aside from M. Gianini, Poppa also allowed me to visit a Jewish family he had known before the war. The Foleiders lived around the corner from us on the Rue de Ruysbroek and had a son named Jacky. Though Jacky was my age, he looked much older with his thick glasses and the formal clothing his

Mindele's Journey

mother made him wear. I liked visiting their spotlessly clean apartment where there was a radio and delicious things to eat. Mme. Foleider welcomed my visits, as she said I was the only child Jacky ever played with. He loved listening to the radio, and he especially wanted me to come Sunday afternoons to hear his favorite program, *Radio Jeunesse.* It became a welcome escape from the sadness on the Rue Ste. Anne, this program about children all over the world and fairy tales from different countries. Jacky and I would make appreciative noises when evil came to a bad end, and applaud every good thing that happened. Because the stories were left unfinished until the following Sunday, we would spend the rest of the afternoon making up our own endings.

Sometimes I saw a woman on the Rue de Ruysbroek I wished was my friend. I saw her come out of a house one afternoon when I was playing hopscotch in the street, and she looked to me as if she had stepped out of the pages of a fairy tale. She carried a tennis racket and was dressed all in white. Her hair was so blond it was almost white. She was the most beautiful woman I had ever seen. I was hardly able to believe she was real, and thought of her as "the angel." On the mornings I didn't have school I looked for her. When she appeared, I stopped playing and watched, mesmerized, as she walked down the street and disappeared around the corner. I wanted to be just like her when I grew up.

Then there was Mme. Charpentier, the blind woman who lived on the second floor in the rear of our house. It was difficult for her to climb the winding narrow stairs to the room she shared with her

Mariette Bermowitz

cats. The old bare wooden stairs were full of splinters. One day when I was in the hallway I heard someone trip on the stairs and ran to help. It was Mme. Charpentier. I gave her my arm and helped her up the rest of the stairs and she let me open the door for her. There was a terrible smell and I was glad she didn't invite me in. It must have been because of the cats. She let them out on the balcony where they jumped down and disappeared over the rooftops. But they often stayed away too long, and then she would shuffle outside on the balcony and call down, asking me if I had seen her cats. I reassured her that if I saw them I would bring them back straight away. I felt sorry for Mme. Charpentier, who at seventy was still selling newspapers on the Place du Grand Sablon, huddling in a doorway to stay out of the draft. She always seemed so sad. I never saw her wear anything other than a long black skirt and a pullover that hung down over her hips. When the weather got colder she covered herself in a black shawl so that only her wrinkled face and blank eyes were visible. I could hear her shouting from the top of the Rue Ste. Anne, *Le Soir, Le Soir, ici Le Soir!* It was a popular newspaper even though during the war it became a propaganda rag for the Nazis. I thought Mme. Charpentier was brave, and told her so one day when I accompanied her home. *Ah, Mon petit Chou,* she said. *C'est la vie, c'est la vie.*

M. Gianini came in one afternoon to tell Poppa that there was a phone call for him. It was les tantes! My beloved aunts were calling! I skipped out the door and over to M. Gianini's atelier, hardly able to believe I would soon be hearing their beautiful soft

Mindele's Journey

voices again. I pressed the phone to my ear, listening to their musical voices telling me all the latest news from Fraiture. Marthe, who had been in Odeigne during the war, was back home. They were now living permanently with M. le Curé. The school was being rebuilt but it would take a long time before the town had enough money to resurrect the home where the sisters had lived.

After they told me their news, they wanted to hear all about what I was doing. I didn't want to tell them about the apartment and how we were living, so I told them about the beautiful quilt we found in the old wardrobe. From then on they called at least once a week. Poppa never asked me about the phone calls. When M. Gianini tapped on the window, that was the signal, and I'd rush off with him without a look back.

Poppa was also reconnecting to those he had been close to before the war, those who were left, like his cousin Vladek who had also lost his family. Vladek was younger than Poppa, and managed to get enough money together to open a barber shop in Brussels. The barber shop was very successful. He invited all of us, Poppa, Mme. Goldman, Sarah, Andrée, the twins, and Jean, to a house he rented near the beach in Blankenberge. An entire month at a resort on the North Sea sounded wonderful, but we had to share the house with another family, so it was very crowded, especially the small bedroom I shared with four other children.

The summer was unusually pleasant for Belgium, with lots of sunshine and soft breezes. I was out walking with Poppa one afternoon and we got separated

77

in a crowd. I will never forget that feeling of being crushed by the jostling crowd. The feeling of no escape, of being lost forever. The police found me sobbing on a bench. I didn't know the address of the beach house and couldn't even tell them where I lived. I remained in the police station for the rest of the day, until Poppa came looking for me.

Everyone seemed to be having a wonderful time except me. I was so afraid of one of the other children—a boy who terrorized me—that I slept on the floor near the open window in case I needed to jump out. None of the adults knew I was sleeping on the floor. They all looked so happy and I didn't want to worry them.

Then one afternoon during our last week, I found myself alone with the boy in the bedroom. He threw me on the bed, and when I saw he was about to put a bottle between my legs, I hit him over the head with the alarm clock. He howled, I screamed, and Sarah burst through the door. Between hiccups and sobs, I told her what happened and she yelled for the boy's mother. He was crouching in the corner crying. When I saw the way his mother was beating and kicking him, I couldn't help feeling sorry for him.

Yet all the misery of that summer was swept aside when we had a surprise visitor at the end of July. It was a day when the normally damp air of Brussels was warm and dry, and even the Rue Ste. Anne got its share of sunshine. I was home with Poppa when we heard a knock on the door. He told me to go open it. It was Maman Thérèse! Maman Thérèse with her round body and beaming face, poking through the door looked like some extraordinary gift. A shiver of

Mindele's Journey

joy rippled through my entire being and I jumped into her arms like a ball through a hoop.

It seemed that Maman Thérèse had heard about the Blankenberge incident when she spoke with M. Gianini, and arrangements were made with Poppa that I would return to Fraiture for the rest of the summer. It felt like Heaven itself had opened up. My heart opened again to Poppa, knowing that he was allowing me to go back to Fraiture.

Maman Thérèse told me later that she would forever remember the day when Poppa had allowed her to take me back for the summer. He had been worried about the cough that plagued him, especially at night when the cold gripped his body like a merciless clamp. And now, after the incident in Blankenberge, he was concerned about my safety. It hadn't been difficult for Maman Thérèse and Tante Marie to convince him that I would be in a safe and loving environment in Fraiture.

At the Gare du Midi Maman Thérèse was holding my suitcase with one hand and trying to hold onto me with the other. But it wasn't easy, for I was so delirious with happiness that I skipped and jumped, enchanted by everything. The people on the platform, food vendors, suitcases being dragged, broken voices dribbling out of loudspeakers, the smell of oil around the trains, all filled me with joy. Yet this was nothing compared to the hissing, billowing clouds of smoke escaping from the massive locomotive. When we climbed aboard I could hardly wait to leave the station.

The journey to Fraiture took several hours. Tante Marie had prepared dinner. Tante Marthe held

Mariette Bermowitz

her arms out like wings ready to enfold me. It had been decided that because of Marthe's poor health she would not return to Odeigne and her position as *maitresse*. I basked in the attention of my "three mothers." Maman Thérèse, with the warmth she emanated, was the heart of the household. Tante Marie, with her intellectual skills, was the mind of the house. And Tante Marthe, with her otherworldly fragility, was the spirit.

Tante Marthe was striking looking, a bit taller than her sisters and quite slender, which made everything she wore look like high fashion. I thought her beautiful. She in turn called me *une adorable petite fille*, which forged a special bond between us. Her gray-green eyes added to the drama of her moody nature. It was a moodiness she might have inherited from her father, an orphan, who had spent a lonely childhood in the servant quarters of a grand house.

While the town of Fraiture was rebuilding itself, the members of M. le Curé's household were settling into their roles. Maman Thérèse was now able to put her home economics education to broader uses, serving exceptional dishes to the priests who visited M. le Curé. He proudly referred to her as "chef in residence." Her reputation grew over the years as her skills became more and more refined. Priests were now volunteering to come to Fraiture to assist in celebrating important masses and events. For these occasions Maman Thérèse researched her special dishes in *L'Art Culinaire Moderne,* a cookbook she called her bible. From this enormous volume I was taught the cooking terms that would foster a life-long pursuit of matters relating to the delights not

Mindele's Journey

only of fine dining, but also the art of presentation. Maman Thérèse had a new garden, much larger than the one behind the schoolhouse. She was in charge of most of the household tasks and she went about doing her chores singing her favorite tunes as if she was in a perennial waltz with life.

Tante Marie prepared her lessons for the fall term and tested me so that I would be prepared for school on my return to Brussels in September. Once a week she held choir practice for Sunday Mass. When no one else was using the church she slipped in to play her favorite pieces on the organ. I always hoped she would ask me to join her, and then I listened intently to her renditions of Bach. When she made mistakes she bit her lower lip to avoid saying something she might regret. It made me laugh to think of Tante Marie using swear words. Tante Marthe didn't have a particular job, she just went around arranging things. I tagged along behind her as she put flowers in vases and folded the freshly laundered towels and linens. She often went to an enormous armoire and made sure everything was stacked in neat piles. She also checked to see if the metal box was safely hidden between some sheets. This was where the week's money was kept, as well as what was left of the family jewelry retrieved from the debris of their former home.

As there was no need any longer to hide my identity, it became known around the village that the little girl who had been there during the war was Jewish. They were curious to meet the brown-eyed child who looked so different from the others. Unlike the war years, I now accompanied my aunts on outings in the village. We passed Yvonne and Zélie's farm and watched the sheep being shorn. Zélie was the only person in Fraiture who had refused to evacuate. She said she wanted to remain with her cows. Yvonne showed me how to milk her favorite cow. On other visits her brother gave me a ride on the back of his motorcycle. He had spent most of the war years in a German prisoner of war camp and was now getting back to farming. He never stopped reminding me that those *sales boches* (lousy krauts) were now paying for it.

I was acquiring a large extended family. There was old Emilie who knew many fairy tales, and Mme. Minet, whose dry goods store was now housed in a makeshift barrack filled with an assortment of merchandise just waiting for me to discover. Mme. Minet had lost her husband in a German labor camp. She always looked as if she had been crying, but what a nice smile she gave me when I chose a piece of cloth. The cloth was for my new outfit. Tante Marthe said, "You should have a pretty skirt made before starting school." She pointed to a striking plaid. "All wool, and it will be so warm for the winter. It will last too. When you grow, we can lengthen it by putting in another pretty pattern on the bottom." In those days, things were made to last. When we outgrew them, pieces would be added to lengthen sleeves and the hems of dresses. She spoke with such conviction that I knew the skirt would be mine forever, growing as I grew. Red plaid has since become my favorite pattern.

We took the fabric to Jeanne the dressmaker, who lived with her husband and children in an old water mill below the village. What an adventure walk-

Mindele's Journey

ing down a steep dirt road through the woods until we came out at the river! Jeanne gave us a hearty welcome and invited us to sit down and eat some of her freshly baked bread with homemade butter and applesauce. Aside from her sewing skills, Jeanne was known to bake the crustiest loaves in the region. The taste lingered on my tongue as I listened to the sound of water clapping against the wooden wheel. Tante Marthe brought me back many times for fittings, and always Jeanne was ready with more fresh baked treats.

Though I could not invite children to come play in the rectory, I became very close with the other Mariette, the girl whose mother was killed so tragically during the war. After her choir practice we often disappeared into the pantry to play. Since we had no toys we invented our own. I showed her the picture postcards I found in the attic, and we cut them up to use as colorful backgrounds on the miniature stage for our paper dolls. When the fair came to town we went to see the gypsies set up their tents. The aunts told me to be careful because there was talk that gypsies stole things, and sometimes children disappeared when the gypsies were around. But I wasn't afraid of them. After Mariette and I stopped to talk to the young gypsy girls, she said I looked just like them. Perhaps that was the reason I wasn't afraid.

The wonderful day at the fair when Mariette and I went on all the rides, sealed in my mind that first summer back at Fraiture. I would return every holiday. Christmas, then Easter, when every flower and bit of grass seemed to shout joy to the world, and of course summer. The long summers when I would sit in the garden and watch the harvest in the fields beyond. Once, I saw a boy kissing a girl from choir practice. Another time I saw M. le Curé holding hands with Tante Marthe. I think that was when I realized she was in love with him. I'm sure he loved her too, in his own discreet way. There was no mistaking the gentle way he talked to her and held her hand when she was sick. When she didn't join us at dinner, he wasn't his usual cheerful self. Her sisters knew of their deep affection for one another, and that nothing could ever come of it.

At the end of the summer it took all their skill to prepare me for the difficult transition I faced in going back to Brussels. But I would be starting a real school for the first time, and I was easily distracted by new notebooks and pens and the wooden box with colored pencils and erasers. I felt reassured knowing that I had everything I needed to be like the other children. And then, because I had told Maman Thérèse I didn't like it when the man upstairs in the Rue Ste. Anne watched me whenever I came out into the courtyard to wash my hair, she gave me a special toiletry bag. "Isn't that a wonderful thing?" she said. "Now you won't have to wash up in the courtyard with the neighbors looking on." I would take my new purse with my initials that maman had filled with toiletries, and go with the other children on the monthly excursion to the public baths.

My new clothes were laid out neatly on the bed, ready to be packed in a brand-new suitcase with lots of little pockets inside. Maman Thérèse had sewn down the pleats of the red plaid skirt so it wouldn't crease.

Mindele's Journey

I was to wear it for my first day in school with the white cotton blouse I had chosen. The old suitcase I had come with had been thrown away as soon as I arrived in Fraiture. There were bugs inside. There had been bugs on my head as well. I had been given a good scrubbing and my old clothes were thrown out. When I went back to Brussels I would have to check for bugs every day so as not to contaminate these beautiful new things.

I also helped Maman Thérèse fill my favorite cookies with mocha cream, and promised her I would share them with others and not eat them all at once. Before I left, Tante Marthe walked me through the village to say good-bye to all the people I had met during that idyllic summer. The excursion was worthwhile because I came back to the house loaded with presents, including lots of shiny coins to start the school year in Brussels. I was taking back with me such a wonderful new suitcase filled with treasures, I almost forgot where I was returning to. I cried the entire morning I was to leave. I kept saying, "How can I talk to Poppa? He doesn't speak French! And I don't like Mme. Goldman. She looks so mean with her white face and gray hair hanging down her back like strings. And Jean looks so strange when he makes those faces and sounds."

It would take the entire journey back to Brussels for Maman Thérèse to explain why *mon papa* needed me back. She promised that one day I would understand how much he loved me. After all, he had allowed me to return to Fraiture, hadn't he? I conceded this was so, but I still couldn't bear the thought of going back to the awful Rue Ste. Anne.

85

Maman Thérèse walked me to school on opening day, introducing herself to Mme. Biezemans, who was going to be my teacher for the next five years at the *Ecole Communale no. 11.* My new teacher came up to the bench where I was waiting and stroked my face. I knew from that moment on that we were going to have a very special relationship.

Before Maman Thérèse left, she reassured Poppa that he didn't have to worry about school, M. Gianini would call her if there were any problems. I watched as she slowly made her way up the street. When she reached the top she took out a handkerchief and waved before disappearing around the corner. I stood there for a while, staring at the empty space where she had been. When I came back into the house it seemed to smell worse than ever.

Poppa had lit the gas fixture in the kitchen and it cast a yellow glow over the grimness of the room. I ran into the bedroom and looked up to the rooftops for a glimpse of my angel, the statue of Gabriel in his shimmering gold coat, and I prayed for the next holiday to come quickly so I could go back to Fraiture. I knew Gabriel would always be there, sending my prayers up to Heaven.

By the time I was eight years old, Poppa no longer had to accompany me to school. It was a moment of triumph, being allowed to take off on my own. It rained almost all the time but I didn't mind. I rarely took an umbrella when I walked to school, though it might be pouring buckets on my way home. And then

Mindele's Journey

the sewers would overflow and the sidewalks would be flooded. On those days I stood in a doorway watching the rain under the streetlamps become rivulets of shimmering crystal. Or I would stop and talk to M. Mombassa at the entrance of the paper mill where he greeted the workers as they came in for their shift. M. Mombassa was born in Kinshasa, the capital of the Belgian Congo, but he had come to Brussels a long time ago. He showed me Kinshasa on the large map that decorated the wall inside the main corridor. I could always depend on seeing his tall frame at the entrance, black as the man on the Banania box in Maman Thérèse's kitchen. M. Mombassa was always the first person I would meet on the way home who would say hello to me, and who listened when I told him about my good grades.

I took my time walking back from school, as I was never eager to get home. I skipped down the cobblestones, stopping in fascination at the shops. The wide storefront windows were always brightly lit, no matter how gray the weather. First there would be the antique shops, then the stores selling books and toys, and lastly the local patisserie where I would mentally devour trays of perfectly decorated pastries and chocolates laid out on the counter. Sometimes I went in and bought myself a treat with the money I received in Fraiture. Then I would feel guilty because I never bought anything home to give to the others. I felt even worse when we started reciting poetry in school with lessons on kindness and charity.

As I grew older I became more aware that we lived in a slum. By the time I was nine I was coming home from school during lunch recess, and from noon to two o'clock I cleaned the house. But everything had gotten shabbier in the three years we'd been living there. Poppa had set up his sewing machine next to the window in the room that served as kitchen and workshop. Under the broken mantelpiece was an old coal stove with pots always containing some leftover food. The table was a wooden board laid across two barrels and covered by a sheet. The sheet hid the barrels, and also the boxes and suitcases of old clothes stored underneath. Poppa's irons were kept warm on the two gas burners that were always leaking and needing repair. In the corner was the bed where he slept with Mme. Goldman. But when they argued, which became more frequent as time went on, she would end up sleeping with me in the bedroom I shared with Jean. I dreaded Mme. Goldman's presence in my bed even more than the bedbugs because she hardly ever washed.

But the bedbugs were horrible. It didn't matter how many I squashed against the sheets, their numbers kept on multiplying. In the morning I would count the new red streaks and scratches on my skin, but eventually they just became part of life, and part of me. I was too ashamed to tell my teacher about them. My aunts knew, of course. When I went to Fraiture, my suitcase would be left outside, all of my clothes immediately dumped into a wash tub and my head checked for lice.

It would be another year before Poppa bought me a new mattress. But it didn't matter whether I had a new mattress or not, because the bedbugs remained. Meanwhile, Mme. Goldman had taken up permanent residence in my bed. I could no longer read under the quilt with my flashlight. My "tent" had become so streaked with blood from those horrible creatures (called *punaises,* because they resembled thumbtacks), that I refused to sleep with the quilt until it had a new cover.

On one of my secret forays into the wardrobe I found a picture of my mother. It was stuck behind another photograph and I almost tore it trying to pull them apart. I knew it was my mother. She was already married to my father because she was pregnant. I sat looking at her for a while, imagining myself inside her, and then I got up and went to the mirror wondering if I could see her face in mine. I felt a terrible sadness not knowing anything about her, and the more I looked at the picture the more intense the feeling became. But then a strange thing happened. I started to feel her presence. I slipped under the quilt and pretended it was her warmth I was now pulling over my head. The quilt had been a part of her, though in a way I was yet to discover. The thought of all those little pieces so lovingly sewn together would accompany me throughout my life, as if she was following me on my journey. Even then, I resented Mme. Goldman sharing my heirloom, and desperately wanted to keep it clean.

In school I had three friends, Yvette, Annie, and Danielle. I liked Yvette Rosenstein a lot, partly because she was the only other Jewish girl in my class, and partly because with her blond hair and sweet face she reminded me of my doll Yvette. But she lived in the wealthy part of town, and when she invited me to her birthday party and I saw her room, a pink palace where dolls lived in a beautiful cream cabinet, I was overwhelmed with jealousy. It wasn't until we had dessert that I felt more on an equal footing, because it was strawberries with crème Chantilly, and it had nothing on the strawberries Maman Thérèse served. Maman Thérèse had taken me to Wepion where the best strawberries were grown, and brought some pots back to plant in the garden behind the rectory. The vines quickly spread into thick green patches where the ruby-colored fruit hung on little stems like gorgeous jewels. I helped her gather the pails of fruit that she prepared for the most exquisite *confiture aux fraises* for miles around. She had saved the best of the harvest to be dipped in melted chocolate and gave me a box to take home to Poppa.

I remained in fierce competition with Yvette for the duration of my time in the *Ecole Communale no. 11*. We competed against one another for the top honors and prizes at the end of each school year. I don't know what Yvette did with her prizes, but my winnings became the beginning of a collection I called *ma bibliothèque*, books with my name below "First Prize" on the inside cover. I didn't dare invite Yvette to my house. I always felt inferior when she talked about all the things she had and where her parents were going on their next holiday. So I talked about the things I owned in my house in the country, like the marionette and the miniature theater, the bicycle, and the tea set.

I was more relaxed with Annie who thought I was very intelligent. Annie shared her sweets with me

Mindele's Journey

when we sat together on the bus during school outings. She had the best comics, *Spirou, Tintin,* which she brought into the schoolyard during recess. We would read and eat sweets and laugh hysterically when we saw boys from the other schoolyard trying to climb the fence to get to us. Annie took ballet. I loved hearing her talk about the ballet classes. She tried teaching me the *pas de deux, jeter,* and *plier,* but I was hopeless. Besides, I knew that Poppa could never afford dancing lessons.

The library, however, was free. I usually spent my afternoons in the library, reading and doing homework before going home. Books were my salvation, and I was determined to read every single volume in the library. I would sit for hours in my favorite corner, losing myself in the stories and tales that allowed me to escape to a distant realm. When I was off in my fantasy world, life on the Rue Ste. Anne seemed just pretend.

When Melle. Vroemans, the librarian, found me reading Greek and Roman mythology in the adult section, she introduced me to the books of a Russian countess, the author known as La Comtesse de Ségur. Exiled in France, the countess had recreated her Russian childhood in novels, describing the lavish world of the Russian aristocracy during the first half of the nineteenth century. Being poor and Jewish, I didn't think I would have been allowed inside her chateau, but I lived the adventures in my mind. I dreamed of the *petites filles modèles* in the Chateau de Fleurville in the French countryside, and longed for their pink satin dresses and crowns of fresh daisies placed on their long shiny braids. I tried to imagine

Mariette Bermowitz

what it must have been like every morning when the countess greeted her children at breakfast. I pictured her touching their foreheads delicately with her long porcelain fingers, while the pastel-colored ribbons she wore as bracelets fluttered from her wrists.

The closest I ever came to that world were the games I invented to entertain my doll Yvette. Poor Yvette! She had been given to me that long ago Christmas in Theux with Sister Reine Marie's family. Her dimpled face was still smiling though one of her legs was beginning to detach itself from the frayed rubber string holding it to the rest of her body. She was very fragile. I had learned how to sew and knit so I could dress her in the latest creations I found in *La Semaine de Suzette* magazines. Mme. Biezemans, my teacher, had contributed a yellow and brown knitted pants suit that included a miniature belt and rhinestone buckle. It covered Yvette's leg, hiding the bad place where she was beginning to come apart.

Mme. Biezemans had given me this gift sometime after Open School Week. She asked me why no one ever came to admire my notebooks and schoolwork exhibited each semester. I started to cry as I told her that Poppa was too sick to come, and my aunts in Fraiture said it was too far away for them to come. Mme. Biezemans tried to cheer me up by promising that my notebooks would be shown to the *Directrice*, and I would certainly be nominated for the prizes at the end of the school year, as I had achieved top honors in all my subjects.

Danielle often came to the library too, and we started walking home together along the Rue de Ruysbroeck. I told her I was Jewish and spent my

Mindele's Journey

vacations in Fraiture. I never spoke about my mother and family members who had died during the war. Poppa told me not to give family details to outsiders. I didn't know very much about our family anyway, except for the discoveries I was making in the wardrobe. I could not explain to anyone what I was remembering, except perhaps to the angel statue above the rooftops. I often confided in him, telling him how lonely I was not to have friends invite me to their homes. I asked him why my mother had to die. To calm myself, and block out the emptiness, I sang like Mme. Goldman did when she was sad, except my songs were loud and joyful. I sang in all the languages I knew—French, Flemish, Yiddish, Walloon, and even the Polish lullaby I remembered my mother singing to me. When the cacophony of sounds streamed through the open window and filled the courtyard, Mme. Charpentier leaned out the window and shouted, "What are you singing about?" *La vie madame, la vie!* I cried.

Feeling very reckless one day, I invited Danielle to my house before she headed up the Rue de Ruysbroeck on her way home. "There are so many things I want to show you!" I said excitedly. She had to ask her mother first, and when her mother agreed, I asked her to come by on the afternoon I knew Poppa and Mme. Goldman would be out. I could hardly contain myself with the thrill of finally having a friend over. But Danielle came with her mother, and as soon as they walked through the door and I saw her mother's face, I knew our friendship was doomed. With a withering glance, Danielle's mother took stock of our apartment. Poppa's sewing

Mariette Bermowitz

machine, the old stove, the dirty windows, the irons resting on the gas stove, the washbasin and pail underneath. She stared at the pail and the wash basin for a few seconds, then held her nose. "Ugggghhhhh," she cried, and ran from the room shouting, *Oh, ces sales Juifs!*

I couldn't believe it. I had tried so hard to clean up the room before they came, making extra trips to the courtyard to wash out the pail. But it wasn't good enough for this woman with her tidy, orderly existence. In the freezing winter months, the pail served as our WC. The bathroom was only a crude hole in some wooden planks in the outhouse in the back. It was quite an undertaking to mount the wooden slats, and many times I would miss the hole because it was so high up. I was cold, my fingers were stiff, and often I couldn't undress myself fast enough. It became more convenient to have a pail near the bed in case Poppa needed it at night. The smell had become ordinary, just another sad fact of our lives.

Danielle remained my friend despite her mother, and never mentioned the visit to my house. After a while I no longer minded not having friends over to visit. I still had the library, and now that Poppa had enrolled me in the Yeshiva I was busier than ever. He wanted me to know about Judaism, especially when he began to suspect that I hadn't given up on my Catholic prayers. I didn't tell him that I went to catechism with Tante Marie every Sunday I was in Fraiture. I wanted to be confirmed and wear a pretty dress like the other girls, but Maman Thérèse said that *mon papa* would never agree to that. It didn't

Mindele's Journey

matter. I knew in my heart how special I was to Him who knew everything.

I didn't like the Yeshiva. The classes were very noisy and most of the students already knew Hebrew. Many of them were being prepared to go to *Erets Izroel,* the Promised Land that had just been opened to European Jews. Cécile and Renée, Mme. Goldman's twin daughters would be going very soon.

Poppa, Mme. Goldman, Jean, and I visited them regularly in the home for displaced children. We brought whatever food or sweets Mme. Goldman could afford to buy. They were only a few years older than me and I thought of them as sisters. Cécile and Renée had spent the war years with a Catholic family not far from where I had been in Banneux. They seemed eager to go to the Promised Land, talking at length about Theodore Herzl and Zionism and the kibbutz where they were being sent. I always felt terrified during these visits, afraid that Poppa was going to ship me off there as well. We often stayed the night, sleeping in the large dormitory overlooking a winding river. While I lay in bed listening to the water splashing against the rocks, I prayed as hard as I could not to be sent to the Promised Land, because then I would never see Fraiture or the aunts again. But as I fell asleep to the sound of the current rushing downstream, I felt in my heart that Poppa would never part with me so randomly.

The night before Cécile and Renée left for Israel, they stayed with us on the Rue Ste. Anne. The three of us slept in the same bed, cramped and tangled in our oversized nightshirts, giggling late into the night as we searched for bedbugs. When they left the next

Mariette Bermowitz

morning in clothes long outgrown, I gave them each some gifts to remember me by. Old books and a beat-up cigar box with postcards of lovers holding hands and street scenes of old Brussels. I gave them sheets of my stationery rimmed with roses and daisies, or swallows in flight, and some recent pictures of the three of us taken in a photographer's studio.

This bounty had been part of the stash of make-shift toys I hid in the credenza in the bedroom along with the wrappings saved from the chocolates Sarah brought when she came to visit her mother, Mme. Goldman. My father liked Sarah. His mood always picked up when she came to visit, bringing fruit and sweet milky chocolates. Jean and I tore open the paper with gray elephants, then the aluminum foil underneath. Long after the chocolate had been devoured the aroma lingered in the foil. I would press it to my nostrils, smelling the remnants and imagining the arrival of the next treat.

I wrote down Cécile and Renée's address in Israel so that I would be able to tell them news of Poppa and me and Jean and Mme. Goldman. I was the only one who could write. Though I had spent many an afternoon teaching Jean what I was learning in school, the enterprise wasn't much of a success. He was such a gentle boy, and when I saw how frightened he was of everything, I began coaxing him out of the house by promising we would go to a Laurel and Hardy movie on the Rue Haute. He fell in love with Laurel and Hardy right away, laughing joyfully, just as he did when he watched me talking to the green mustached faucet in the courtyard outside our window. On the way home we held hands and talked

Mindele's Journey

about Laurel and Hardy, and Jean made his strange faces. People stared, but I just squeezed his hand as hard as I could and laughed with him as if I hadn't a care in the world.

Before reaching the Rue Ste. Anne we stopped in Wittamer, the bakery on the Place du Grand Sablon where little cakes and tarts positively shimmered behind the window. Row after row of twisted, fluted, curled chocolate creations beckoned from glass cases. On the shelves below were puff pastries bursting with custard or praline mocha cream, beside blueberry, raspberry and strawberry tarts. Each name more mouth-watering than the next. My favorite was the cream-filled puff pastry swan. With coins from Fraiture I bought two swans filled with crème patissière. Jean and I sat and stared at our reflections in the gilded mirrors of the bakery, watching ourselves as we indulged in those edible luxuries.

Although Poppa and Mme. Goldman argued a lot, there were times when they seemed almost happy. Which made me happy too, because that was when she slept in the other room with Poppa, and I had the bed all to myself again. Often when I was alone in the bedroom I opened the wardrobe to look at the beautiful clothes that had belonged to my sister Esther. The wardrobe was big enough so that I could step inside. There were so many boxes, so many reminders of lives that now rested only in things. I sat in the corner where the quilt had been, and when I closed the door almost all the way, the strange smells took on a life of their own. I would imagine my mother with a handful of mothballs, or have a vision of Esther daubing perfume onto a handkerchief, stuffing papers and photographs into her patent leather pocketbook.

On one of my excursions into the closet I discovered the black crepe dress. It was hanging under the fur coat. Even in the dim light I recognized the red embroidered flowers carefully sewn on the front panel. Esther had been wearing the dress in her engagement picture taken with her fiancé, Jean. There was still a whiff of her perfume on the dress. I stepped out of the wardrobe and took off my skirt and blouse. Then, ever so carefully, I slipped into the soft perfumed folds of the black dress. It hung around me like a magnificent ball gown. As I looked at myself in the mirror again, I imagined I saw Esther's face staring back at me. From that day on I kept the dress and photo hidden from the other things in the wardrobe, so that not even Poppa would find them. I felt they belonged only to me, just as I knew my mother's quilt belonged to me. And though I hardly knew it yet, in protecting my heirlooms I was safeguarding my stories, my history, my survival.

Maybe because Mme. Goldman was sleeping with him again, Poppa started feeling better. Or maybe it was because of the bowls. I came home from school one day to find her putting strange little glass bowls on his bare back. I watched as she took a lighted match and swished it around inside the glass before placing it on his skin. It made a popping noise, and then his skin swelled up into little mounds inside the glass bowl. It was frightening to see those little purple

Mindele's Journey

mounds swelling up on my father's bony frame. He moaned as Mme. Goldman went on with her swooshing. Her hair was now combed and folded into a neat bun held in by lovely combs on the back of her head. With her hair swept off her face it was possible to notice her fine features, her skin white as alabaster.

Mme. Goldman was also cooking now. I never cared for her chopped liver or chicken soup, thinking it greasy, but she had a knack for gefilte fish. Her pickled cucumbers were also a success. They could be seen from the street marinating in large glass jars on the window sill. No one was allowed to touch them until Mme. Goldman pronounced them ready, which was only when the brine turned an opaque shade of gray. Jean and I used to go to the market with her to help carry the baskets of food. I didn't like it when she chose the live carp for her famous gefilte fish, and found it best not to look, just concentrate on the result. There were few dishes of hers that I liked. Maman Thérèse had spoiled me. For how could I forget the succulent chicken, the duck and paté, the *boudin blanc*, the venison that graced M. le Curé's table?

Aside from Mme. Goldman's renewed attentions, Poppa was working full time, which in itself made him feel good. He had also reconnected with old friends. They were all in the clothing business, and dressed as if they were going to a party, with handkerchiefs in their lapel pockets and a comb hidden in a pocket, just in case. I've never seen my father

Mariette Bermowitz

as happy as when his bunch of cronies came to visit. They *kibitzed,* talked shop, talked about their plans for the future, the hope of finding lost family members, and *Eretz Izroel.* When they talked about women they lowered their voices so I shouldn't hear. But by then I knew Yiddish again, and was mesmerized by their discussions.

Mme. Goldman made tea for these reunions. I loved being included in this group of men who made my father laugh. Poppa had a nickname for each one, so I never called them by their real names. My father being of a diminutive height and his best friend taller by a foot, they resembled a comedy team and were referred to as *De Lange und De Kleine* (the stretched one and the little one), which they enjoyed very much. Two of Poppa's other friends were Vonssele because of his mustache, and De Rőete for his dazzling red hair. I was in love with De Lange. Not only did he tell me jokes and buy me candy, but he taught me how to roller skate in the Bois de la Cambre, a lovely park on the outskirts of Brussels. The whole family went, Poppa, Mme. Goldman, and Jean. They sat in the café surrounding the rink while De Lange and I waltzed around on skates, oblivious to the thunderous sound of the metal wheels. He held me tightly by one hand as I waved toward the family, enthralled as much by the dance as by my partner.

I was to find out what real lovers were like when Sarah, joined by her beautiful cousin Etka, came to the Rue Ste. Anne. The sun had finally peeked through the dusty gray sky hanging like a tarpaulin over the city for weeks. Spring was in the air. It even

Mindele's Journey

blew away the stale odors of the hallway. Poppa, his cousin Vladek, and Der Rőete were drinking tea in small glasses, pouring some of the hot liquid into the saucers to cool it off. This was accompanied by a slurping sound before the plate was emptied of its amber color. Little poppy seed cookies were stacked on the table, filling the room with their fragrance. Not even Poppa's cigarettes bothered me.

I sat in the little chair I had claimed exclusively mine so it would be kept clean, and watched them closely. I was to write a story for school, telling the class how we spent Sunday afternoons in our house. There were certain things Poppa told me never to talk about, which I wouldn't have wanted to share anyway, like how our living quarters resembled those in the Charles Dickens story I read in the library. But I could write about Poppa's friends. The laughter and perfume. Vladek's elegant suit. The way Der Rőete's red hair caught a beam of sunshine through the window. I remember admiring the sun in his red hair when there was a knock at the door, and when he opened the door he stood still as a plaster mummy. It was the two lovely cousins, two of the most beautiful women he had ever seen, he would say later. Sarah, Mme. Goldman's daughter, had blond hair and blue eyes. Etka was just the opposite with black hair down to her shoulders and large almond-shaped hazel eyes. Der Rőete stuttered as he introduced himself, and then Vladek bolted toward the door as if he had been stung by a bee, and Vonssele introduced himself as well, bowing before the beauties.

The room seemed to shrink when the women entered. The men gave up their seats and stood

101

awkwardly with their hands in their pockets. Poppa offered cigarettes around. Then it was decided that they would all go to the Bois de la Cambre to join Mme. Goldman and Jean who had gone to the Café Métropole for the best *café Liégeois* in Brussels. I stayed home to write my story for school.

That day was the beginning of Etka's many visits to the Rue Ste. Anne. De Rőete had fallen madly in love with her. Poppa's cousin Vladek was in love with Sarah. Sarah still lived in Liège and worked in a jewelry shop. After the war her husband had been arrested for having collaborated with the Germans, and upon his release he disappeared, leaving behind his young wife and child. No one ever heard from him again. Sarah had been questioned by the police, but was cleared of any suspicion when the story came out how she helped her Jewish family and friends to survive. Sarah was now preoccupied with raising her daughter Andrée. She was also concerned about her mother and Jean living with my father in Brussels. She had actually brought Etka with her on a rescue mission to take them back with her that Sunday in Brussels, but Cupid had intervened.

Vladek, a successful businessman with the means to impress the ladies, took charge of everything. On weekends when Sarah and Etka came up from Liège to visit with us, they found flowers and chocolates upon their arrival. There was always a special treat for me as well, but what I enjoyed most were the outings in the Bois de la Cambre, or afternoons spent on the terrace of a café. I always tried to sit next to Etka because her perfume reminded me of Esther. I thought Etka looked just like my sister in the photo-

Mindele's Journey

graphs. On the way home, Etka held my hand when Der Rőete walked ahead with Vladek. On one of those occasions I told her about Esther, and was surprised to learn Etka had met her and my mother before the war on a visit to Liège. Etka assured me that, yes, Esther was very beautiful and so was my mother, pregnant with me at the time. She promised to tell me more when I got a bit older so I wouldn't forget.

Meanwhile Vladek and Der Rőete were now traveling to Liège in order to spend entire weekends with their sweethearts. When Poppa told me Etka would not be coming to Brussels for a while I couldn't help feeling betrayed. But then we were invited to visit Etka in Valenciennes, France, where she lived with her parents, Malka and Samuel. Malka was Mme. Goldman's sister. I learned how Etka's family survived the war at the Passover Seder, when everyone was sitting around the table telling stories. During the war years they were living in the cellar of their lingerie factory, helped by loyal and trusted employees. With money hidden in a secret vault, after the war they were able to rebuild the business, which was now headed by Etka and her brother George.

Valenciennes was a gray and dreary city in northern France famous for the delicate lace sought after for the bridal gowns of Europe's upper classes. It is said the icy blue in Watteau's paintings was inspired by the color of the sky in Valenciennes after the winter rain washed away the clouds. The city's textile industry attracted skilled foreigners from as far away as Poland, like Etka's parents. Early in the century the brutality of the Cossacks and the pogroms, and then the Revolution, had driven them from their shtetl. They took nothing

Mariette Bermowitz

with them but the clothes on their backs and the gold jewelry sewn into the lining of their coats. Samuel, Etka's father, had an uncle, Moishe, who had made it to France and was dealing in cloth. The family seldom heard from Moishe. Then finally a letter arrived addressed to his nephew Samuel, convincing him that France was the place to be. Etka showed me his letter dated 1919.

Dearest Samuel and family:

I haven't been able to write to you sooner because I have been so busy setting up my shop. I finally found a place with large windows to attract all the ladies in the neighborhood. Everything I make is for the ladies! You should see the quality of the materials and the lace! What patterns, what colors, what variety! It is unbelievable that I should have such *mazel,* especially with the beauties who come in. *La Crème de la Crème,* I tell you, who wear only the best, and whose perfume could drive a man crazy.

They come in with their chauffeurs in motor-driven carriages. *Oy,* what a racket it makes on those cobbled streets. But never mind. It's quiet at night and romantic with the gaslights lining the streets. I only wish I could find a suitable girl who'd want to spend her life with me. Maybe you could tell the rabbi. Never mind. I have plenty of company for now. I have a wonderful apartment. I cook, I shop, and I spend money. You wouldn't believe the markets, the fresh fruits and vegetables. Like you've never seen in your life!

Mindele's Journey

And how are you? I read about the political situation in Poland and I worry about you. I hope and wish from the bottom of my heart that you will leave soon. You will always have a place with me. Of course, we have our problems here too; lots of *tsurres* (problems and pain) after the war. But not like where you are. Those *mishigines* with their ideas and brutality will not come to a good end, I tell you. I could write you a book but I want to send you this letter so you know I'm alive. Write me, and tell me everything about the family and especially how you and Malka are doing.
Your loving uncle, Moishe

A month later Samuel arrived in Valenciennes with his wife Malka, sister to Mme. Goldman. They found Uncle Moishe living in two small rooms that faced a courtyard. This was only the beginning of their disappointment, but there was no going back. It wasn't that uncle Moishe had lied, "only exaggerated a little," according to him, and they knew his heart was in the right place. After much protesting, Samuel and Malka accepted the bedroom. Moishe would sleep in the kitchen.

Little by little, life according to Moishe was revealed to the new immigrants. Not only did he exaggerate a little, but he had acquired some very Gallic tendencies. The most obvious was an appreciation for expensive French wines, especially Bordeaux. He had a few bottles hidden in a box and opened one the night of their arrival. Not being wine drinkers, they didn't understand how anyone would be

Mariette Bermowitz

so crazy for a drink that left such foul odor on your breath!

When confronted by the bleak situation they found themselves in, Samuel asked Moishe what happened. *Voos hot passiert?* Little by little, the story of Moishe's financial problems came out. Those fancy "ladies" he mentioned in his letter, well, he had been taken in by one of them. Perfume, fancy clothes, money, the works! Moishe looked away as he recalled the devilish allurements of the world and his inability to resist beautiful women. But Samuel, a survivor of pogroms, soon had the situation under control.

"Listen, Moishe, do you still have the shop?"

"I do, but it isn't so big and it hasn't such fancy customers."

"Never mind. We are going to figure something out. First we rest then we go have a look at this shop of yours."

Within weeks Samuel had a plan. The shop was certainly not what he expected, but with a major cleaning and Malka's organization, only good things would happen. After all, wasn't he a talented tailor, and his darling Malka the best seamstress in the world? Not only was Malka the best seamstress in the world, she was also the best cook. Uncle Moishe soon found that the most incredible *mazel* to come into his life was when Malka took over his humble kitchen. One thing he had not exaggerated about was the refined palate he had acquired as a bachelor and connoisseur of good wine and good food. Malka found his little kitchen with its country table and chairs and wooden cabinets had a certain charm. It

Mindele's Journey

wasn't long before she was conjuring up some of her best dishes.

Malka never forgot that first day in the open market in Valenciennes. It looked like a painting to her. There were rows upon rows of greens, oranges, reds, purples, and yellows wanting to be touched and tasted and admired. Slowly she made her way down the covered stands with Samuel and Moishe following behind, delighting in the sounds she made with each new discovery. Moishe charmed the vendors with his courtesy, and they returned home with baskets filled like horns of plenty. That first meal she cooked was a celebration of their freedom, their plans and the *Raboyne Shaloylem* who granted them such love.

Malka felt great pride whenever Samuel recalled how her chicken soup had a reputation in the shtetl, and how she had won his heart with her cooking. When someone tried to bribe her into handing over her secret she would say, "Would David tell Goliath? Would Delilah not make Samson wonder a little? And what about Scheherazade and Esther?" Now in this kitchen, in this new country, she could show off the talents that made her Samuel so proud. Moishe had all the spices she needed lined up in little metal containers on the shelves. She thought Moishe was pretty organized when it came to important things. Malka placed the chicken in a pot of steaming water, removed all the foam that accumulated, and then added the vegetables. Carrots, turnips, celery, dill, and her secret spice, an onion speckled with cloves. Salt and pepper would come later. When Malka emerged from the kitchen with her steaming chicken soup, both Samuel and Moishe once again thanked the *Raboyne Shaloylem* as they sat around the wooden table, which had suddenly taken on a new grandeur.

After dinner they talked late into the night. "Moishe, there is no way that any of us can ever go back to Poland. It's madness there now with the Russian Revolution. Our families are hounded constantly. It's like when the Cossacks came on horseback and threatened to kill us." Samuel's voice broke at the memory. He put a hand over his eyes to hide the tears. Malka put her arms around him. "Samuel, enough is enough. We are here. We have a future and we will succeed."

Moishe agreed. With their talents they were going to turn that little shop into a gold mine. The money and gold hidden in the lining of their coats would be put to good use. They were going to buy cloth, lace, materials. Moishe knew the suppliers and he spoke French, which would make all the transactions so much easier. Samuel would design and cut while Malka, with her flair for beauty, would assemble the most exquisite ladies lingerie Valenciennes had ever seen.

Samuel took out the old bedding that had served to pack up their belongings when they left Poland. It was their *pereneh*, a soft down feather quilt, undeniably the most precious of all the items in a household. This one had been made by Moishe's mother. Moishe cried when he saw it. He saw his mother's face, thought of her hands stitching the pieces of cloth together. He had thought the past was forgotten, cut out of him like the country and customs he had rejected. But now his nephew and his nephew's darling wife had rekindled love and hope. Samuel, noticing how still his uncle had become, put an arm around his shoulder and said, "If only this *pereneh* could talk. We would have stories to take us into the next century."

It was in this *pereneh* that Malka and Samuel fell asleep, but not before Samuel nestled in the warmth of his beloved and shared great pleasure with her. Etka came into the world soon after, her brother George two years later. Their business became the most well-known purveyor of fine lingerie in Valenciennes. Etka and George made an even greater success of it when their parents retired. And so the stories continued around the Passover table.

Poppa and I accompanied Mme. Goldman and Jean to Valenciennes many times. Poppa seemed happy that we were treated as part of her family. He had a photograph taken with Mme. Goldman in a professional shop on the Rue Haute. Her forehead gently grazing his, they looked like they were in love. His smile with the gold tooth was devastating. With her hair neatly piled up on top of her head, she leaned into the camera so that the jewel on her lapel could not be ignored. It was a gold brooch with little diamonds surrounded by rubies. Poppa had bought it for her when his tailoring started to bring in money.

Now that Poppa was making more money, I didn't understand why we didn't move out of the Rue Ste. Anne, away from the smells, the broken furniture, the gloom. When I asked him why, he said it wasn't time yet and I should be patient. Maybe where we lived connected him to the past. The unforgettable sadness he couldn't talk about, yet took refuge in. But he surprised me with gifts as well. He believed in gold and bought me what he considered would not lose value, a gold ring and a gold chain. "Better than in the bank," he said. He also warned me about governments and the lies they told. Then Jean, who often listened to my father's lectures, surprised everyone by saying, "I believe communism is here to stay."

A naah ist immer a naah. "A fool is always a fool," Poppa answered, smacking his lips in disapproval.

On my birthday he gave me a *Mogen David,* the Star of David, with my name on one side and the word *mazel* for good luck on the other. I never wore it except when he asked me to, and then I put it under my blouse so no one would see it. I think Poppa knew what I was thinking, but he was waiting for the right time and place to tell me what he thought of my behavior. He wasn't getting brilliant reports from the Yeshiva either, and withdrew me from the school after the headmaster called him in. He had to take a day off from work to learn that his darling daughter had put thumbtacks on the teacher's chair. He made me go and apologize. I told my father that a *dybbik* made me do it. I hated the Yeshiva anyway. I hated it when the students looked at me when I couldn't answer in Hebrew. Whenever a girl approached me to play or look at my books, I pushed her away, saying, *Laisse-moi tranquille.* "Leave me alone." I was afraid to learn Hebrew. If I learned Hebrew they might send me to

Israel. I was afraid Mme. Goldman would send me off to a kibbutz to join her twins, Cécile and Renée.

I didn't want people to know I was Jewish. I didn't want to see people turn around when I spoke Yiddish with Poppa. I didn't want to be known as a dirty Jew, *sale Juif,* as Danielle's mother had called me. I knew that being Jewish only meant suffering and being set apart from the others. I didn't want to know about Theodore Herzl and Zionism. I didn't want to go to a kibbutz where I would be one of the orphans who were repatriated. I wanted to be surrounded by the love I had known with the aunts in Fraiture. I lived in fear of losing them. Of being sent into the unknown, all alone and without ever being able to go back to the world I knew and loved.

My father later told me that of course he never even considered sending me away. I was the only thing he had left that gave his life meaning.

I was happy when we went to Valenciennes. Etka made me feel special. The way she squinted and arched her eyebrows, even wiggling her nose, made it seem she was listening with her entire face. I told her all my school stories, even the one about the Yeshiva. And when she laughed I knew I had conquered her heart.

I couldn't wait to get to Valenciennes and see the family waiting on the station platform. Sarah and Etka stood so close together they looked like one person, a tussle of blond hair and black, with skirts swept up by the steam engine as it slowed to a halt. What a treat getting into the car and stopping in front of an imposing house. I rushed in and threw myself on the plush sofa in Malka's parlor. Then George would come in, followed by his wife and children, everyone kissing and hugging the visitors from Belgium. I felt part of the family, even though the children didn't want me to play with their toys. I usually ended up in Malka's kitchen with a coloring book, but I didn't mind. The kitchen was a special place to me anyway. There was a black and white tiled floor and doors opening onto a terrace filled with potted plants. Embroidered white curtains framed the windows and tall armoires with piles of neatly arranged dishes with floral patterns lined the walls. Malka was a true homemaker. A *balabusta*. Even though she had a domestic, she insisted on doing her own cooking. I always made sure to be in the kitchen when she prepared our meals, helping her peel, scrape, taste and smell as she shifted her pots and pans about on the stove. Sometimes Etka would come in to taste and give her opinion, and I'd tell them about Maman Thérèse and "our" kitchen in Fraiture.

I loved running back and forth in the hallway, sliding down the polished wooden floor in my socks. Malka was proud of the fact that she polished it herself every week "to make the wood talk," as she said. I never heard the wood speak, but the fragrance in that corridor had its own language.

Our sleeping arrangements in Valenciennes were very unusual. Poppa insisted I sleep in the same bed with him and Mme. Goldman, but he didn't tell me why. When I asked him, he didn't answer. So I found myself sleeping between the two of them

Mindele's Journey

with my head facing their feet. I hated it. I told Etka that my father snored and let out smells at night so that I couldn't sleep. I made it sound much worse than it really was. And when Etka laughed and told me to come sleep with her, I found that it paid to exaggerate.

I couldn't stop talking to Etka or looking at the beautiful things arranged on her dressing table. She let me try on her dresses and shoes as well as all the trinkets in her drawer. What I appreciated most was the way she listened not to my fear of being sent to Israel, but my secret dream of being just like La Comtesse de Ségur.

When we returned to Brussels I hid the presents from Etka, the coloring books and colored pencils and paper dolls, in the wardrobe. At the time they were more precious to me than Poppa's gift of the *Mogen David*. Since Mme. Goldman had returned to my father's bed, I only had to share my domain with Jean, and he preferred the warmth of the kitchen most of the time anyway. One day, seeing him huddled near the coal stove like an animal seeking refuge, I brought him some of the butter cookies filled with mocha cream I'd saved from my last trip to Fraiture. I told Jean that I hadn't exactly helped Maman Thérèse bake the cookies, but I was her apprentice all the same. She allowed me to taste the food at the bottom of the pots after she had emptied them out. She said it was a lesson in taste appreciation, something fine chefs learned early on. She entered the names of recipes in a special notebook, and I was to copy the rest from *La Véritable Cuisine de Famille par*

Tante Marie, which she kept next to her prayer book on an old oak shelf near the kitchen stove.

My lifelong adventure with *La Véritable Cuisine* thus began underneath the perfectly scrolled handwritten notes of Maman Thérèse. The first of those recipes was for the cookies I now shared with Jean, *Petits Beurres fourrés à la crème.* I watched Jean's face transform from its usual grimace into a smile as he took the cookie and put the whole thing in his mouth. "How does that taste?"

He picked the crumbs off his lap and said, *Oh oui, c'est bon, c'est bien bon.*

"Are they better than those at the Wittamer Patisserie?" I teased.

Without pausing he stuffed another cookie into his mouth. *Oh oui, c'est meilleur, c'est meilleur mais j'aime aussi Wittamer.* He still wanted to go to Wittamer.

One of Etka's presents was a box of stationery with borders cut to look like the lace of Valenciennes. In the letters I sent to her, aside from describing my explorations of the city and boasting of winning first prize in poetry recitation, I mentioned my mother's quilt, and said that the bedbugs had come back despite the new mattress. Etka knew about the quilt and promised to have it cleaned on her next visit.

As the days grew shorter and Poppa suddenly started paying attention to my whereabouts, saying he wanted me home earlier, I was afraid the news of my explorations in Brussels had gotten back to him. On my last walk in the Parc Royal with Jean we held hands and meandered through the patchwork of fallen leaves. Then we ran, kicking up a delicious smell of earth and musk. Jean laughed,

Mindele's Journey

and as I looked at him laughing, for some reason I felt like crying. I didn't know why. It was just such a perfect moment, that day in the Parc Royal, and yet it felt like the end of something. It was dark when we returned to the Rue Ste. Anne. The streetlamp lighter was turning on the flame in the gaslights with his big stick. To me it looked like lights going up on a stage and at any moment the actors might appear. I took a bow in the haze of honey light and grabbed Jean's hand as we skipped down the street singing, *Nous sommes au théâtre! Nous sommes au théâtre!* "We're in the theater!"

Our merriment quickly died as soon as we came into the house. Poppa was sitting at his sewing machine, making a thunderous clattering sound as his foot worked the treadle. The air, as always, was stale with cigarette smoke. I looked at his back hunched over the table and thought how thin he was, emaciated really. His face reminded me of the pictures he kept in a drawer. The horrible pictures of people who were no more than skeletons, their eyes so deeply recessed they looked almost hollow. I watched him now, gripping a seam so tightly I was afraid the bones in his hand might crack. Frail though he appeared, Poppa was still one of the finest tailors. His friend Jakobowicz said that my father's work was much in demand on the Rue Haute, which was hardly surprising, as he approached the making of a suit as an artist would a painting. First, there were the sketches, then swatches of material, canvas lining, padding, fillings, and finally paper patterns that hung on the wall. Sometimes the patterns got wet from the humidity and he had to cut new ones.

115

When he held them up they made me think of a human being in the making. He placed the material on the table and carefully traced a line around the pattern with a piece of chalk. Next came the canvas that was to fit between the cloth and the lining. "That's what makes the difference between a man and a mensch," he would say. When I asked him what it meant, he said, "Well, a man will buy a suit that looks good on him, but a mensch wants to tell the world that it was his tailor who made him look so good."

Sometimes, this attitude created problems for my father. He was such a perfectionist that before he could complete a suit, the customer had to have at least three or four fittings. Poppa would mold a little canvas here, a little canvas there, "To give a lift where nature forgot," he said, laughing at the innuendo I was too young to understand. I will never forget the day I came home during one of those fittings when the conversation between Poppa and a customer had reached cataclysmic proportions.

"It's not necessary," said the customer, a rather large man whose body didn't seem to have any definition except for a billowing midsection. He had no neck, and his head sat on his shoulders like an ostrich egg. My father wanted to readjust what nature had left out, and was trying to convince him that padding the shoulders would proportion the fit.

"No, I don't want any stuffing!" the man shouted.

His voice was so loud I could hear him clear out on the street. I came inside the house just as my father shouted, "You *putz*, you! I'm trying to make you look like a *mensch*!"

Mindele's Journey

All hell broke loose. I felt sure that if my father hadn't been so small and frail, he would surely have landed through the window along with the stuffing. Instead, the frustrated customer only said, "Use it on yourself, you midget *putz*!" and almost knocked me down as he stormed out the door.

Poppa collapsed in a chair and lit one of his *Boule d'Or* cigarettes. *Gai kaken ahfen yam!* "Go take a crap in the sea," he muttered. It was one of his favorite expressions. Jean giggled and twisted his hands together. Poppa looked at him through the haze of cigarette smoke and shouted, *Golem vu du bist. Schveig Shtill!* "Idiot that you are, keep still!"

Stung by the unfairness of attacking Jean, I shouted, *Paskudnyak!* "You're a mean person!" Poppa looked at me with hurt in his eyes. "That's how one talks to a father?" he said, and Mme. Goldman started to cry. I cried with her.

Trying to cheer us all up and make amends for his horrible mood, Poppa suggested an outing to the terrace of the Métropole Hotel for ice cream. The hotel on the Place de Brouckère with its terrace that went all the way around the corner was one of my favorite places in Brussels. I loved the comfortable straw chairs, the heating ventilator under the canopy, the chance to watch the passersby. As soon as we arrived I excused myself and headed straight for the bathroom. Whether I needed to go there or not was immaterial. It was the walk down the hall with its plush rugs past the huge potted plants fanning the red sofas lining the walls. The bathroom itself was something out of my wildest dreams. A polished marble floor, porcelain sinks with swan-shaped

117

Mariette Bermowitz

faucets and gilded mirrors decorated with angels. At the Métropole, I could almost forget the Rue Ste. Anne with its putrid odor of backed up sewers.

I ordered grenadine, the ruby syrup and mineral water drink I had loved when I visited my friend Louise at her family's café in Fraiture. Now, watching the people go by on the Place de Brouckère as I sipped the luxurious concoction through a straw, it was almost heaven. Poppa watched as I twirled my glass, creating a storm of bubbles, and looked as if he was going to cry. But instead he said brusquely, "Let's order some food. It's getting cold here."

The following week Poppa seemed to be feeling better. He tried his best to *kibitz* with Mme. Goldman, but she would have none of it. I don't think she had forgiven him for having called her son a golem. The atmosphere in the apartment was tense, and I was glad when he decided to take me with him when he went to visit his friend Jakobowicz, the actor. They had known each other in Poland, and always joked and told stories. Jakobowicz performed in the Yiddish Theater and everything about him was theatrical, from his booming voice and peeling laughter, to the way he held his imitation tortoise shell cigarette holder. I was very impressed by his shiny gold tooth and the silk ascot he wore instead of a tie.

Poppa relished getting dressed up for these visits. Being somewhat of a dandy, he had made himself several suits that he wore for going out. Today he had chosen the blue pinstripe and his perfectly sized tan felt hat. The silk handkerchief so carefully poised in his lapel pocket matched his tie. Before we left he went into his secret hiding place, a cupboard

Mindele's Journey

only he had access to where he hid his stash of *Boule d'Or* cigarettes, and took out a small bottle of Chanel No. 5. I watched him remove the crystal stopper and put his nose to the scent, then dab it under each ear.

I thought Poppa smelled like a movie star. I was so proud of him as we walked down the sunlit streets. It was a glorious fall afternoon, unexpectedly warm. Usually by now the cold winds had begun to sweep through the city, bringing rain and unhinging the few remaining leaves off the trees, but today the breeze was soft and mellow. Jakobowicz lived quite a distance away and we had to take a trolley. Since the weather was so fine, instead of catching the trolley at the far end of the Place du Grand Sablon, Poppa and I walked to the next stop, past all the beautiful shops. As we walked, Poppa gave me instructions on what to say and not to say, because Jakobowicz had also invited a very special lady friend. Not wanting to speak Yiddish in public, I didn't answer. Poppa stopped to ask what was wrong because it wasn't like me to be so silent. But I just shook my head, and we continued on to the trolley stop.

The beautiful yellow trolley opened in the back so you could stand and look out at the city. Though Poppa knew I loved standing at the back, he led me inside the car with the other passengers. We sat down in a waft of Chanel No. 5, and Poppa started talking louder and louder. I cringed, still refusing to say a word in Yiddish. Then he leaned in closer to me and held out his finger. *Nem,* he said, "Squeeze my finger." I innocently took his finger and squeezed it. It was like a trigger. My father, the perfumed dandy, let out the biggest fart I had ever heard. I couldn't

119

believe my ears. The sound reverberated through the entire trolley car and heads turned, aghast. People got up and changed their seats. My father was quietly laughing to himself.

It was the last time I didn't answer him in Yiddish. But when we got to our destination there was to be an even bigger embarrassment, for the "lady friend" of Jakobowicz was really a setup for my father. His buddy wanted him to meet someone better than Mme. Goldman. And there was no chance of my saying the wrong thing, for I couldn't speak at all. Though I hardly liked Mme. Goldman, it was inconceivable that this other woman, this perfect stranger, might take her place. Though nothing came of the meeting, something had changed. Some fragment of security, of well-being, had slipped away and I knew nothing would be quite the same again.

Meanwhile, the relationship between Mme. Goldman and my father continued to deteriorate. They mostly argued about money, hurling nasty words at each other, sometimes even throwing things. Yet when the house was quiet, the tension felt almost worse. And when Mme. Goldman took up her mournful singing again, I fled to the outhouse. Huddled in a heavy coat and sweater, with nothing to protect me from the cold but flimsy clapboard walls, I stayed there for hours reading my books. Once, I accidentally left a book on the bench, and by the time I came back to retrieve it, pages were missing. Someone had used it as toilet paper.

Etka and Sarah came in November to take Mme. Goldman back to Valenciennes for a visit. We hadn't seen them for months. Mme. Goldman had finally

Mindele's Journey

gotten over her fear of trains. Knowing that a train had taken her husband and two of her six children to the death camps, she had been afraid to travel alone. She hated the deafening noise of the locomotive, its massive wheels clattering on the rails. But now she seemed ready to go on with her life, whatever that was, and Poppa no longer had to accompany her to Valenciennes, which had begun to feel like a chore to him. For me it was a great disappointment, as I had loved our trips.

Luckily, Sarah and Etka still came to visit. They entered our dark little apartment like rays of sunshine. They brought candy, chocolate, my favorite rolls sprinkled with poppy seeds, cold cuts, coffee, tea, desserts, and jars filled with Malka's preserves. It was life in all its abundance, a joyful celebration of giving and sharing. While Etka had decided that Der Rőete wasn't meant for her, Sarah announced she would marry Vladek in the coming year, which meant another celebration to look forward to.

Sarah went off with Vladek and Etka stayed the night. She had come laden with special gifts, new sheets and pillows and a rose colored quilt. The freshly made bed looked as sumptuous as any of those where the princesses slept in the books of La Comtesse de Ségur. Meanwhile, my heirloom quilt had been tied up inside a big bag to take back to Valenciennes for cleaning.

That night in my room, Etka told me the story of the quilt. I closed my eyes while she talked, and began to imagine Etka's voice was the voice of my mother. I pictured my mother's face from the photograph I'd found in the wardrobe. When Etka said my mother was a mail-order bride, I imagined her saying, "*I* was a mail-order bride leaving on a journey to marry a man I had only seen in a photograph." In the morning, Etka said I fell asleep against her shoulder and mumbled in my sleep. Perhaps I was talking to my mother.

Etka returned to Valenciennes with Mme. Goldman and Jean. I would have gone if it hadn't been for school and not wanting to lose my place as the best student in the class. Not even the gloom of a Brussels winter could dampen my spirits when I won first prize in the writing contest. It had been sponsored by the ASPCA, and I wrote about the cats of Mme. Charpentier who kept the old blind woman company. My prize was *Djibi, the Little Cat* by Felix Salten, which I proudly took to Fraiture that Christmas vacation.

When the train pulled into the station and I climbed down with Maman Thérèse, there was Tante Marie and Tante Marthe waving and running down the platform to greet us. I felt like I had returned home. The Christmas tree, the embroidered white tablecloth, the antique plates on the old Flemish sideboard, the lace curtains at the kitchen window, drinking my first champagne and falling asleep in M. le Curé's office to the sound of Tante Marie playing Schubert, this was my true home. The home where I knew I was loved. Where evenings were spent talking and singing as we sat around the table in the living room, while the wind moaned outside and the logs crackled in the old stove. Tante Marie sang at her mending as Maman read her favorite gossip magazines about royalty and Tante Marthe

Mindele's Journey

wrote letters. Amid this cozy warmth, I finished reading my new book, *Djibi,* and entertained them with recitations of the poems I had memorized for class.

I returned to Brussels at the start of the new year with a suitcase full of clean clothes and chocolates and *Petits Beurres* with mocha cream. That was the year Poppa's cough became worse. Sometimes his coughing woke me up in the middle of the night and often I couldn't get back to sleep. There would be an explosion of choking gasps, then the slow dribbling cough, repeating for endless hours till dawn. He was smoking four packs of cigarettes a day. Ashtrays overflowed with butts. His fingernails were discolored with orange-brown stains. Practically the only time he put his cigarette down on the wooden edge of his sewing machine was when he was convulsed with wheezing and coughing. The sewing machine table was pockmarked with cigarette burns.

Mme. Goldman was once again sharing my bed. And along with her unwelcome presence, the bedbugs had returned with a vengeance. Sometimes I pulled coats out of the wardrobe and slept on the floor. The coats smelled of mothballs, but I preferred mothballs to the itching, bleeding wounds of a bedbug assault. The pile of dirty laundry in the corner didn't smell good either. Mme. Goldman hardly ever went to the laundry anymore. Sometimes I put my head in the credenza to breathe whatever fresh-smelling clothes remained from my last holiday in Fraiture. And then I thought of Maman Thérèse with her lemony scent, hanging clothes on the line stretched between two flowering hazelnut trees.

123

Mariette Bermowitz

At the start of summer when Maman Thérèse came to pick me up, Poppa seemed relieved. After telling her how grateful he was that I would live in the country for a few months, he insisted on giving her a ring. I don't know what its value was, but she didn't want to take it, saying, "Monsieur, you can rest assured that Mariette will always be taken care of. And if you need anything at all, we will be there for you as well."

I didn't know how ill Poppa really was. Then in the fall something terrible happened. I came home from school one afternoon to find him sitting on the bed with the tin box he kept hidden behind the wardrobe. He was sweating profusely, his fingers roaming around the box, frantically looking for something. "Where *is* she? Where *is* she?" he shouted.

Mme. Goldman had taken the money and jewelry and gone to Valenciennes without telling him. Somehow my father and I got through the rest of the evening. But a few days later I had the feeling something was wrong and decided not to stop in the library after school but go straight home. It was already getting dark as I hurried down the cobbled street, trying not to look at the shadows moving against the wall, hearing my father's gasping cough in every step I took. Finally I reached the apartment and saw none of the lights had been lit. It was empty. I sat down in the dark and sobbed, wondering if Poppa was ever coming back.

I don't know how long I sat there alone in the dark before M. Gianini knocked on the door and told me my father had collapsed in front of the house earlier that day and was taken to the hospi-

Mindele's Journey

tal in an ambulance. M. Gianini had just come from the hospital and assured me that Poppa was OK and we would visit him tomorrow. I stayed at my friend Jacky's house for a few days, and then Poppa came home. Mme. Goldman and Jean came home too. Etka brought them back along with the quilt, all fresh and newly cleaned.

I never saw Etka again. A few months later Poppa and I left for America to live with Tante Rifcha in Brooklyn. Mme. Goldman eventually went to live with her sister Malka in Valenciennes. Sarah and Vladek went to distant relatives in Rio de Janeiro. Poppa wanted a fresh start. And a fresh start could only happen in America. No matter that he hadn't seen his sister Rifcha since 1922. Already I didn't like her. She sent us packages from time to time filled with her daughter's used clothing. None of it fit me. I hated the thought of wearing secondhand clothing anyway. We gave it all to the local Hebrew school for the orphans.

Amid the shock of leaving Belgium, I got my first period just shy of my twelfth birthday. The sight of blood on the sheet terrified me. I had a terrible stomachache too, and didn't know what it was from. I thought I had done something to myself in my sleep so as not to leave Belgium. Poppa was out, so I sobbed to Mme. Goldman, begging her to take me to the hospital before I bled to death. First she slapped me, then she hugged me, explaining that I would become a woman in America.

A week before our departure the aunts came to Brussels to say good-bye and to take me shopping for new clothes and plenty of stationery for all the

125

letters I would be writing. Being in their company and the pleasure of so many new things almost made me forget what was coming. But when they left, and I watched them walking up the Rue Ste Anne for the last time, it didn't matter how many times they said they would always be there for me, waiting till I came back. I didn't know when I'd ever see them again. It was too unbearable to contemplate.

We left Belgium a few days before Christmas. It was snowing. On the way to the station I stared forlornly at the ribbons of flashing lights and glittering holiday decorations. The Gare du Nord was swarming with people. The platform was covered with a steel-gray wetness that soaked through my boots. It was packed with travelers dragging carts full of luggage, many of them loaded with children on top. As we made our way through the crowd I held on to my belongings tightly, but I could not hold back the tears. I was leaving my world and everything I knew. Afraid of losing my suitcase, I gripped the handle with all my might. It was terribly heavy, yet its weight was not as important as protecting the treasures I had gathered in the few months before our departure.

Inside was the leather bound book Mme. Biezemans had given me on my last day in school. I worshiped Mme. Biezemans who had allowed me to sit on her lap, which she never did with any of the other students. I thought her incredibly beautiful with her silver-colored hair and red lipstick, and the fragrant white powder she dabbed on her smooth skin. Under her gentle loving tutelage I had become insatiably curious. She reminded me of that as we said good-bye, when she handed me a book filled

Mindele's Journey

with the poems, watercolors, and farewells my classmates had prepared, their farewells written in extravagant calligraphy highlighted in gold. She also gave me a bound collection of the comic books I loved, *The Adventures of Tintin* and *La Semaine de Suzette*, dated 1938, the year I was born. A dedication in feathery script inside the front cover read, *A ma chère petite élève Mariette pour qu'elle ne nous oublie jamais.* "To my darling little student Mariette, so that she may never forget us." The adventures detailed in the illustrations had been a constant companion during my childhood. It was the canvas against which I had created my reality, transferring that imaginary world into my daily existence. And soon it would become even more of a connection to the past, soothing the emptiness of the months to come.

I would also miss the librarian, Melle. Vroeman, who was kind to me during all those hours I spent at the library reading and doing my homework. For a going-away gift, she had given me brand-new copies of my favorite books. *The Last of the Mohicans, David Copperfield,* several of the *Heidi in Switzerland* novels, an illustrated text on Greek and Roman mythology, two of the idyllic novels by La Comtesse de Ségur, and several Tintin adventures. I put a photograph of my friend Annie wearing a white gauze tutu inside one of the books.

My little suitcase couldn't possibly hold all the treasures I wanted to take with me to America. Poppa didn't mind my taking Yvette and her trousseau, but he told me I couldn't take my entire book collection, forty in all. I would soon outgrow them, he said, and besides, he didn't have the strength to carry

127

them. But little did Poppa know that I had inherited the skill of our nomadic ancestors who placed their worldly goods inside the bedding they took on long journeys. While my most cherished books went into the suitcase, the others were safely hidden in my mother's quilt we were taking to America. As Poppa was about to examine the bulging bedding, I exclaimed, "Oh Poppa, don't touch it. Isn't it going to be a wonderful thing to keep us warm in America!" He put his hand on my head and said with tears in his eyes, "I know Mindele, I know."

I cried when we boarded the train. Poppa was silent, absorbed in his own web of thoughts. We were now homeless wanderers. It was clearly stamped on our passports, *Apatride*, without a country. I looked out the window, and when I saw someone waving a handkerchief in my direction, I waved back. When the train started to pick up speed and the platform disappeared into the haze of snow, I made a silent vow to return. *Je reviendrai.* Someday when I could travel by myself, I would come back. *Je reviendrai.* The thought consoled me. As I said the words over and over again to myself, *je reviendrai, je reviendrai,* they seemed to merge with the rhythm of the train. I stopped crying and stared at my breath on the window, then at the snow-laden trees fleeing past. And then I looked up into the milky white sky and silently vowed to God, *Je reviendrai.*

Brooklyn 1959

I had been up late studying for my college exams and had just fallen asleep when the phone rang. At first I ignored it, thinking it was the alarm clock. Then I realized the ringing was coming from the kitchen and stumbled over to the phone. It was the hospital calling. "Please come immediately. Your father will not survive the night."

I knew it two weeks ago when the ambulance took him away. He was coughing and choking nonstop. Coughing fits that beat his body like a hammer, as if to shatter whatever remained of his fragile bones. His eyes bulged with fear. *Ich starb Mindele, Ich starb.* "I'm dying, Mindele. I'm dying." The emphysema had punctured so many holes in his lungs they could no longer hold up.

I threw on a coat and ran down Hegeman Avenue in my slippers, oblivious to the cold and the icy sidewalks. I didn't know what was more frightening, the dark ominous shadows of the deserted streets or what I would find at the hospital. By the time I got to his room, out of breath and dripping with sweat, he was already gone. My stepmother, Molly, who had been summoned earlier, said he died only minutes ago. The oxygen mask still covered his face. I sat down and held his skeletal hand one last time. His face,

Mariette Bermowitz

haggard and worn, would now be still forever. Our journey together had come to an end.

He lay in a simple pine coffin at the I. J. Morris Funeral Parlor of East Flatbush. My aunt Rifcha came up from Florida and we sat Shiva for a week. Her four daughters were there and it was almost festive. The table was overflowing with fresh fruit and cakes and sandwiches. The friends Poppa had made in the synagogue across the street came to pay their respects. They had so much to say about their *kleine Abele,* their term of endearment for their diminutive shul member. It was from them I learned how proud he was of me. They said he boasted I spoke seven languages, read ten books a week, was the smartest kid in school and was probably going to be a diplomat because of my big mouth.

My father had become somewhat religious in the last few years of his life. I don't know if he really believed in God, the *Reboyne Sheloylim,* but I do know that he measured his life according to certain tenets. "Don't ever trust a government," and "What is meant to be, is meant to be." *Voos ist beshert ist beshert.* He was not an educated man but a practical one, earning his wisdom through the tragedies he endured. I think he believed they redeemed him. He was called to participate in the Minyan, the prayer that can only be said when there are ten participants. He didn't miss a week, and according to his buddies there, he said the prayers in such a way that the *Reboyne Sheloylim* must have heard it. When I sat on the stoop in front of the house, I could see him in the synagogue on the other side of the street, proudly standing under his shawl, rocking to the tune of his inner song. When he returned from shul those Friday nights, he had a look of peaceful acceptance.

Mindele's Journey

My father never talked about the past. Like so many Holocaust survivors, he was silent about what happened in the war. American Jews didn't want to identify with what went on in Europe. It made me feel we were tainted, marked by fate as the sacrifice. They called us greenhorns. We were foreigners without a country. The Jews they didn't want to be reminded of.

During that week I was sitting Shiva, newly orphaned and feeling totally alone in the world, Tante Rifcha's youngest daughter, Esther, came up and hissed in my ear, "You know what you did, don't you? You killed your father for sure." With a sweep of her fur coat, she turned and flounced back to her sisters on the other side of the room. I stared at her in dumb silence. What did she mean? Did she mean the Italian Catholic boy who wanted to marry me? Or was it the weekend I went off with a boy my father didn't approve of? Or did she find out what I did with her husband, Roy. My eyes smarted with tears. I remember telling my father I wanted to marry a Catholic boy. Poppa's face had turned ashen. He said, "*Meine kinde*, I have lost them all, and if you marry him, I will sit Shiva for you too." Six months later he was dead. It has been hard not to think I was responsible.

Arrival in America, 1951

Nine years earlier the two of us boarded the *SS America*. We had spent two glorious days and nights in Paris right before Christmas. The entire city was festooned with lights and decorations for the holidays, and it distracted me from thinking too much about Brussels, or the Christmas I was missing with les tantes in Fraiture. It was hard not to think about the sweet-smelling fir tree in the corner of their dining room and not being there to see it. Then we came aboard the grand American ocean liner, a floating palace of sparkling lights and luminous garlands strung across the upper deck, and I forgot for a moment what I was leaving behind.

My father left me alone in a cabin with a Mrs. Maloney, saying he would be in another cabin for men only. Never mind that Mrs. Maloney was kind and friendly, calling me a sweet little girl. I burst into tears. I didn't know how I would ever find Poppa again in the endless maze of corridors. I sobbed even harder as the reality hit me that I was leaving my country and everything that was dear to me. Mrs. Maloney sat me down and put her arm around my shoulder, assuring me everything would be fine. When she realized I didn't know English, she said in broken French that it would please her to teach me my first words, as English would be my language from now on.

English might be my new language, but I could still write in French. I had so many new things to write about in my journal, addressing each entry to les tantes, who would become lifelong witnesses to my journey in the New World. I went into great detail about the Christmas party in First Class. All the children had been invited and given gifts. Mine was an elongated plastic doll with a blond wig. I almost gave it back. Nothing could ever replace Yvette and her

Mindele's Journey

wardrobe of custom-made outfits. Then I wrote about making a fool of myself at dinner when I ordered both the ham and the turkey, and all the vegetables, because I didn't know what the words meant.

I couldn't take my eyes off the women in First Class. So exquisitely dressed! All heads turned when the captain entered with a beautiful woman on his arm. She seemed covered in diamonds and emeralds shimmering in the light. I thought she was an apparition from one of my fairy tales, and I had been transported to a magical world. I would never want *les tantes* to know how dowdy I felt in the new fuchsia-colored dress they had made for me in Fraiture, which now seemed so old fashioned.

Toward the end of the trip the weather took a turn for the worse. As the waves smashed angrily against the lower decks, my period came on with a vengeance. I was ill with cramps and vomiting, but I didn't want Poppa to know. I think Mrs. Maloney must have told him anyway, because he looked at me differently after my "illness." From the tone of his voice I could tell that he knew the little girl he was taking to America was no longer a child.

Before leaving Belgium, my teacher, Mme. Biezemans, had shown me a picture of the Statue of Liberty in a geography book and said it was a gift from the French people. We read the long poem about liberty written on a plaque welcoming people like Poppa and me to our new country. Yet the statue floating on the water was more magnificent than I could have imagined. My teacher said the sculptor had used his mother as a model, and it felt that much more meaningful to me to think that someone's mother was welcoming us as we sailed into New York Harbor.

As the *SS America* eased into the dock there was a sudden burst of applause. We had arrived. I stumbled down the gangplank with my suitcase and Poppa grabbed my hand. I had forgotten how heavy all those books were. But I was stepping into the new world, and with my very own possessions.

They were waiting for us near the gate. Though Poppa hadn't seen his sister in thirty-eight years, he knew her immediately. She waved to us in the distance, and he ran toward her like the young man he had been when she left Poland all those years ago. They fell into each other's arms and cried. They stayed huddled together in this tearful embrace until my cousins stepped forward to greet their uncle Abele. I stood to the side with my suitcase until Poppa suddenly remembered me, proudly pushing me in front of him, saying, "This is my child. The only one left." He started to cry again.

One by one, they came to kiss me. Other than her diminutive height, Tante Rifcha didn't look like Poppa at all. Her face was angular, but she was as round as a butterball. When she pressed against me for a kiss I could feel her corset like an armor plate. Unlike their mother, her daughters were tall and blond and wore long fur coats. The drive from the pier on Manhattan's West Side to Brooklyn seemed to take forever, with Poppa and his sister doing more crying than talking. I sat in the back with my cousin Rochelle who was my age, and I gave her the plastic doll I received at the party on the ship. Rochelle had noticed the doll when I opened my suitcase at cus-

Mindele's Journey

toms and said how pretty it was. Les tantes said that if someone admires one of your possessions, it is polite to find a way to give it to them. They said this was an old tradition. I was more than happy to place the skinny plastic doll in Rochelle's pudgy hands. I had never seen such a fat child before. She had a double chin and thick stumps for legs, and the buttons on her coat looked ready to burst. I immediately disliked her, which I am not very proud of, but perhaps it had something to do with all the skinny children I knew during the war.

Brooklyn in the 1950s

Tante Rifcha owned a four-family house on Osborn Street in East New York, Brooklyn, between New Lots Avenue and Linden Boulevard. It was mostly a Jewish neighborhood then, with identical semi-detached two-story dwellings. On warm evenings people would sit on the stoops staring at the world going by or talking to the neighbors. Everyone knew everyone else's business due to the narrow alleyways that allowed close examination of apartments and conversations when the windows were open.

Tante Rifcha lived upstairs with her husband, Max. I will never forget how the smell of soap and wood polish instantly put me at ease when I walked into Tante's house that day. She was a *balabusta*, a real homemaker, though a bit tyrannical about cleanliness. Her kitchen had all the latest appliances, including a refrigerator. I had never seen a

Mariette Bermowitz

refrigerator before. There was no need for one in Fraiture where the cellar was always cool. And on the Rue Ste. Anne we hardly had more than a stove. But the biggest surprise was the living room, crowded with collectibles in mirrored boxes dotting the walls. When I asked her what was in the beautiful Chinese cabinet against the wall, she opened it and laughed as she turned the dial and a picture appeared on a screen. I was looking at my very first television set. This was beyond my wildest expectations. In Brussels we didn't even have a radio.

That first night I slept in the small bedroom next to my aunt's. Poppa slept in the basement apartment where Tante stored her old furniture. I didn't like being separated from him, or sleeping in the bed where I was told my grandfather had died. Grandpa Joseph, also a tailor, had come to the States with Tante Rifcha in 1922 before she was married. Poppa never saw him again. Grandpa Joseph lived with Tante Rifcha until his death. In his picture on the night table he looked like a sage with his white beard and long black frock coat. Until we came to Tante Rifcha's, I hadn't even known that I had grandparents. But now I was beginning to sense that I had more family than I had ever imagined.

The loss of grandparents I had never known didn't make me nearly as sad as realizing that not only would I not see my beloved *tantes* in Fraiture, but no one would understand me when I spoke French. I would no longer hear the language that connected me to everything I loved. The thought propelled me out of bed and over to my suitcase for one of my Comtesse de Ségur books. If I wasn't able to speak

Mindele's Journey

French, at least I could read it. Then I recited my prayers and fell asleep, trying not to think I was lying in the very bed Grandpa Joseph had died in.

In the days that followed, I familiarized myself with my new surroundings. There was not a wardrobe to be found. The wardrobe in Brussels had been our only nice piece of furniture. I missed its fragrance. I missed not being able to explore its contents and lose myself behind the dark wooden doors. In America there were closets built into the wall. The heat came up through radiators, the lights were run by electricity, and the sinks had both hot and cold water. There was even a toilet in the bathroom! I got used to these luxuries far more easily than I got used to the food, most of which seemed to come out of cans—even the vegetables. The strawberries were fresh, but they were tasteless, and were served with sour cream. I missed my *fraises de Wepion à la crème Chantilly*. Then I thought of Maman Thérèse, who would have offered her grief as a sacrifice to her favorite saint, Sainte Thérèse de Lisieux. There were so many sacrifices I had to make here where the meat was overcooked and soda was served with every meal. I did like Tante Rifcha's rugelah though, which was always piled high on a special porcelain plate in the kitchen. Freshly baked sweets were the only thing that gave me a feeling of well-being.

I walked to school in my new American sneakers. It was not a very pleasant walk. Unlike Brussels with all the lovely shop windows to gaze into, my school in Brooklyn was surrounded by factories and auto repair shops. The speech therapist taught me English. She knew a smattering of French from her holidays in France and Belgium, and I felt safe with her. Mr. Feingold, the grocer, couldn't get over it when I came in with my aunt's grocery list and spoke to him in Yiddish. In that neighborhood the only ones who still spoke Yiddish were the old people.

Poppa was at home sitting on the milk crates outside his store, smoking cigarettes and laughing at Mr. Feingold's jokes. Tante Rifcha's husband, Max, found him a job as a tailor in a shop where they were all survivors from Europe. My father was back in his element speaking Yiddish. It wasn't a fancy shop like the Rue Haute, and there was no need for custom work, but he made a living.

When I was thirteen, a year after we arrived in Brooklyn, Poppa married Molly. Shortly before, we had moved into Tante's empty apartment on the ground floor. I heard about the news when I came home from school and found Molly in the kitchen piling dishes in the cabinets. Poppa was holding a flowered dish. He said, "Mindele, this is Molly, my wife." I was shocked. I wanted to snatch the dish from his hand and throw it on the floor. Later, I learned that Tante Rifcha had arranged the whole *shiddach,* as it was called in Yiddish.

I didn't like Molly. She was a short woman who pursed her lips when she talked, and the glasses she wore gave her eyes a filmy look, as if they had been dipped in egg yolk. She had a whiny voice and I couldn't bear being in the house with her. If I wasn't in my room with the door locked, I was down in Tante Rifcha's basement. I loved spending time in the basement. The furnishings were nice, placed there when Tante Rifcha redecorated her apartment

Mindele's Journey

after her first husband died of cancer. He had been a furrier, and she always thought the dye they used to treat the furs had caused his illness. Her second husband, Max, was a tailor. He set up a workshop in the back of the basement for rush jobs he finished in the evenings. But he never went to the front part of the basement, so I was able to feel that the front part was all mine.

I was much happier in the basement than I was upstairs. The kitchen had a maize-colored enamel stove and a hidden cache in the wall for storing potatoes. A rainbow of odd-colored glasses and multi-patterned dishes shone through the glass panes of the cabinet doors. Tante only used those dishes on Passover, and boasted to her neighbor, Mrs. Friedman, that she didn't have to bother changing dishes for the holidays. In the living room was an old piano that played sheet music, and hidden away in the corner was an old sewing machine garnished with frayed lampshades. I especially loved the enormous velvet brocade sofa, even though it was faded and moth-eaten. Sometimes I did my homework at the long table, seated on one of the mismatched chairs, or I played tunes on the piano, or just rummaged through the closets looking at blouses, yellowing tablecloths, boxes of buttons and the rest of Tante Rifcha's castaways. It was my dream space, where I made believe I was still in the Old World I loved. In the peace and quiet of Tante's closets, I could make believe I was still back there. Then I'd hear Poppa shouting at the top of the basement stairs, "Mindele, where are you? Come eat! Molly is waiting!"

139

Mariette Bermowitz

Molly was a terrible cook. I pretended I was sick when she served the meat stew. I'm sure it did nothing to endear me to her, but I couldn't help remembering the *Boeuf Bourguignon* simmering for hours on the coal stove in Maman Thérèse's kitchen. In those days, no one had to call me to the table. The aroma of caramelized onions, carrots and potatoes sputtering in wine sauce, the smell of parsley, thyme and bay leaves, pulled everyone in the house away from work and into the kitchen. I don't think Molly would have understood Maman Thérèse and her garden of herbs, or how she toiled for hours over her lettuce and climbing string beans and baby carrots. They came from different worlds.

At least when I started junior high school, I had Mr. Blum's candy store on my way home. With the American milkshake I finally found something that thrilled my taste buds. Mr. Blum let me sit in the wooden booth in the rear of the store to savor this delight, and it was there I accidentally found a stack of old comic books hidden underneath the bench. Not only had I found ambrosia worthy of the gods— but also a library. Mr. Blum allowed me to stay and read as many comics and drink as many milkshakes as I wanted. He never charged me the full amount, telling me that I would repay him when I graduated from college. Unfortunately, I was never able to pay him back, because dear Mr. Blum passed away before I ever got to college.

Even though I now spoke English, I could not get rid of my French accent. My friend Sharon said it was a real tease, and boys would pay attention to me. "Oh, come on," I said, not knowing what she meant.

140

Mindele's Journey

She grinned. "Why don't you try it on Alan Greenberg and see what happens?"

Alan Greenberg was the cutest boy I had ever laid eyes on. He had blue eyes and blond hair and always wore a Brooklyn Dodgers baseball jacket that showed off his husky frame. My opportunity came when we were playing punch ball in the school yard. Thanksgiving was coming up and some of the girls had been talking about having a party.

As we were talking, "Alan-the-dream" started walking toward us. Sharon practically pushed me against him. I said, "Hi, Alan. How *arre youu*?" and asked him when I could come and watch him play baseball. Then I don't know what got into me, as I hadn't even asked permission, but I invited him to a party at my house over the Thanksgiving holiday. Alan said he would bring some other boys.

Tante Rifcha said we could have the party in the basement as long as we left everything neat and clean. I promised her we would leave it even better than the way we found it. I was delirious at the thought of my first party, and would have promised Tante anything she asked for. What a relief I didn't have to ask Molly, who probably would have said no just to spite me. For the next few weeks as a favor to Tante, I carried an enormous pot of chicken soup to her daughter Esther's house on Friday afternoon before sundown. Esther hated to cook. She always had a cigarette in her mouth, and complained about her children and the mess they made. Those two little kids never seemed to stop whining and crying. But I babysat, and I carried the heavy pot of soup over, and I listened to Esther's complaints,

141

Mariette Bermowitz

all for the privilege of throwing a party in Tante's basement.

As I counted the days before the party I dreamed about Alan Greenberg. I saw myself wearing his baseball jacket with the bold lettering of his favorite team on the back. I coaxed Esther into giving me an advance on my babysitting money so I could buy soda and candy. I cleaned the basement, even sweeping the hall and stairway. I would have cleaned Tante's whole apartment had she asked me.

The big night finally arrived. Poppa, with Molly shuffling behind him, came down to check the basement to see if everything was in order. Molly whined, "I don't think you should let these children have a party by themselves. They're going to break things and make a mess." I stuck my tongue out when their backs were turned.

Then my father said, "Well, let's see what happens."

For me, it was already a miracle, knowing that Alan would soon be arriving. When the bell rang upstairs, my heart turned over and I was too excited to move. But it was only Sharon. Then more guests arrived, and finally Alan waltzed in, as handsome as a movie star. I couldn't take my eyes off him. Someone played an Eddie Fisher song. Eddie Fisher, who was going to be singing in person at the Paramount on Flatbush Avenue. We danced and listened to the Ames Brothers, Tony Bennett, Perry Como, Nat King Cole, Peggy Lee, and the Hilltoppers.

I worried the music was too loud and they'd hear us upstairs, and sure enough, it wasn't long before Molly's head appeared, and then Poppa and Tante

Mindele's Journey

behind her. Poppa shouted, "The music is much too loud! We want you all out by ten o'clock!" It was no use telling them that life *begins* at ten o'clock. Molly, a triumphant gleam in her eye, said, "Your father and I are going to sleep soon and we don't want to hear any more music!" I lowered the volume, but I was afraid the party was ruined. What had been mere dislike for Molly now turned to loathing.

Someone suggested we play spin the bottle. I had never heard of the game so Sharon explained it to me as we all sat down in a circle with an empty Coke bottle in the middle. When it was my turn I made a wish, and watched in horror as the bottle slowed down in front of a pimply faced boy. Did the power of my longing keep it going a few more inches, so that it came to rest before Alan? As he bent his face toward mine, our lips touching, Eddie Fisher was crooning in the background, *Many times I have wanted your kisses / I've dreamed of it so often / at last it's come true.* I was transported into bliss. Molly and everything else was instantly forgotten.

In the days following the party I tried in vain to get Alan's attention during baseball practice in the schoolyard, staring through the fence in rapt attention, even learning a few baseball terms, but Alan never looked my way. Along with my disappointment over Alan, I lost my refuge in the basement. I was sitting at the long wooden table doing my homework when Tante Rifcha came in and announced she was renting the space to a friend who just got divorced. I must have looked crestfallen because she said gruffly, "You have your own bedroom upstairs."

Mariette Bermowitz

I was banished from a make-believe world where memories of the past melded into the present. My little bedroom upstairs could hardly compare to my former hideaway. I moved my bookcase back to the bedroom, but I could no longer read my French books while cocooned in the sagging sofa, propped against velvety pillows smelling faintly of mothballs. Nor would I be able to try on the clothes in the closet, or fiddle around on the piano, imagining I was Tante Marie playing Schubert.

Molly was always in the kitchen when I came home from school, opening and closing doors, rattling pots and pans, vacuuming or using the sewing machine. After she finished cleaning, and I thought surely she was going to put away the vacuum, she would inspect the surfaces she had already dusted. Only then would she put the monstrous vacuum back in its place behind the kitchen door, ready for next time. Even with the door closed I heard everything from my bedroom down the hall. Yet for some reason the rat-tat-tat from the sewing machine bothered me most of all, which was strange, as the sound of my father's machine on the Rue Ste. Anne never fazed me. Molly seemed to enjoy making her own clothes, and my father must have appreciated that. All the clothes she made were cut from the same pattern, straight and simple, hiding her figure.

There was no doubt Molly was another *balabusta*. Before marrying my father she gave him an ultimatum: she would not go out to work. Taking care of the home was all she wanted to do. I couldn't think why else my father married her. When she cooked she used a big pot, making enough to last the week.

144

Mindele's Journey

Her creativity was limited to daily additions of carrots, peppers, or potatoes. On the weekends there would be chicken soup. Poppa ate very little. A few chicken wings and he was full. He always stared into the distance when he ate, holding his soup bowl between his bony hands. He didn't use a spoon but slowly slurped the liquid the way he drank his tea, letting it cool in the saucer before drinking it.

I wondered what he was thinking. Did he feel as lonely as I did sometimes? Did he miss our outings in the Bois de la Cambre? Or sitting on the terrace of the Métropole Hotel eating pastries just like the rich people? Did he ever think of his friends in Brussels, or of Mme. Goldman? I never asked him what he was thinking, and now I wish I had. He seemed resigned to his fate. Although they were only in their fifties, I thought my father much too old to have any romantic ideas, especially not with frumpy Molly, who never wore makeup and put a net over what remained of the permanent she had done when they first met. How odd though, to see the green negligee rimmed with a feather boa draped on the chair at her vanity table. I tried it on one day when she was out, and posed in front of the mirror admiring myself, thinking how grown-up it made me look. Then I pictured wearing it at the Métropole Hotel, sitting with Alan Greenberg on the terrace and sipping that wonderful café Liègeois. But then I remembered he would have been wearing his Brooklyn Dodgers jacket and probably talking about baseball.

My bedroom windows faced Mrs. Friedman's kitchen and Mrs. Shulman's living room. Mrs. Friedman's telephone conversations were a welcome distraction from my homework. I heard everything she said, which was mostly complaints about the sister who lived with her. When Molly went to visit Mrs. Shulman, I overheard her talking about the mess in my room. It made me so angry that I took to slamming the door to my room whenever I heard Molly coming. But that was Osborn Street. Everyone knew each other's business. You heard it as soon as the weather turned warm and windows were raised. As soon as the yellow forsythia bloomed in otherwise barren cement courtyards.

Molly wasn't all bad. There was a time in junior high when I really liked Molly. I had come home from school beaming with pride after the music teacher said my performance at the student assembly had been absolutely wonderful. I sang *La Vie En Rose.* The teacher was surprised someone my age had even heard of Edith Piaf. Little did she know how many hours I had practiced in the mirror. I didn't know who Piaf was until she appeared on the *Ed Sullivan Show.* She looked so frail in that simple black dress, so tiny all alone on the stage with only the microphone for support. The camera came in for a close-up of her face and she started to sing. I couldn't believe my ears. It was the most thrilling sound I had ever heard—and it was all in French! Poppa and Molly didn't know what she was singing about, but I did. I sat glued to the screen, mesmerized as much by the words as her voice, tender and longing, bringing out all my longing for the language I hadn't spoken since I arrived in America. I was filled with *le mal du pays,* the aching for one's country. Which for me was Fraiture, and the warm embrace of Maman Thérèse,

Mindele's Journey

Tante Marthe, and the memory of Tante Marie's elbows resting on the old oak table as she filled the long winter evenings with soft melodies.

Edith Piaf brought French back to me. Now I had a *raison d'être*. I identified with her small stature, her expressive mannerisms and I wanted to sing just like her. I practiced tilting my head and clasping my hands around the microphone like she did, finishing with arms out in an agonizing prayer. I wrote *La Vie En Rose* in bold letters on a large cardboard and hung it above my desk so it would be the first thing I'd see in the morning when I woke up. Although no one around me spoke French, I would not have to give up my language after all. Songs and books were within my reach and there was a promise of *La Vie En Rose* to look forward to. Piaf's song of yearning for a lasting love was my song too now.

Tante's friend, the divorcée in the basement, found the lyrics to the song in a magazine. She laughed when she heard me sing, "He's mine, I'm his, throughout life." *C'est lui pour moi, moi pour lui dans la vie.* She may have laughed, but I truly meant it. I had found my ideal at fourteen. Piaf's song would beat in my heart for the rest of my life.

The music teacher sent my name to a radio program called *Ted Mack's Amateur Hour.* I would be singing my "song of songs" on the radio! I felt the angels smiling down on me as I ran home from school, my feet barely touching the ground. Molly was in the kitchen as usual, and when I blurted out the wonderful news she looked at me as if she didn't understand. But how could Molly possibly understand? She didn't know anything about Edith Piaf or *La Vie*

En Rose. To Molly, Piaf was just a French singer we heard on TV. Molly didn't know anything about me either. She never asked about my life in Belgium, or what it was like back then for my father and me. To her, Europe was "the old country." She was only concerned with her relatives, an unmarried sister and brother in Paterson, New Jersey, and meeting up with other Bialistockers, the town in Poland where they were from.

But then Molly surprised me. She wanted to know what kind of contest it was and all the details, and ended up saying she would take me to the recording session. It was the first time she had ever taken an interest in me. I was about to give her a hug when she turned away. But I think she was smiling. Just that little bit of attention was enough to make me think *La Vie En Rose* might actually be a possibility in our house. I thought so again when Molly took me shopping at the store where she used to work, and helped me pick out a lavender dress with matching shoes. Maybe Molly cared about me after all. Poppa didn't quite understand what all the fuss was about, but he gave her the money for my new clothes.

By the day of the contest I had practiced my song so many times that I didn't feel at all nervous. I thought I had captured Piaf's longing to perfection. It gave me goose bumps to pretend I was Piaf, bringing the beauty of the French language to America. Molly was in a very good mood. She was all dressed up too, minus the usual hairnet and wearing a dress that flattered her figure and revealed a hint of bosom. She wasn't that bad looking when she made an effort. The excitement of the concert must have

Mindele's Journey

rubbed off on her too, because she said, "Sometimes I miss not going out to work." I was silent. I thought how wonderful it would be if she did go back to work. Then she wouldn't be at home every day when I came home from school.

On the subway ride to Manhattan I went over the song in my mind, but it was such an adventure to leave Brooklyn that I couldn't concentrate. And then I thought, what if I forget the words? By the time we reached the radio station I was in a panic. I wanted to take Molly's hand, but she was busy asking directions to Ted Mack's studio. There were swarms of people in the crowded hallway. Studio hands pushing cameras and equipment around, people yelling, and all I wanted was a quiet place where I could calm myself before I had to go on. We finally made it to the waiting room and sat with the other contestants. My heart pounded when I heard my name called, and my stomach felt queasy, but when I stood before the microphone and thought of Piaf, suddenly I wasn't nervous anymore. I sang with all my heart and soul, *C'est lui pour moi, moi pour lui dans la vie.* Someday I too would find someone to love me.

Though I didn't win the contest, I had crossed a threshold. Singing Piaf on the radio had identified me as French, at least in my mind, and certainly in my heart. Now, walking past store windows, I kept looking at my reflection, imagining myself with short hair like Piaf. Of course, even with short hair I'd still have to wear the new lavender dress for graduation from junior high. I'd never be able to buy a sophisticated black sheath like Piaf wore. Well, if I couldn't have a new dress, at least I could have a new hairdo.

Mariette Bermowitz

I agonized over the decision whether or not to cut my hair. What a struggle it had been to keep my long hair clean and pretty! It had taken such a long time to grow, and braiding my hair was a ritual. I did it with my eyes closed, parting the hair just so, dividing it into three equal parts, then holding it tightly while bringing the silky strands into perfect alignment. Les tantes said it would be easier to keep my hair clean if I kept it braided. Maman Thérèse always checked for lice when I came from Brussels, and washed my hair with a special soap. When it was dry she braided it with lovely new ribbons or barrettes for the tips. Sometimes she circled the braids around my head like a halo. But no one in America wore braids.

I set off for the local salon with my baby-sitting money. The hairdresser tried to discourage me, saying I shouldn't pay attention to how other girls wore their hair. "You're much prettier with braids than they are with short hair," he said. I didn't tell him about Piaf, or the girl who called me a greenhorn. "It's time for me to look American!" I sputtered.

He sighed, and with lightning speed he cut off my past. I almost cried when I saw myself in the mirror. I didn't look like Edith Piaf at all. Just my own scrawny self with a limp mop. I felt a strange lightness on my head as I carried the braids home in a paper bag, but my heart was heavy.

As soon as I came in the door I ran to look at myself in the full length mirror. Sideways, front ways—all the ways showed me what a horrible mistake I had made! But as the tears welled up I remembered the blue silk gown I had borrowed from Tante Rifcha's closet in the basement. I locked the door

150

to my room and took out the dress. Such a beautiful dress with lace across the front and midnight blue panels that shimmered in the light. When I put the dress on I still didn't look anything like my idol, Edith Piaf, but I saw there were possibilities and I was consoled.

What should I do with my braids? The box lined with flowered material and matching ribbon would be perfect, but it was where I stored letters from les tantes. Every month I would retrieve the eagerly awaited blue envelope from the mailbox. The red and white air-mail border always stood out from the plain white ones. Tante Marthe's delicate handwriting was like medieval illuminated text. I would hurry into the privacy of my room, slide under the covers, and drift back to what I had come to think of as the enchanted world of my childhood in Fraiture.

"To our darling girl." *A notre chère petite feye.* I loved being called *pitite feye,* a Walloon term of endearment. The Walloon dialect had a lilting rhythm like a melody. Les tantes had taught me songs and all kinds of wise sayings that were lessons to be remembered throughout life. In turn, I told them Yiddish sayings of my father, carefully avoiding the rude expressions he was so fond of like *shmuck* and *putz.* Les tantes thought I was unique in being able to speak both Walloon and Yiddish, but I never thought there was much difference between the two, especially when it came to wise sayings.

The summer began abysmally, with Tante Rifcha throwing my cousin Anne out of the house. Perhaps I was more upset than I should have been. Anne never paid much attention to me. She was pretty, and I liked the way she dressed in stylish, flattering clothes, unlike the other women in the neighborhood. Her husband, Ben, worked as a pattern cutter in the garment district and brought home his clothing samples. She was a head-turner alright, and the way she walked you could tell she knew it. I pictured her smoking cigarettes in one of those long holders as she lay back on a satin-covered chaise-lounge.

Anne may have brought some much-needed glamour to our street, but I didn't like going up to their apartment to play with her daughter. Rochelle was horribly spoiled and selfish, always bossing me around. She had so many dolls and books, and made sure I knew they belonged to her. I pretended not to care. I brought the Comtesse de Ségur books upstairs to show Rochelle, taking special delight in showing off my knowledge of French. At last, here was something Rochelle didn't have. But then Rochelle started ordering me around again, asking me to start her bath. I was seething. I went into the bathroom and turned only the hot tap on. How she would scream when she put her chubby leg in the boiling water! Sure enough, a few minutes after Rochelle disappeared into the bathroom she screamed at the top of her lungs, "She wants to kill me! *She wants to kill me!*" Tante Rifcha rushed in from across the landing and forbid me to ever go into Rochelle's room again.

Now it was June, and so hot that as soon as I came home from school I opened the windows in my bedroom to air it out. Right away I smelled the putrid garbage in the alley. Then I heard Tante Rifcha yelling upstairs and went up to see what was going on. Anne was packing a suitcase. Rochelle was sobbing in

Mindele's Journey

the corner. Suddenly Tante Rifcha grabbed Anne by the hair and dragged her to the landing. I couldn't believe it. Tante kept calling her a whore, yelling, *kurvah! kurvah!* Anne was holding onto her hair and screaming. Rochelle looked terrified. Then to my horror, Tante pushed Anne down the stairs. She slid down a few steps and grabbed hold of the railing. Such violence! I had witnessed heated arguments in Brussels between Poppa and Mme. Goldman often enough, but never anything like this. I ran back to my room and stayed there until Poppa came home. I was never able to look at my aunt the same way again.

That night at dinner Molly explained the whole sordid story to Poppa. It seems that Anne was having an affair and planned to leave her husband. Tante loved her son-in-law, Ben. To make things worse, Anne's lover was someone in the family. Despite everything, I felt sorry for Rochelle, who was being taken away from her father and grandmother. She wouldn't be around anymore to torment me, but somehow that didn't matter.

That summer Tante arranged for me to spend the vacation working for a family at Budd Lake in New Jersey. My father was agreeable and Molly was probably glad she wouldn't have to deal with my "fresh mouth" for two months. I would be paid fifty dollars, which was a good deal of money at the time. Tante's friends, the Lipchitzes, gave me an allowance of a dollar a week, but that would hardly cover the notebooks, clothes, and typewriter I would need for high school in the fall.

I went over to meet the Cohens the week before we left for New Jersey. The front room was littered

Mariette Bermowitz

with toys. Clothes waiting to be washed or ironed were piled on chairs. Mrs. Cohen looked haggard, as if she was barely able to take care of herself, let alone three children. Marsha, the oldest, was fourteen like me, but she was in a wheelchair. Mr. Cohen would only come to New Jersey on weekends. Aside from taking the children to day care at the clubhouse, I would be expected to vacuum and wash dishes. I almost blurted out that I wasn't a housekeeper when Marsha wheeled herself up and took my hand. "Not to worry," she said. "I have lots of great Nancy Drew books." They were my favorite. I think I learned English as fast as I did only because I couldn't get enough of Nancy Drew.

The house at Budd Lake was dark and badly furnished, but I could forget it when I was down by the lake wearing my new American pedal pushers, enjoying the way boys looked at me. I didn't like the way Mr. Cohen looked at me. When he came up that first weekend and shook my hand, he held it too long and tickled my palm with his middle finger. I never wanted to be around the house when he was there, and stayed down by the lake with Marsha, watching the boats glide off to the horizon.

Marsha introduced me to Philip, who lived in one of the grand houses on the other side of the lake. He looked very sporty in his light blazer, just like the tennis star I once admired in a magazine. And he spoke French! I fell in love immediately. I didn't want him to know that I was only the Cohens' summer helper from Brooklyn. I wanted him to invite me over to his beautiful house across the lake. But just then a blond came up and pulled him away. "Adieu," he

Mindele's Journey

said, waving. It took weeks for me to get over the disappointment.

At the end of the summer when I was more than ready to go home, something terrible happened. I had woken up in the middle of the night to use the toilet, and was only half-awake when I stumbled into the bathroom in my baby-doll nightie. I didn't even notice the light was already on. Suddenly there was Mr. Cohen wearing only his pajama top. He grabbed me and tried to pull my nightie off. Then he pulled my hand down to touch the swelling member between his legs. I screamed. He let me go.

I wondered if Marsha knew about her father. I couldn't bear to look at Mr. Cohen in the morning. He was talking to his wife and telling the children to finish packing their bags, acting as if nothing had happened. I couldn't imagine driving back to the city with him in the car. Luckily, Mrs. Cohen had made plans for me to go back with a neighbor who lived near me in Brooklyn.

Except for smelly sidewalks where the August heat had melted the tar, everything on Osborn Street was the same when I got back. I said hello to the neighbors fanning themselves on the stoops and mouthed a silent hello to the single lone tree in front of the house, its branches sagging in the sweltering air. Then I went straight to my room, barely greeting my father. I didn't want him to know about Mr. Cohen. I wished there was someone I could talk to, but I didn't know who.

Tante Rifcha opened up a bank account in my name and insisted I deposit my entire salary—the whole fifty dollars. She wouldn't listen when I told

155

her I wanted to buy a typewriter. But Poppa came to the rescue and bought me a secondhand one. He also bought me a pink radio. I discovered Elvis Presley on my pink radio. I put it on top of the Belgian lace doily les tantes had sent me along with a fresh batch of the Côte d'Or chocolates they knew I loved. Oh, how I missed those quiet, cool summers in Fraiture! Instead of televisions blaring in the courtyard, Tante Marie would be playing Schubert at the piano.

By the time I started high school that fall, both Piaf and Budd Lake seemed a distant memory. When Dr. Schwartz, chairman of the French Department, learned that I was a native speaker, he referred me to the foreign language office where I began tutoring other students in French. It was like coming home. Dr. Schwartz even dressed like Poppa did when we lived in Belgium, with a handkerchief sticking out of his lapel pocket and a matching tie. When Dr. Schwartz spoke to me about the family he lost in the war, he had relatives in Antwerp that had been deported, I told him about mine. I hadn't shared my story with anyone since leaving Belgium and the relief was almost too much for me. I started to cry as I remembered Fraiture. Dr. Schwartz offered me his handkerchief, then gently put his arm around my shoulders and said, *Bienvenue en Amérique.*

The foreign language department was a haven during my high school years. I was able to speak French every day, as well as read French literature, and I felt very special with all the attention I got from the teachers. From my first year in high school, I knew that I wanted to be a French teacher.

Mindele's Journey

There was no question of my joining after-school activities, because Tante Rifcha said I had to work. She found me an office job where I learned the switchboard, but I liked my second job at Woolworth's on Pitkin Avenue much better. I worked at the cosmetic counter, where I learned the magical power of nail polish, lipstick, and eye makeup.

With Passover approaching, I helped Tante Rifcha with preparations in the basement kitchen. In Brussels I had refused to go to Hebrew school. But in Brooklyn, where all my high school friends were Jewish, I had become curious about my religion and was now interested in understanding the Haggadah. I was even beginning to like my aunt. She was strict and bossy, but I respected her, and dutifully carried the pot of chicken soup to my cousin Esther every Friday afternoon. It was a long walk, but I usually stayed for the Sabbath dinner with my cousin and her husband, Roy, and baby-sat for them afterward when they went out.

One evening when I was babysitting, I saw a man looking in through the Venetian blinds while I was doing my homework. I was frightened until I realized it was only Roy. Then they came in, and Esther disappeared into the children's room. I got into the car with Roy, who was going to drive me home. I wondered why he was heading the wrong way, going toward Rockaway Pier. He said he wanted to show me how pretty the water looked from the dock. How odd, I thought. I didn't know that Rockaway Pier was where couples went to make out. Roy parked away from the streetlight, but there was a full moon so it

Mariette Bermowitz

was very bright anyway. He put his arm around my waist. I felt my whole body go stiff.

"You know why I brought you here?"

"No, I really don't," I said, more curious than frightened.

He unzipped his fly. "I want you to feel it," he said, grabbing my hair and pulling me down on him. I didn't know what to do. I resisted briefly, and then gave in, overwhelmed by feelings beyond anything I'd known before.

At fifteen, I became the obsession of a thirty-two-year-old man who was my cousin's husband. The situation terrified me. Yet I longed for his touch. I knew I was getting myself into an inextricable mess but I had nowhere to turn. It was sinful, according to everything I had learned in Fraiture in catechism class. I would be damned to the eternal fires of Hell. There was no M. Le Curé to confess to and besides, I wasn't Catholic. I rationalized that perhaps that fact alone would absolve me of complete damnation. I felt trapped in the affair with Roy. I didn't want to babysit for them anymore, but my aunt insisted I go. I couldn't say anything to Esther, and Roy always took the long way home.

And yet for the first time I was feeling a sense of my own power. I was starting to be aware that men were staring at me when I walked down the street. I liked it, but I hated it too. I hoped no one in the family would find out what Roy and I were doing, especially not Esther. Yet how could she not have known? Didn't she wonder what took Roy so long to come home? She was pregnant at the time and looked worn out. Her house reflected the emptiness

Mindele's Journey

that must have filled her heart. She smoked as many cigarettes as my father did, and hardly ever laughed. She didn't seem to have any interests. There were no pretty curtains on the windows, or colorful splashes of life anywhere. There was no seductive fragrance of any kind. I saw her as a dull housewife who had given up her individuality to the overpowering presence of her husband.

I always felt that Esther disliked me. I had felt it on the pier when they all came to meet the ship the day Poppa and I arrived in America. Poppa and Tante Rifcha were locked in each other's arms, while my cousins kept their distance. Esther, in particular, had looked at me in a way I found disturbing. I never understood why I felt the same way about her. The feeling grew more intense as I became a pretty teenager.

Clearly her husband was a womanizer, but she would have her revenge. When Poppa died she said it was my fault. And even before that she said secretarial school was good enough for me and I didn't need college, and furthermore, I wouldn't amount to much anyway since I was so boy-crazy. I did have lots of boyfriends. Roy had given me plenty of practice. I was learning how to survive in America. I sometimes thought how it might have been had I remained in Belgium, but in America, my awareness of the mysteries of sex were revealed early with this older man. After seeing the beautiful Italian actress Gina Lollobrigida playing opposite the French actor Gerard Philippe in *Fanfan La Tulipe*, I decided that she would be my inspiration and he my ideal man. It didn't take long before I acquired pouting lips

159

and deep set eyes dramatized with thick mascara. My wardrobe had changed as well. I paid for my clothes with the money I made working different jobs after school.

I also started a club with my girlfriends called the Avons. They loved the association with the French word *avons*, meaning "we have" what it takes. I designed the club jacket, navy blue with the white logo Avons highlighted on the back. It was a thrill to have created an identity, and I wore my jacket the way boys in *A Stone for Danny Fisher* wore theirs, zipped halfway with their hands in their pockets to make them look tough. I reveled being called "toughie." This outrageous mix of Brooklyn street smarts and European exhibitionism was irresistible to the boys and to some of the male teachers as well, especially my biology teacher. Although the high grade I received in his class was the result of diligent study, I knew how easy it was to charm him.

I became aware that academic success superseded everything else, more so after my cousin's remark that I wouldn't amount to anything. No one in the family seemed to care that I was a member of Arista, the academic honor society, or that I averaged top grades. When I brought my report card home, Poppa didn't even look at it. He told me to sign it. I became quite adept at copying his interesting scribble. He never learned the Latin alphabet and could neither read nor write except for the Hebrew lessons he needed for his Bar Mitzvah. In Belgium, I was the one who read all the letters and filled out documents and papers when requested by the government. Although he never said so, I knew that my

Mindele's Journey

father was proud of me. He didn't say much, but he revealed himself in subtle gestures, such as the blessings he administered on the High Holy Days. I will always remember the way his bony fingers quivered on my head as he chanted Hebrew prayers, invoking the God of his ancestors to keep safe this only child left to him.

I wondered that my father never questioned why Roy paid so much attention to me. There were driving lessons, tutoring in chemistry, the day trip back to Budd Lake without Esther, and the way he hovered over me at the Passover Seder. I was mortified when he rubbed his leg against mine under the table. But in the clinking of glasses, communal singing and rejoicing, no one seemed to notice.

Then I fell in love with Marvin. At last there was an end to Roy. The high school placement officer had sent me for a receptionist job and I was immediately hired at the old-age home on Sutter Avenue. I didn't think I was going to stay very long because of the way the manager was flirting with me. I dreaded another Roy episode. But when I volunteered to work on Sundays they put me at the switchboard. Now I had a clear view of the lobby. I enjoyed being there on visiting days when the elderly residents gathered with their families in the lobby. Some of them befriended me. They called me pretty girl, *sheine meidele,* and loved speaking Yiddish with me. I was especially fond of Mr. Pfeffer, who often came to chat and read aloud excerpts from his Jewish paper *The Forward* to see if the "wonder kid" really did know Yiddish. I was in deep conversation with Mr. Pfeffer when Marvin, the spitting image of Louis Jourdan

161

Mariette Bermowitz

in *Gigi,* sprinted past the desk. It was, as the French would say, *le coup de foudre*—love at first sight.

I loved the way Marvin moved, slow and easy on his feet like some gorgeous jungle animal on the prowl. He had jet-black hair and dark eyebrows that framed his green-gray eyes. He was tall and slender and his shirt was unbuttoned more than it needed to be, showing off his chest. When he introduced himself, I lathered on my French accent.

"Yeah, I heard you came from Belgium and that you speak French."

His "yeah" was so sexy. After work he took me to the local luncheonette. I felt so intimidated by his looks and the way he talked that all I could do was listen. But after a while, I relaxed enough to tell him that I was going to college and didn't intend to work at a switchboard all my life. Marvin didn't seem to be particularly interested one way or another. He talked about his family, his younger brother, his Hungarian father and mother, and his love of jazz. I listened without offering any information about my past. Tante Rifcha told me that nobody would be interested in what happened in Europe, especially not the boys I would be going out with. So I never told Marvin.

I spent hours dressing for our first date. Marvin was taking me to the Circus Lounge on Flatbush Avenue to hear Dave Brubeck. I tried on one dress after another, hoping that one would make me look older and sexier. When I put on the new pair of spiked heels, Poppa frowned and said he almost didn't recognize me. He didn't make much of an effort when Marvin came to pick me up. He remained seated,

162

Mindele's Journey

expecting this suitor to make the proper moves. I was pleased to see them shake hands and to hear my father say that he expected me home before midnight. It was a sign that he cared.

That first date was exceptional in every way. I floated into the club feeling like a movie star, holding onto the arm of the most beautiful man in the world. When he told me *I* was beautiful, I silently thanked Gina Lollobrigida for teaching me how to display cleavage. The club was dark and smoky and smelled like the inside of a box of stale perfumed handkerchiefs. I loved the low lights, the tables covered with candles, the costume jewelry glimmering everywhere as women moved about. But I especially loved the feeling of being part of this grand adventure into adulthood. After a few sips of the cocktail Marvin ordered, I was euphoric. But it was the sound of the piano, its swooning languor that made the evening a touchstone in my life. Marvin had introduced me not only to alcohol but to Dave Brubeck.

After two dates we got into sex, except in those days it was called heavy petting. No one wanted to get pregnant and there were other ways of enjoyment, with lots of touching in the right places. I waited for Poppa and Molly to visit her brother in New Jersey to invite Marvin to my bedroom. I surprised him with my awareness of things sensual. I didn't dare talk about my experience with Roy, but it had freed me of my inhibitions. Marvin may have intimidated me with his good looks and smooth talk, but not when it came to intimate caresses. Making love made me feel wanted and needed, just like I felt when I listened to Elvis singing.

Mariette Bermowitz

Marvin took me to meet his family. Pampered by an overprotective mother, he was used to attention. "A gift from the gods," she called him. His parents had come from Hungary before the war and the extermination of the Jews there. I never told them what happened to me and my family. I wish I could have. But there was a feeling of Europe in that apartment that I related to, from the lace doilies on the table to the lingering fragrance of the Hungarian meals his mother prepared. While I was never invited to join them for dinner, I did get to hear his brother play the saxophone. According to Marvin, jazz was America's gift to the world.

Home on Osborne Street began to feel like a place where I was just passing through. Poppa was always tired after coming home from work. He didn't like the subway ride and the long hours in the shop where he did assembly-line work. Gone were his glory days on the Rue Haute and his reputation as a master tailor. But he surprised me one day by bringing home a piece of silk paisley material and another in beige wool. It took him over a week to sew me a magnificent new suit. He had lined the jacket with the paisley material and made a matching blouse. He didn't exactly tell me, but I knew he wanted me to feel special. And maybe it was also a way for him to show off his skills.

Poppa didn't like Marvin. When I asked him if it was because Marvin was older, he answered with a snort of disdain, "I just don't trust Hungarian Jews. They aren't good to their women." Was it past experience or the fact that his child was growing up and perhaps leaving soon? When Marvin came to pick

Mindele's Journey

me up for a date, Poppa always managed to disappear. But he was waiting up for me when I got home. I would open the door and there he was, grinning, sitting on the bathroom toilet, which faced the front door. He was making sure Marvin knew that I had a curfew and that someone cared when I came home. But I think he also enjoyed seeing how embarrassed I was.

I started to go out with other boys I met in my classes, mostly to delude my father into thinking I no longer cared for Marvin. The truth was that Marvin no longer wanted an exclusive relationship. He told me one Sunday when I returned home from work. I had waited for him in the lobby of the old-age home for almost an hour. He always came to walk me to the bus, which stopped underneath the elevated subway not far from the home. It was a deserted area where I didn't feel safe. I never dared ask him to drive me home in his father's car. Those occasions were reserved for when we went to jazz clubs and necked afterward. But that Sunday he didn't show up. Mr. Pfeffer had come down to the lobby and insisted on keeping me company while I waited for Marvin. He even tried to comfort me when he noticed the tears I couldn't hide. I think he told me not to trust "those Hungarians," but maybe it was only Poppa's warning I was remembering. Poor Mr. Pfeffer volunteered to escort me part of the way to the bus stop. He could hardly walk, gripping his cane and stumbling on the uneven sidewalk. Yet the smile on his face showed how much he enjoyed helping his favorite damsel in distress. He talked about the wife he had loved and the children who hardly came to visit. I murmured sympathies, but really only felt the ache of my own heart. When we reached the street corner he turned back. I gave him a hug and told him I would be fine. Then I remained at the bus stop, waiting and hoping against hope to see Marvin running up with an excuse for his lateness.

When he called later, before I could tell him how I waited for him in the lobby, anxiously expecting him to appear, he announced that he no longer wanted an exclusive relationship. He still wanted to see me but he would be going out with some of the college girls he was meeting. "But you're still my little tiger," he cooed.

He knew how to play my emotions the way a cat plays with a mouse. "My father doesn't want me to see you anymore anyway," I said. "Did you know that he sits on the toilet with the door open when you bring me home just to embarrass you?"

Marvin answered, "If we go out again, I won't walk you to the door, then." There was something triumphant in the way he said it, as if he knew I would accept him on any terms. And I would. I had placed myself on the altar of unrequited love. I needed to be consumed by *passion.*

The opportunity came about soon enough. The following week, I told him I had a date with someone else that Saturday night. I was hoping to make him curious, but he turned his back with a shrug of boredom. Then, as if he had thought it over, he turned around. I was hoping for a sign of jealousy, but he had something else in mind. When my date brought me home, Marvin would be waiting for me in his car down the block.

Mindele's Journey

I was no stranger to subterfuge, having learned it from Roy at Rockaway Pier. I may have been a model student in high school, but outside of the classroom was another matter. There was something I liked about subterfuge. Maybe it was because of the games I had learned to play in Belgium when the nuns told me to hide in a basket so the Nazis wouldn't find me. Or when they called me Mariette de Jésus so no one would suspect my true identity.

All through my date I would dream about meeting Marvin later. My date would leave me at the door, and I'd wait until Poppa thought I was asleep. Then I quietly slipped out to meet my *passion*. Marvin was waiting for me in his car parked at the end of the street. I loved the way he called me "Tiger," then grabbed me and threw me into the backseat as if I were a rag doll. I couldn't wait to feel his body against mine, smell the masculine fragrance of his skin, touch the smoothness of his muscles, and linger in the moment as time stood still. Then I'd go back home with my secret, back to my room, and life with Poppa and Molly.

One night it was more French farce than *passion*. It was the weekend Poppa and Molly had gone to New Jersey to visit her brother and stay overnight. I had already made a date but told Marvin that my father would be away. He said to give him the key to the apartment and he would wait for me at home. I never considered the perversity of the suggestion. I was thrilled, exhilarated. I couldn't wait for my date to bring me back home. When I got to the apartment, Marvin was nowhere to be found.

167

Mariette Bermowitz

The next morning Tante yelled for me to come upstairs. I hadn't had a chance yet to call Marvin and find out what happened. My heart was thumping as I went up to "face the music." I waited for my aunt to start accusing me, but to my surprise, she said, "Did you hear anything unusual when you came home last night? Max heard a noise in your apartment and went down to check it out."

I called Marvin as soon as I could get away from Tante. He said when he heard my uncle come into the apartment he ran to the bedroom and hid in the closet. "I thought I was going to suffocate in the closet from the smell of those mothballs!"

I laughed, enjoying the thought of Marvin trapped in the closet. Not long afterward, he asked his mother to invite me for a weekend in the Catskills at their bungalow colony. Did this mean he really cared for me after all? That none of the older girls he was dating pleased him as much as I did? Of course, it was out of the question that I would tell Poppa about the invitation, but I was determined to go. I asked a girlfriend to call the house and invite me to spend the weekend with her family.

"Let me speak to her mother," Poppa said.

"She doesn't speak Yiddish," I lied. Poppa was reluctant to let me go, and I felt guilty for lying to him, but I was in love. I even bought new perfume and a new outfit to wear. The week before we left I was so excited I could hardly eat.

As soon as we arrived, Marvin left me with his mother and took off to play baseball with his friends. Why couldn't he have taken me for a walk first and shown me around? This wasn't turning out as

168

Mindele's Journey

I expected. But when he came back later and took me out for lunch, all was forgiven. How could I have known that Tanta Rifcha's stepson, Ben, would be staying in the same bungalow colony with his wife and kids? What terrible luck that we would be in the diner at the same time! Ben stopped at our table and said, "Mariette, what are you doing here?"

"Please don't tell Tante. My father doesn't know I'm here!" But he told her anyway. When I came home, I saw Tanta Rifcha looking out from the upstairs window. Her hair was uncombed and she looked as mad as one of the Furies. I shuddered to think what I was in store for.

"Come up here immediately!" She sounded as angry as she did the day she threw her daughter Anne out of the house. Her hands with the chipped red nail polish gripped the banister. "Where were you this weekend?" she shouted.

I nearly tripped up the stairs. But I didn't care anymore. "I was in the Catskills!"

She pointed her finger at me like a saber, shrieking, "Go down and see your father!"

Poppa was sitting at the kitchen table with his head between his hands, staring into the distance. He pulled himself up and came toward me. He seemed no more than a hollowed shell about to crumble. I couldn't bear to look at him, and as I turned away he lifted his hand and smacked me with fingers that felt as sharp as steel. His voice quivered. "Why do the bad have to survive and the good die?"

I was cut to the quick. Then, as if he realized what he had said, he threw his arms around me and broke into sobs. We remained locked together in grief.

Then I took the handkerchief from his pocket and wiped his tears as if he was a child in need of solace. He looked like a wounded sparrow. "It's so hard for me to be both your father and mother. I tried and failed."

"No, Poppa! You didn't fail! I'm sorry I lied to you." But nothing I said made him feel any better. I went to my room. Poppa would probably go out to smoke. He would sit on a milk crate outside Mr. Feingold's grocery store and talk to the neighbors. I had no one to talk to. I wanted to cry but the tears wouldn't come. I wanted to wipe Marvin out of my mind and make him disappear along with the ache in my heart. But it was useless. I kept hearing Edith Piaf singing, *Je l'ai dans la peau.* "He's inside my skin." I took out the box with the letters from les tantes. *Chère pitite feye.* Maman described the marigolds she planted to keep the bugs away. The carnations, roses and lilies were growing in abundance and would make bouquets to put in M. le Curé's church on Sundays. The doves were impossible with their gurgling so early in the morning. When would I ever be able to go back?

When I returned to work at the old-age home I heard my dear Mr. Pfeffer had died. The family wanted an autopsy. I couldn't bear to think of poor Mr. Pfeffer on a slab in the morgue. I would miss him terribly. Every time he saw me it was, "Well, pretty girl, how are you doing?" *Noo, sheine meidele. Vee geitz?* "I'm fine, Mr. Pfeffer, I'm fine," I always said. And I was fine. I graduated fourth in my class and was admitted to Brooklyn College. I proved them all wrong. Tante Rifcha had said, "My daughters were

Mindele's Journey

secretaries—why do you want to go to college to be anything else?"

"All my friends are going to college and I'm going with them!"

"Don't expect your father to help you—he's in poor health."

"Don't worry about me—I can work." I swore that I'd never become a secretary or a housewife spending my days sitting on the sofa, smoking cigarettes and watching soaps like my cousin Esther did. My cousins thought I was boy-crazy, but they didn't see me during those long hours I spent alone studying in my room. They didn't know me at all.

I was eighteen now, an American citizen with a bank account. That had been my aunt's idea, which I appreciated now. Molly said it was about time that I contributed some money for household expenses. I pretended not to hear. Then she said, "You could at least help your father out." I knew Poppa wasn't making much. That night I slipped some bills into his jacket hanging in the closet. The next day the money was on my night table. He never said anything about it, but he winked at me at the dinner table.

Poppa never told me how he felt about my going to college, but he beamed when I spoke about my plans. He had never learned how to read or write. He came from the Old World, where trades were handed down from father to son. Only religious scholars were allowed into the realms of learning and higher knowledge. Times had changed too quickly for him. First he had to run from Poland, then from Belgium to an America where he still felt like a stranger. The week before I started classes he presented me with a

171

Mariette Bermowitz

wool jacket he had made. He stroked the velvet collar and cuffs and said, *Zoll zein mit mazell.* "Let it be with good luck." His eyes were filled with tears. I saw that I had made him proud.

☆ ☆ ☆

I met Simon in my junior year when we sat next to each other in English class. He had dark brown hair and soft brown eyes, and when he looked at me it was hard to pay attention to the lessons. We were studying Marlow's *Doctor Faustus.* The professor read aloud the passage where Faust says, "Was this the face that launched a thousand ships?" He asked Simon to continue reading. Simon looked mortified. I almost burst out laughing. But he picked up where the professor left off, and as he read his voice grew more confident, more resonant, as if he was inspired by some inner fire. "Her lips suck forth my soul... Come, Helen, come give me my soul again...And none but thou shalt be my paramour!"

Simon looked up and flashed his beautiful eyes at me. He walked me to my next class and I gave him my phone number. When he gave me a book of Khalil Gibran's love poems, I gave him a record of Beethoven's Sixth Symphony. I told him about André Gide's novel, *La Symphonie Pastorale,* which had left such an impression on me in French class, and he took me to hear Van Cliburn play Rachmaninoff. The concert was at Lewisohn Stadium in Manhattan. People from Brooklyn usually stayed close to home, especially those in my neighborhood. But with Simon I was stepping out. He was the first man who

172

Mindele's Journey

ever showed me any kind of devotion. The afternoon when we walked in the Brooklyn Botanic Garden he kept stopping to kiss me. He said my perfume drove him crazy. We never did anything other than kissing. As a devout Catholic he didn't believe in sex before marriage. I wrote to les tantes about my Catholic boyfriend, wanting them to know that in my heart I was following the teachings I learned in catechism. I thought it would make them happy.

When Simon proposed, I said yes, because he was the gentlest, sweetest man I had ever met. I wanted to have Simon over for dinner, but I dreaded telling Poppa that he was Catholic. So I said nothing, and Simon came to Sabbath dinner. It was the first of many. Poor Simon! All those Friday dinners being subjected to Molly's leaden matzo balls and reheated noodle puddings. I made Simon promise not to tell my father about his religion until my father got to know him better. They weren't able to understand each other very much anyway, as Poppa still spoke only Yiddish. Simon knew a smattering of the Yiddish expressions, which were rampant in Brooklyn vernacular, and tried his best. I was in charge of translating their conversations, and I was hardly ever truthful. Simon was deeply troubled. He said that if I didn't tell my father about him, he would.

That weekend I asked my father to take a walk with me. It was a lovely summer evening. I was grateful the humidity had let up. His steps were slow and hesitant, and he breathed with difficulty. I thought he knew how Simon and I felt about each other, but I was still terrified to tell him that Simon wasn't Jewish. Still, it had to be done. I summoned all my courage and blurted out, "Poppa, Simon and I love each other and we want to get married. I also want you to know that he isn't Jewish!"

My father's face turned ashen. "*Meine kinde.* I have lost them all, and if you marry him, I will sit Shiva for you too."

I was shocked. My father died later that year. Cousin Esther said I killed him. I have tried not to think that somehow I was at fault. But the guilt remains.

I couldn't believe Poppa was gone. Sometimes I imagined I still heard the sound of his slippers shuffling down the hallway, or his hacking cough. I saw traces of Poppa everywhere. I saw the nicotine stains on the edge of the bathtub, reminding me of his night vigils on the toilet seat waiting for me to come home. I saw the outline of his elbows pressed against the table top, the outline of his back against the pillows on the sofa. I felt the blessing of his hands above my head. I kept seeing his face before me, smiling and laughing, or crying. And over and over again, I saw him dying.

Within a month of his passing, Molly had disposed of all his clothes. I helped her empty out the closets. Poppa's beautiful suits and hats were given away to his friends. At the back of the closet I found an old pair of shoes. The leather was cracked and discolored. I remember when he asked Mme. Goldman to buy them for him. It seems they had the same shoe size. My father, who seemed so big when I was a child,

Mindele's Journey

was in fact a very short man who couldn't find shoes to fit him. What he found in the boy's section was not elegant enough. But he had seen a pair of shoes he thought were ideal in a women's shop on the Rue Haute. He kept them in a special place by his work table. I remember watching him sketch, then cutting patterns and choosing swatches of material. I saw my father as an artist. When he tacked his finished cuttings to the wall, they looked like paintings to me. Mme. Goldman would make him a cup of tea and they would sit down together. He poured the hot tea into the saucer to cool it off, then put a cube of sugar between his teeth and slurped the liquid with delight. When he went back to work, Mme. Goldman went back to her singing. She rocked herself as she sang, her arms folded over her ample bosom, her long stringy hair hanging down to her waist. She sang Polish and Yiddish songs that recalled her homeland. As I carefully placed Poppa's old shoes on the pile of clothes being discarded, I could almost hear her singing, *Brent, my shtetele brent.* Burning, my homeland is burning.

Arthur

Poppa had liked Arthur. I might add that he even considered Arthur a potential son-in-law. Not only was he Jewish, but he spoke Yiddish. "That's a *mensch*," my father said, after meeting him only once. He liked that Arthur brought me candy and flowers and had introduced himself properly. Arthur waited for Poppa to offer him a seat. He smoked with my father

Mariette Bermowitz

and laughed at his jokes. Poppa was also pleased to hear that he had a well-paying job as a talent agent. He didn't quite understand what that involved but he thought he would no longer have to worry about his daughter's future. I never told him that Arthur was already married. At thirty-six, Poppa suspected that Arthur might have been married before, but it didn't really matter. *A gitte mensch,* he said, nodding.

I was relieved when Poppa accepted Arthur, as it put a stop to his constant reminders about Simon. The only problem was that except for the "*gitte mensch,*" Arthur was not the man Poppa thought he was. I had met Arthur when the college office sent me to his dental office to interview for the job of assistant. The hours were long but the salary made up for it. Arthur offered me the job within a few minutes of our meeting, later saying that I was irresistible with my French accent. I was fully aware that he was just as taken with my choice of sweater and tight-fitting skirt as he was with my accent. We became lovers within weeks. I was in the darkroom developing X-rays when I heard him come up behind me. He put his hands on my waist and pulled me tightly against him. I didn't resist. His breath smelled sweet, his cheek felt warm against my hair. But Arthur was married. His wife wanted to go into show business; hence, he was an aspiring talent agent on the side. I lied to Poppa about Arthur, but it didn't matter. My father never found out that Arthur was married. He died before I ever had to confess that dreadful truth.

Not long after Poppa's death, Molly decided to live with her sister in Florida. Our lives changed so quickly after Poppa was gone it was like a windstorm had come in the night and swept the past away. I felt shattered inside. I didn't know what I was going to do, or what was to become of me. I wanted to finish school, but where was I going to live? Tante Rifcha had gone to Florida the year before. My cousins wouldn't talk to me. Arthur was in Manhattan living with his wife. I thought of visiting les tantes and Belgium, but I had no money for a trip.

Arthur saved me. One day when I went to work I found him waiting for me at the door. He had closed the office and announced we were going to go look for an apartment for me. He said he couldn't leave his wife, but neither would he abandon me. We found a small studio not far from the high school where I had started student teaching. It was on the first floor overlooking a tree-lined street. There were always people going to and from the subway station on the corner. I loved the street sounds floating up to my window, making me feel part of the movement and activity below. Hearing other people close by also made me feel less lonely. Though Arthur had promised me love and protection, he never stayed beyond a certain hour. There were just so many excuses he could offer his wife for coming home late. I met her once in the office when she happened to be in the neighborhood, or so she claimed. From the way she looked at me I wondered if she suspected him of having an affair. I had seen that look on Tante Rifcha's face. It was a look of utter contempt and it cut through me like a blade. But if I had any misgivings about my wrongdoings, they didn't last long. I didn't like Arthur's wife. She was the daughter of a prominent doctor, and Arthur said she was always

Mariette Bermowitz

reminding him that it was due to her money that he was able to set up his dental practice. I thought her haughty tone and obvious dislike of me justified the way I felt.

I found our illicit relationship both exciting and familiar. At times it reminded me of Roy, other times of Marvin. Roy came to visit when he found out where I lived. Luckily, Arthur happened to be there at the time and he told Roy to leave. He made sure that Roy knew never to cross my threshold again. The scene was pure melodrama. I took great pleasure in watching Roy's mustache twitch and beads of sweat dribble down his forehead. Arthur had claimed me as his. And I followed his guidance and supervision like a dutiful child. I no longer had to worry about where I was going next—I had arrived. I lived in a beautiful apartment, dined in elegant restaurants, and my clothes were from Saks Fifth Avenue. Arthur sent me flowers that came all the way from Hawaii. He bought me jewelry from Cartier and a mother-of-pearl cigarette holder. Sometimes I caught my reflection in the mirror of one of those elegant places where we dined, and I hardly recognized myself. Young, beautiful, on the arm of an admiring man, it was all I wanted to be. I loved the way I was greeted by doormen and by the maître d' at Quo Vadis, the Four Seasons, and La Brasserie. Arthur never took me to Sardi's because that was where he always took his wife. I didn't ask questions about his life with her. But sometimes I wondered what it would be like if he could spend the night with me. Then his wife found out about us.

Before taking her away on holiday, Arthur had left his car with me. It was a Vauxhall, a British import,

178

Mindele's Journey

and perfect in every detail as with all of Arthur's possessions. I couldn't drive, but one night a friend offered to drive me to a club outside the city. I must have had too much to drink because I left a small purse inside the car and completely forgot about it. Arthur's wife found it. Maybe subconsciously I wanted her to find it. But then she hired a detective to find out what Arthur was doing when he wasn't with her, and Arthur had to fire me. But he still paid the rent, put food in the refrigerator and sent presents. Our idyll was over but the relationship wasn't. To stay clear of any further snooping by the detective, we met in secluded places like the cemetery opposite the school where I was a student teacher.

For me, there was nothing more addictive than forbidden desire. Arthur and I played a game of promises, deceit, and illusion. Arthur would call me from a public phone booth. He called me at night when he took the dog for a walk. Long talks, when he wanted to know what I was wearing, how I was sitting, and that sort of thing. I wondered if Arthur went home to satisfy his wife after our steamy exchanges. When Arthur wanted me to date other men, I did, but then he insisted I tell him every detail. I did at first, and then I started inventing things to please his imagination. I wanted him jealous enough to consider the possibility of leaving his wife.

Right before spring break, my last semester at Brooklyn College, Arthur presented me with two envelopes. The first contained a credit card and a round-trip ticket to Belgium. He said I wasn't to open the second envelope until I was on the plane. I was so moved I couldn't say a word. A ticket to

179

Belgium! Suddenly I saw Poppa holding my hand as we boarded the train and left Brussels.

"Will we ever come back?" I asked.

"Over my dead body, over my dead body," he repeated over and over.

Poppa never wanted to go back. After ten years of separation and a lifetime of changes, I was going back home. Arthur had made my dream come true. I could not have loved him more for it. I could not kiss him enough, or stop holding his hand against my face. He was laughing with me. Then he wiped the tears smudging my makeup. He said it made me look so sad.

Brussels 1960

I had never been on a plane before. When Poppa and I came to America it had taken five days of travel by sea. And now, in less than a day, I would be back in Brussels. I could hardly believe my good fortune, or Arthur's generosity and love. I was going home, back to the place I loved. Tante Rifcha had never understood why I missed the moody skies over Belgium. We had so many arguments about my dislike of Florida, the overbearing sunshine and humidity. I had grown up in the mist and rain. Tante Rifcha couldn't conceive of a world that was hidden, mysterious, romantic, leaving so much to the imagination. And now I was returning to that world, to the family that was waiting for me.

As soon as we were aloft I took out the second envelope. Arthur had said it was a hotel reservation.

Mindele's Journey

He loved keeping me guessing, and then offering me an unusual gift. He said my look of childlike joy fulfilled him. But now I felt like crying. Arthur had booked me a room at the Métropole Hotel for my first night in Brussels! He remembered. He had listened when I told him about my childhood and what the Métropole had meant to me. I was glad that les tantes were not going to be at the airport. In a few days I would take the train just like old times. Thoughts tumbled through my mind like jumping beans. Would les tantes recognize me? Would they still consider me their *pitite feye*? I hoped they wouldn't mind that I was staying in Brussels before coming to see them. Brussels! Would I even recognize the city where I had walked as a child, or would I wander the streets like a stranger? But how could I forget the Rue Ste. Anne or eating mussels at the Grand Place?

When at last the plane landed it was pouring, the rain like pellets of gray metal striking the windows. The runway was aglow with multicolored puddles under the glare of airport lights. I was in bliss as I stepped out into the rain, that ever-present companion of my childhood. I was back in the past. Feathery mists in the morning, then drops that turned into sheets of rain crashing down onto the cobblestones. I remembered how I used to love meandering down the alleys and impasses that surrounded the streets where we lived, where the color of the stones seemed to mix with the gray of the sky. It was like entering a black-and-white photograph where the edges of things were defined only by the contrast of light and dark.

181

Mariette Bermowitz

At customs everyone spoke either French or Flemish. It was music to my ears. How long ago since I had heard Flemish! The only Flemish I remembered was the poem I had once recited in school, *De Lach Van Moeder.* "A Mother's Smile." I was so excited, it was all I could do not to blurt out to the customs official stamping my passport, "See, I was born in Belgium. I've come back. It's been such a long time. But I'm back!" I had come back as an American, with an American passport.

On the way to the hotel, the taxi driver spoke Flemish. I thought about telling him I knew *De Lach Van Moeder,* which had made my teacher cry when I recited it in class, because she knew how my mother had died. Instead, I let my mind drift. I took in the early morning light, the cobblestones, and the old buildings that looked so small compared to New York.

We pulled up to the Métropole Hotel, a Belle Époque masterpiece that had survived the wars that ravaged Europe. An ageless splendor, a feast of lights and columns festooned in nineteenth-century finery. Before going through the opulent door, I glanced at the terrace. No one was sitting under the canopy to watch the rain fall. Poppa and I used to sit on the terrace on warm Sundays before his friend De Lange took me roller-skating in the Bois de La Cambre. Afternoons of pure indulgence, when we were able to forget that we lived in a squalid working-class district. I always ordered my favorite drink, grenadine, that unforgettable ambrosia of ruby syrup and mineral water. I remembered how Poppa stared at me when I slowly sipped the liquid through a straw, then

Mindele's Journey

lifted my glass to inspect the passersby on the Place de Brouckère through a filter of red. He watched me silently as I twirled my glass, creating a tornado of bubbles, and sometimes he looked as if he was going to cry. We sat on straw chairs that circled the terrace and watched the world go by.

The straw chairs were gone now, replaced by sturdier seating, and there were now heating ventilators above the tables. Inside, little seemed changed. Persian carpets and glistening brass, crystal chandeliers and marbled walls still graced the halls. Arthur had reserved a luxurious room for me. I thought I was still dreaming the next morning when I woke up in such fragrant sheets, surrounded by soothing blue-papered walls. And so quiet compared to Brooklyn! I showered and went down for breakfast. The rain had passed, but felt no farther away than the somber clouds overhead. I gleefully ordered croissants and café au lait, and reveled in the strawberry jam. I was indeed back in my native land, remembering how the smell of strawberries grown in neat little kitchen gardens perfumed the air, particularly the ones behind the stern stone houses of the Ardennes.

But in ten years, the contours of Brussels had changed. Tall buildings and new hotels had transformed the city into a modern mecca, etching a different skyline onto the medieval city. I walked past the upscale shops lining the wide boulevards and tried to find the Rue Ste. Anne. It was a test of my inner guide to see if I remembered the route. I had mastered those streets as a child, walking alone in the rain on the way to the library after school, and I had no fear of getting lost now.

Mariette Bermowitz

Still, I had to ask directions to La Grand Place, which was in walking distance of the Rue Ste. Anne. I turned into a narrow cobbled street where time had stood still, and came out at the Place de la Chapelle on market day. It was as if a painting of Breughel or Bosch had suddenly come to life; the ruddy complexions, corpulent bodies, the tattered clothing of the pushcart vendors shouting their wares, crying children, the odor of fried potatoes and mustard, and the tiny coral shrimps heaped into newspaper sheets that resembled horns of plenty. This was medieval Brussels, where Gothic church spires hovered over slanted rooftops, and houses were wrapped in time-worn ivy. Past the church with its jewel-like windows and stone embroidery resting under an impassive gray sky, was the headquarters of the Belgian Communist Party, modern and out of place. Its red flag was hanging from the first-floor window, hammer and sickle bending into the folds with the wind. I had seen it so many times from the trolley window when Poppa and I went to visit his friend Jakobowicz.

Nothing had changed on the Place du Grand Sablon. The antique shops bloomed around the square like faded flowers. The fountain in the middle was still there, solid and stern with barely a trickle from its spout. I remembered as a child how I used to climb into the empty stone basin and passersby told me to get out. The fountain was opposite the patisserie Wittamer where Jean and I made faces in the mirror as we delighted in homemade vanilla ice cream served in silver cups. I went in to buy some chocolates. I told the salesgirl what a refuge Wittamer had been to me as a child, how wonderful it was to come

Mindele's Journey

back. She wished me *bienvenue* and put an extra chocolate in the bag.

The Rue Ste. Anne began a few houses down from Wittamer. Cathedral bells rang out as I reached the entrance to the narrow street. I felt as solemn as if I was visiting a graveyard. I saw myself as a child roaming the Impasse St. Jacques, buying candies in Mme. Marie's store, notebooks in the *papèterie* and milk in the *épicerie*. I walked slowly, breathing in the stones, revisiting the sounds of old until I reached the end of the street where we had lived, No. 8, Rue Ste. Anne. The house looked empty. There was a sign in the window. *A vendre.* I had planned to ring the bell, ask to come in perhaps. Tell them I had once lived there. I thought that maybe I could have seen those rooms again. Now I felt locked out, robbed of something I couldn't name. I rang the bell at No. 10. There was no answer. I rang again. The old door creaked open and there stood M. Gianini in his canvas apron that hung below his knees. His face was sprinkled with plaster dust like a ghostly clown. I was too overwhelmed to speak.

Ce n'est pas possible, mais c'est Mariette! He hugged me, saying he would recognize me anywhere because no one with such pretty brown eyes ever lived on the Rue Ste. Anne. It seemed as if time had stood still in the shop. Everything was the same as I remembered. He made me sit down while he kept on repeating, *Ma petite Mariette, tu es revenue, tu es revenue.* His hands resting on his generous abdomen were as white as the statues surrounding him. I remarked how empty the Rue Ste. Anne was, how gray and silent. M. Gianini bemoaned the fact that

Mariette Bermowitz

except for the stones, the street was no longer the same. Mme. Marie had died and the candy store was closed. He told me Mme. Goldman hadn't remained very long at No. 8 after Poppa and I left. She had often come into the shop to make phone calls to her family in Valenciennes. That was how he learned she was planning to go back there for a while, though she was hoping eventually to be reunited with her twin daughters in Israel.

While M. Gianini made coffee, I looked out the window and saw the back of my old house. Then I leaned out to get a better look. The drain pipe hung loosely from the roof. Mme. Charpentier's balcony was falling apart. I remember how she used to go out on the balcony and call to her cats.

"All gone," whispered M. Gianini with a sigh.

I imagined a faint odor of coal and cat urine in the air, but it was soon dispelled by the fragrance of coffee. I gazed back into the room and saw the stool and the phone beside it in the corner. The very same stool where I used to stand to call les tantes. M. Gianini noticed where I was looking and asked if I would like to call them. What a sweet, kind man. I told him I was going to see them the next day. He walked me to the door and I took his picture, promising that I would write.

I took one last look at the old house. The windows were covered with a thick sheet of dust. They resembled hollowed eyes, their stare drowned in sadness. I knew that I would never see the house again. No. 8 Rue Ste. Anne was where my childhood memories were stored. But soon they would be scattered when the demolition crew took away the walls and

186

with them, the vestiges of the people who once lived there.

I walked past Mme. Marie's candy shop and said hello to her memory. When I reached the Rue de Ruysbroeck, where I had spent so many afternoons playing with my friend Jacky, I looked up to see if his old apartment was occupied. There was a "For Rent" sign in the window. High above the rooftops I recognized the golden dome I used to see from my bedroom window. The angel Gabriel was still there, pointing his hand toward heaven.

I arrived early the next morning at La Gare du Midi and was swept into the crowd moving toward the trains. I was overwhelmed with memories. The day when Poppa and I ran from the Rue du Lavoir, fearful of being picked up by the Gestapo. Then there was the day we left Belgium for good, "never to return." Poppa had never wanted to return, but he was with me now. I could see his skeletal face and sad eyes looking at me everywhere I turned.

But I had come back. I had a seat by the window, just as I did when Maman took me to Fraiture for the holidays. The rain had washed the sky, leaving an immense horizon of clear blue. The tender green of spring was beginning to color the landscape. I felt renewed as I settled into the comfort of my upholstered seat. And now I was going to the town of Hour in the Belgian countryside where les tantes and M. Le Curé were now living. Would they still call me all those endearing names?

Mariette Bermowitz

I was shaken from my reverie by the announcement that my stop, Namur, was next. As the train glided to a halt, I noticed a tiny lady running down the platform, waving a handkerchief in the air. It was Tante Marthe dressed in a stylish coat and hat. She was waving to me just as she had when I was a tearful little girl leaving for the unknown. She knew I would recognize the gesture that had been her last good-bye.

There they were, the three of them, Tante Marthe, Tante Marie, and M. le Curé standing behind as if to hold them up. I dropped my suitcase and ran with open arms. What a tearful reunion! Their voices were even more lilting and melodious than I remembered. Tante Marthe couldn't stop crying as she held her damp handkerchief against her nose and repeated, *Mon Dieu, mon Dieu, bénit soit-Il, te voilà.* "My God, blessed is He, you are here." What a surprise to find myself the same height as my aunts. They gushed at what a beautiful young woman I had become, so stylish, so self-assured looking in a black suit. I didn't know what to say other than to comment on how beautifully dressed *they* were. They looked so dainty and delicate wearing their latest custom-made coats and hats, described in detail in their last letter. But I would have recognized them anywhere. M. le Curé looked imposing in a long black robe. He had gained weight and reminded me of the man and child in a painting by the Italian Cimabue with his bulbous nose and ruddy complexion.

M. le Curé went to get his new car, a sleek and sparkling beige Opel. He loved beautiful cars and never let the ones he owned get too old. I had many

188

Mindele's Journey

photographs of myself as a child smiling behind the wheel of a Citroen, his favorite car at that time. Now I chided M. le Curé about his choice of an Opel instead of a Citroen. He smiled, pleased that I remembered. Once we settled inside the car, les tantes kept asking questions about my life in America, saying how sorry they were about my father dying so young and how proud they were of my school results. Did I hear from Mme. Goldman, they wanted to know? She had called them for help before her departure for Valenciennes and Israel. Tante Marthe wanted to know about the hotel in Brussels, whether I ate well, was I tired, did I visit the Rue Ste. Anne? Between my excitement in answering their questions, I caught glimpses of endless pastures, rolling hills, and the crisp radiant light flooding the land.

Maman was standing in the doorway of the house as the car pulled up. She had stayed behind to prepare the Sunday meal, a feast for my homecoming. It was past the usual noontime when everyone sat down to eat after mass, but this was a special day. When she saw me, she took off her apron and ran to the gate shouting *nos pitite feye, nos pitite feye!* I was laughing and crying as I hugged her, rejoicing in her warmth and the familiar fragrance of cooking that clung to her.

The stone house in Hour dated back to the mid-nineteenth century. It had always served as a parish house, which meant it was more elaborate than the surrounding farmhouses. The property was bordered by shrubs and a gate with a latch as old as the house. A sign outside the front wall read No. 12 Rue du Paradis. It certainly looked like paradise. A parcel

189

Mariette Bermowitz

of heaven with a lawn covered in springtime flowers. Espaliers pear trees climbed the walls, there was a hothouse filled with grape leaves, and in the back, a garden bursting with freshly planted vegetables and herbs. Les tantes had their quarters on the left, a living room and large kitchen with windows facing the garden. M. le Curé's office and sitting area were to the right of the vestibule. In the entrance hall a large clock ticked away the time, and when it chimed, rich warm tones resounded throughout the house. There were four bedrooms on the second floor. Les tantes occupied the one facing the front to the left, and M. le Curé the one to the right. I was to sleep in the one facing the back with a view of the garden and the distant field where sheep grazed. The last room had a small bathtub and toilet hidden behind a curtain while the rest of the room was used for storage. An ironing board stood by the window so that Maman could see the garden while ironing. It was a world that hadn't changed its ways. Like the century that preceded it, old clocks like the one in the vestibule dictated the rhythm of life. Seasons were honored, each in its own way, by loving adherence to customs and traditions.

No sooner had I taken off my coat than I was led to my bedroom. The window was open to let in the spring air. I looked out at the lush countryside. The light was just as I remembered it, bright, intense, and magical. Maman called my attention back into the room when she began pointing out the antique furniture that had survived the war. So much had been lost in the bombardments, but here was the credenza that had belonged to their family

190

Mindele's Journey

and the wardrobe made of solid oak. I still needed a footstool to reach the bed with its thick frame and high mattress, but what an invitation to wondrous dreams. The bright white sheets and pillow cases were all embroidered. Maman said that the weather had been kind enough to allow her to spread the sheets on the grass before hanging them to dry, so I would be able to smell the perfume of the earth as I slept. The satin quilt was the same one that had covered me as a child. The feathers had since been cleaned and the cover exchanged for the soft peach that matched the color of the flowers on the wallpaper. The *pot de chambre* was in the nightstand and the pitcher with fresh water for the morning was on the washstand. Nothing had changed from ten years ago. It was just as it had always been.

The dinner table was set with the fine blue china for special occasions. As a child, I had climbed a chair to peek into the china cabinet and study the blue scenery of flowers and insects decorating the plates. Tante Marthe once showed me the 1830 date stamped on the back. I couldn't imagine anything that old could still be so beautiful. Unfortunately, much of the china had been lost during the *Offensive des Ardennes*. Tante Marthe had decorated the table with ferns and leaves and colorful eggs surrounded by miniature straw animals. She knew how to set a table and always said, *On mange d'abord avec les yeux, après tout.* "One eats with the eyes first, after all." Not only was the table a feast for the eyes, it was a feast for the palate. All the dishes had been my favorites as a child. Les tantes beamed with love as I sighed over each course that was served. There was the

Mariette Bermowitz

chervil soup, the *boeuf bourguignon* I dreamed about in Molly's kitchen, fava beans in a nutmeg-flavored sauce, *les fèves du marais à la noix de muscade,* the mache salad with Maman's incomparable dressing— she said her secret was a dab of fresh cream in the vinaigrette, and crème caramel for dessert. All this was accompanied by one of M. le Curé's finer bottles of red wine from the cellar.

We talked about the war. As Maman spoke about Fraiture, she kept saying, "Do you remember?" about this or that. Then Tante Marie would interrupt, asking, *Tu te rappelles Mariette, tu te rapelles?* Tante Marie had retired from teaching and was fully occupied in the rectory taking care of the new library and fund-raising for the church and school, the house, the garden, the birds in the aviary, the grapes in the hot-house, the harvesting in the fall, and then the preserves. It was endless. Maman proudly showed me the small room where she kept that year's assortment of jams, jellies, soups, and vegetables neatly labeled in jars and laid out on the shelves of the same *garde manger* I knew as a child. Wandering around the house, touching familiar objects, was to be reacquainted with old friends awaiting my return. Before falling asleep that night, I kept hearing les tantes, *Tu te rappelles Mariette, tu te rapelles?* "Do you remember?" How could I have forgotten!

It seems everyone in town had heard about the return of the little Jewish girl hidden by les tantes during the war. *La petite juive cachée pendant la guerre.* After mass on Easter Sunday, I was introduced to so many inquisitive faces eager to meet "the Jewish-American phenomenon." Les tantes said I didn't have to join

192

Mindele's Journey

them for mass, but I was curious. I was glad to be seated in the front pew between Tante Marthe and Maman. Tante Marie was at the organ. She looked the same as she always did when she played the organ, as if she was in a trance, playing to celestial beings. The music mingled with the fragrance of incense, which floated above the altar where M. le Curé was holding a chalice. Behind him, Christ was dying on a cross. At that moment, it seemed to me that Jesus was simply another Jew who had been sacrificed. Though I did not mention this to my little aunts, only remarking how beautiful the mass had been, I was left with a feeling of overwhelming sadness.

The week was over much too soon. Maman gave me two jars of her famous strawberry jam and several boxes of Côte d'Or chocolates. I promised them I would return. *A bientôt! A bientôt!* I shouted out the window as the train slowly pulled away. My heart pounded with joy to think I would be coming back.

My father

My mother

My brother Zelik, my mother, my father, my sister Esther, my sister Rebecca

Mindele's Journey

Esther and her fiancé Jean

My sister Esther

My brother Zelik and me, age 2

With my father at Blankenberge 1945

Mariette Bermowitz

With Cécile and Renée

At Fraiture, age 6

Poppa and Mme. Goldman 1948

Maman Thérèse 1963

Fraiture, late 1940s

Mariette Bermowitz

*With les tantes in the garden,
Fraiture 1944*

Marthe, Thérèse, Marie

*M. le Curé, les tantes,
Sister Cécilia*

*With Louise,
Fraiture 1948*

*Age 12, before leaving
Belgium*

Sister Cécilia, Banneux

*Sisters Cécilia and
Clotilde*

Mariette Bermowitz

Age 19, Brooklyn

Alan Bermowitz

Student at Brooklyn College

Hour, Belgium

*With M. le Curé, les tantes,
Hour 1975*

Mariette Bermowitz

In the Bazaar, Shiraz, Iran 1976

Tomb of Hafiz in Shiraz

Alan

I was standing outside the college library waiting for my friend Evelyn and her boyfriend Mike. Evelyn and I had been friends since we first met in a French lit class. We were almost inseparable, along with a third friend, Nicole, also a French lit major. Aside from a common language, we shared a history entangled in the events of the war.

Evelyn and her parents had survived the Holocaust in Poland, and they lived in France for years after the war before coming to Brooklyn. But they were never able to assimilate. Nicole's father was Jewish. He had married a French woman and spent the war years with her in Paris pretending to be a Catholic. They eventually came to Brooklyn to be with his Jewish family, but he died not long afterwards. I shared many stories with these friends as we sorted out the reasons for the sadness and loneliness of our parents. We did this in keeping with the literature we were studying, applying the existential dilemma to our present condition. We knew we were different from the other students. We were the children of parents whose tragedies we were trying to escape. But we remained Europeans, drawn to the French intelligentsia of post-war Europe with all of its angst and romantic possibilities. All of which we

Mariette Bermowitz

admired to the extent of fashioning ourselves to resemble heroes and heroines of French literature, but especially movies. It was therefore understandable that Evelyn, with her gorgeous mane of blond hair, resembled the Italian actress Monica Vitti, possibly to please her Italian boyfriend. Nicole, with her exquisite figure and features, was her own very special creation, and attracted the older men on campus. I loved Edith Piaf more than ever but continued to model myself after Gina Lollobrigida.

Evelyn and her boyfriend finally arrived, followed by someone I had encountered on the stairs once. He was running up so quickly that he almost knocked me down. I was struck by his good looks and turned around to stare at him. And now here he was again, wearing loose-fitting trousers and a navy blue turtleneck sweater, standing against the railing lighting a cigarette. His dark hair and dewy eyes reminded me of the French heartthrob, Alain Delon. Actually, his hair was so curly he reminded me of a Michelangelo, of paintings I had seen in art books. Then he smiled at me and my heart shifted.

His name was Alan, an art student who had recently had a show on campus. I told him I'd seen him on the stairway once, but he didn't remember. We avoided looking at each other directly, as if afraid to give too much of ourselves away. Evelyn asked why we were talking to the air. Alan laughed. His laugh had a pleasant husky sound, very seductive. Then he asked me where I lived, and would I like the four of us to go out sometime.

That Saturday afternoon they picked me up in Mike's old Chevrolet convertible. At first, with

Mindele's Journey

his curly black hair and hazel-gray eyes, I thought Alan was Italian like Mike, but he was Jewish. In Bensonhurst, Italians and Jews were neighbors and seemed to be made out of the same mold, except of course, for the traditions that set them apart. Long after Alan's parents left the old neighborhood, he remained attached to his warm and expressive Italian friends.

Alan and Mike wore shiny jersey shirts, and Evelyn was her usual gorgeous self behind a pair of dark sunglasses. I appeared at the door in one of my Lollobrigida outfits, tight-fitting white linen pants, a sleeveless red and blue striped tank top and white backless high heels. Alan just stared at me. What a sight we must have been, driving through the streets of Brooklyn in that funny old Chevrolet convertible.

Alan called me a woman, the first time anyone had called me a woman, but before long he was calling me baby. After only a few dates we found ourselves in my bed, making love to the sounds of Miles Davis and Sarah Vaughn. Alan was slender and almost ethereal looking with skin as white as porcelain. He claimed it was the only fragile aspect of his being, something he inherited from his delicate mother. Afterward, we smoked cigarettes and he read aloud his favorite passage of Dante's *Inferno* in Italian. As he read, the cigarette smoke curling upward, the music of the Italian language cradling his words, I imagined myself in the Renaissance with this god-like being the heavens had sent my way.

But for now I was caught between Alan and Arthur, and for a while it was like being in Dante's *Inferno*. I told Arthur I was seeing another man, but he said it didn't matter. It wouldn't have to change anything between us. After all, he was still married. He and his wife had even adopted a child at her insistence. Arthur felt I still needed him. For my part, it was hard to refuse the rent and the bills being paid, and the generous gifts. Arthur was right; I did still need him, not only as a provider but as a father figure.

Lying to Alan took its toll on me. I dreaded telling him I lived a dual life. How could he possibly have understood? I wondered myself how I could love two men at the same time. Yet they were so different. Arthur made me feel secure and loved, whereas Alan was passionate. He was young and mysterious, possessed by ideas, constantly thinking, reflecting, questioning. It was easy to imagine why he had been interested in astrophysics until the chairman of the Art Department came upon some of his doodling and convinced him to change his major to art. According to Alan, it was all about the mystery of the universe anyway. Being in his presence was like being admitted to a special world, removed from the banality of everyday life. Sometimes I was afraid he was too deep, that his intelligence was beyond me. I worried that I couldn't keep up with him and his Schopenhauer and Stravinsky, his Kerouac and Ginsberg, his interest in advanced mathematics and surreal art. Then the neighborhood kid would surface, the boy who loved the Brooklyn Dodgers, basketball, jazz, the blues, and comic books. And besides, he thought I was not only beautiful, but smart too. I thought he was brilliant, if somewhat moody and unpredictable.

Mindele's Journey

We had both graduated by then. I was going to teach French in a local high school and he got a job as a caseworker for the Welfare Department. Alan hated his job and was terrified that he would be drafted. I was in turmoil, as I didn't know how to soothe his angst. I began to wonder about our relationship.

That summer I made an unexpected trip back to Belgium to be with les tantes. I needed to be in Maman's garden, surrounded by the serenity of her world, the world that had saved me as a child. Alan wrote an endless stream of letters describing his vision of our future together and how much he loved his baby. He signed his letters, "My love for you is forever." I missed him more than I thought I would, and began to feel I belonged with him. I told les tantes Alan was the one. They made me promise to return with him, if we were married, of course. I had already made up my mind that Alan would be my husband.

He met me at the airport with a bouquet of flowers. When I came through the gate he clasped me in his arms as though he was never going to let me go. In the taxi back to my apartment, I saw that he looked haggard, as if he hadn't eaten or slept. He told me how anxious he had been while I was gone. He couldn't understand why I went away for two months when he loved me so much, when he was so worried about being drafted. Didn't I care to be with him, by his side one last time before he went off to the army? "You still want to marry me, don't you?" he said. "Of course," I assured him, holding his hand tightly.

207

Mariette Bermowitz

But when he told me he had already chosen our wedding date, my sense of unease returned. I remembered the letters where his fear of being drafted billowed into paragraphs of screaming panic. He sounded like he was on the verge of a nervous breakdown. And was I really prepared to give up my freedom? His emotions were so intense, his moods so changeable. Yet finally, it just didn't matter anymore. I had been captured by the dreamer, the artist who pointed the way to a world of ideas and beauty. I felt that Alan had recognized something special in me. He said I was different from all the American girls he met. I knew more about life certainly, but there was something else that had intrigued him, the pain and self-doubt he claimed I was hiding behind my smile. His perceptions hit a chord. I felt I couldn't lie any longer, especially not to myself. I would have to tell him about Arthur.

Arthur was still calling me and occasionally we had lunch, but we were no longer lovers. Now that I had a teaching job I was paying my own way. I almost considered Arthur as family. After all, he had known my father, and Poppa had been very fond of him. I had a vision of Alan and Arthur becoming friends. But he found out about Arthur before I had the chance to tell him. Mike and Evelyn knew about Arthur, and Mike felt it his duty to reveal the truth to his buddy. This was soon after I came back from Belgium, at the beginning of the new school term.

Things had been going very well. Alan was declared 4F, and we were going to be married in October. He got out of the draft by drinking gallons of salt water to elevate his blood pressure. He fainted

Mindele's Journey

during the physical and they hospitalized him for hypertension. Then one day, Alan was waiting for me outside my building when I came back from school, and the look on his face made my stomach turn over. As soon as we were inside the apartment, he shouted, "Is it true that you're having a relationship with an older man?" He grabbed me by the hair and raised his hand as if to strike me. "How could you, how *could* you when you know how much I love you!" he cried.

The bitter taste of tears filled my mouth. For the rest of the day I tried to explain about Arthur and what he meant to me. I implored Alan to meet him so that I could prove to him that Arthur and I were only friends, that he was like family. Finally Alan cradled me in his arms and held me close, and Piaf's song played in my head.

> *Quand il me prend dans ses bras, il me parle*
> *tout bas*
> *Je vois la Vie en Rose.*
> *Il me dit des mots d'amour*
> *Des mots de tous les jours*

Eventually the two men did meet. Arthur and I remained friends for a while, then lost touch. I heard later he divorced his wife and married a much younger woman.

My wedding to Alan was a sweet affair. I wore a pink silk dress made in France. We were married in my new in-laws' apartment. It was filled with flowers. From the moment I met Alan's mother, Tillie, I knew that she and I would be friends. I loved her name, her gentleness, and her abundant laughter, which seemed to fill everything with her goodness. Louis, Alan's father, reminded me of the actor George Raft. With his gambling habits he was even like some of the characters Raft played. It was a small gathering. Aside from Alan's family, only a few of our closest friends were invited.

How I wished Poppa could have been there. He would have approved my marrying a Jewish boy and having a proper Jewish ceremony. A ceremonial chuppah was set up near the windows and chairs lining the walls, leaving the middle of the room empty so that it looked like a ballroom. Food was heaped on a table at the other end. Tillie had prepared most of it herself. Poppa would have loved her for sure. She looked like him in so many ways, especially her small frame and sad brown eyes. No doubt these were the very qualities that had drawn me to her from the beginning. I think she felt it and understood my longing for the family I no longer had. She never asked me why I hadn't invited my cousins to the wedding. But I didn't want them there. I didn't think they would have come anyway. The last wedding in that family, my twenty-year-old cousin Phyllis marrying her first rich man, was a ten-thousand-dollar production in a big synagogue.

Molly came to my wedding. She called me when she came in from Florida and I invited her. She had been my father's wife and that entitled her to a certain acceptance. I think I wanted her to tell my aunt and cousins about the wedding no matter how she might have described it. I wanted them to know I was getting married. Molly looked wonderful. She was fit and younger looking than when I'd last seen her. She

Mindele's Journey

said she had met a new man in Florida and was hoping to marry him. He would be her fourth husband. Some women collect men. Molly had made a career of it. But at my wedding I thought of her as Poppa's wife, and almost looked for him to come join her in the celebration.

Alan looked handsome in his light brown suit. Up until the last minute I wasn't sure he was going to make the effort. He hated anything fitted around the waist, or jackets that made him look acceptable to "the establishment," as he called it. In those days I enjoyed his rejection of all things *bourgeois*. I thought his baggy trousers, disheveled hair, and turtleneck sweaters bohemian and romantic. He reminded me of French artists, especially Modigliani, whom he was always talking about, going so far as to sign one of his letters *Modi*. After we were married, I imagined myself a bit like Jeanne, the woman who loved him. I didn't think about the sacrifices she had made, of course. To my mind, I was simply entering the rarified life of an artist.

Alan's rebellious streak showed up immediately after the ceremony when he got drunk and insisted on being photographed wearing a hat like Modigliani, a cigarette dangling from his mouth. He delighted in the effect he was creating, and we all laughed. But inwardly I was expecting a different beginning to married life.

He moved into my studio apartment, a small room with what was called an efficiency kitchen built into the wall. Arthur had furnished it with a red convertible sofa and Danish modern side chairs. I was into Danish everything then, including dishes and

Mariette Bermowitz

kitchenware. But the pictures hanging on the walls, prints of Raphael and El Greco, were my purchases. I thought they lent a colorful romantic touch to the room. Our space may have been small, but not our enjoyment of one another. We loved and laughed and talked endlessly about art, music, and literature. I told him about Jacques Brel and Françoise Hardy, and he told me about Coltrane, Dizzy Gillespie, and Howlin' Wolf. We talked about Kerouac and Allen Ginsberg with Alan's best friend Ted, whose philosophical rants kept us going for hours into the night. I went to museums with my artist husband who taught me about the classical triangle in Poussin's paintings, the magnificence of Renaissance paintings, the humanity in Cimabue's work, the incomparable Rembrandt, and the timeless *Guernica.*

But it didn't take long before it began to feel like we were living in a closet. Alan was overloaded with social work cases and overwhelmed with the daily confrontations of misery. He felt frustrated by his inability to rescue those who had fallen by the wayside. Abused mothers, orphaned children, the mentally ill, the wounded, the scarred, those rejected by society. Before we were married he had shown me the chalk drawings he had done of the derelicts living on the Bowery. The drawings were powerful. Alan was amused when one of the men had chased him, threatening to kill him. He kept the drawings in a large folder, a record of the underworld, the oppressed. At times I thought he was drawing himself, as if his models had possessed him.

We moved to a one-bedroom apartment in the back of a new building on Ocean Parkway. We were

Mindele's Journey

finally able to buy a bed. I bought a fancy red bedspread, which made such a splash in the otherwise drab little square room. The living room window overlooked endless rooftops that stretched all the way to the Verrazano Bridge floating on the horizon. At night it looked like a sparkling necklace mingling with the stars, and made up for the dullness everywhere else, especially the lack of green, which was reserved for the apartments in the front of the building.

Then Alan quit his job as a caseworker. It was too consuming. He couldn't stop talking about his work when he came home, engulfing us both in the nightmare of bureaucracy and the impossible challenges of redeeming "man's inhumanity to man." I felt that it was up to me to let my husband pursue his life's calling. Like so many women of my generation, I was willing to enable the man I loved to pursue his quest. I recognized Alan as a man with indomitable talent and feeling. I think too, that underneath it all, in supporting Alan I was trying to make up for not having done more for my father. If I hadn't been a good daughter, I would be a good wife.

It was ironic for an artist to set up a studio on Ocean Parkway, the ultimate Jewish middle-class neighborhood. An unappealing landscape but for the trees running the length of the parkway. We couldn't see them from our windows, but our neighbors across the hall had the front view and all the light. They barely spoke to us. They never said hello when we met in the hallway. We could not have been friends anyway. Our furniture was not compatible. I had a glimpse of their apartment once through the

Mariette Bermowitz

open door—French provincial and a crystal chandelier. They reminded me of my cousins. My cousins would have liked the lobby with its sconces, mirrored walls and plastic palm trees. Alan always took the back entrance to avoid the onslaught of nouveau bourgeois bad taste.

We set up the studio in the L-shaped part of the living room, which was actually an extension of the kitchen. It was adequate for an easel, a full-length mirror and a table for paints, paper, and for stretching a canvas. The light was just right and the Verrazano Bridge in the distance lent a majestic quality to the view outside the window. I loved coming home from my teaching day to the smell of oil paint and a work of art in progress. My husband was often so absorbed that he barely noticed me coming in. I watched him applying colors, blending textures, moving in and out to focus on the subject, stepping like a dancer. When Alan asked what I thought of it, I told him that it was like the poetry of André Breton transformed into color. He liked that.

The best part of the day was always dinnertime. If there was one area in which I felt competent it was cooking. Maman Thérèse had sent me recipes, which I tested on my appreciative husband. I was introducing him not only to the greatness of Belgian cooking, I was bringing the joy I had known in Fraiture to our table. Les tantes had sent me several tablecloths, including a lavishly embroidered one for the holidays. I perfected Maman's *boeuf bourguignon, endives au jambon, poulet à l'estragon,* as well as her favorite dessert, *crème à la vanille.* We didn't need fancy furnishings. Our apartment was filled with fragrance

214

Mindele's Journey

and music and conversations that celebrated love and life.

Every Friday night we visited Tillie and Louie who lived close by. Probably one of the reasons we moved where we did was to be near them. I couldn't tell whether Alan loved his father. There was little exchange between them. But he did admire his father's craftsmanship as a diamond setter. He occasionally went down to Canal Street near Grand on his jaunts to the Bowery where the diamond shops were clustered together. Louie worked above the store beside longtime cutters who were not only his friends but his partners in gambling. Alan took many pictures of those incredible faces and hands bent out of shape by their craft. But above all he loved his mother. He was her favorite son even though he gave her so much trouble. She told me about the time he kicked the rabbi who was tutoring him for his Bar Mitzvah. His younger brother, Robert, who was studying astronomy, was shy and very lovable.

Friday nights were always special. It was Tillie's shining moment when she catered to her family, preparing simple yet flavorful dishes. She ordered meat from a kosher butcher and made the best hamburgers I had ever tasted. She talked a lot but always listened intently to what was going on in our life. She made her own dresses and proudly showed the care taken in finishing the inside of the garment. Poppa always told me you could tell a good piece of clothing by the way it was finished. How I wished Poppa could have known Tillie. He would have been proud that I ended up in such a loving family. He would have *kvelled*.

Mariette Bermowitz

Then Alan shaved his head. When I came in he was sitting in the bathroom, staring at the dark curls strewn about the floor and looking as if he was going to cry. I screamed, "What have you done!" and then I cursed him. I couldn't believe he had shaved his head in order to get out of going to his cousin's Bar Mitzvah. He told me he didn't want to go, but I thought I had convinced him to come with me. It was his family, after all, and I thought he had an obligation. But he couldn't stand what he called the circus-like atmosphere of family gatherings. He said it reminded him of George Grosz paintings where fat women tried to look like teenagers and teenagers tried to look like older women. Still, I thought I had convinced him to go. I was in the bedroom getting dressed. He wasn't speaking to me. It was very quiet in the apartment and I wondered if he had gone out. I would not have believed he could do such a thing to himself. But I wanted him to come to the Bar Mitzvah anyway. He wouldn't listen. I finally left by myself, as I didn't want to disappoint Tillie. He took no notice of me when I came home later that evening. I was fuming because I'd had to lie and make excuses for him. He was working on a new painting, a surreal landscape outlined in outrageous strokes of color. All of his anger was splattered on the canvas.

The apartment got smaller as the art got larger. After teaching all day I would come home to his clutter and mess, to paint tubes littering the table, canvases and stretchers all over the place. Worst of all was having the floor covered with a tarp and sketches taped randomly over the walls. But my domain was the kitchen. Cooking was my way of relieving the

Mindele's Journey

stress of the day and getting into my own creativity. At first, the smell of paints mingling with cooking odors felt compatible, almost romantic. To me, mixing ingredients in a bowl was no different than Alan mixing his colors. But that was only until the smell of turpentine overcame the aroma of a simmering sauce, so that all I could smell was a nauseating vapor. It was unbearable living the way we were. We had to move. But where could we go with only my salary to keep us going? It never occurred to me to tell Alan how frustrated I was.

I had taken a job after school teaching evening classes and came home too exhausted to talk. At first I thought I had taken the job for extra income. Then I realized it was because I wasn't looking forward to coming home anymore. For months he had been engrossed in a series of paintings. Then one afternoon I came home and he had taken them all off the stretchers. I asked him why, but he was silent. I didn't know if it was because he didn't want to tell me, or if it was because he didn't know why he had done it. I didn't understand, but it made me feel like our life was falling apart.

Things got better when les tantes invited us for the summer. I didn't think Alan would want to go, as he usually wanted to stay home working, but he surprised me. We flew to Brussels the day after school ended. He was looking forward to seeing the place he had sent all those letters to the summer before we were married. He knew the address by heart and I loved hearing him repeat it, practicing the French pronunciation like a schoolboy. He laughed and howled like a wolf because les tantes' last name was

217

Leloup, which means wolf in English, and *Hour*, the name of the town where they lived, seemed to fit. The Hour of the Wolf. I told him there was actually a lot of superstition surrounding wolves in the folklore of the old days.

Tante Marthe and M. le Curé met our train. I was overjoyed that I was bringing the man I loved to the place and the people that I loved. But Alan was anxious. He hesitated on the platform, and when I took his hand his palm was moist. I had forgotten how lost one can feel not being able to speak the language. "Don't worry, I'll translate for you," I said, thinking to reassure him. But he looked even more disturbed, as if he was suddenly realizing that he was giving up all his authority. Had it been a mistake to bring him? But here was Tante Marthe holding out her arms, her smile like a ray of sunshine poking through the clouds. She gave Alan a warm welcome, though when he turned to shake hands with the priest, I saw the way she was sizing him up.

Maman Thérèse and Tante Marie were standing at the front door when we arrived. They darted toward the car, unloading bags and suitcases while asking questions about the trip, then suddenly paused to hug the newlyweds. Maman Thérèse managed a quick whisper, telling me how handsome and *gentil* my husband was. Tante Marie giggled like a little girl, not quite knowing how to address Alan. After a quick deliberation with Marie, Maman Thérèse looked at Alan and said, *Bonjour Monsieur Alain*. Alan laughed, delighted to be called *Monsieur*. I was glad to see that he had relaxed. His eyes were eagerly taking in our new surroundings. I thought how strange it must be

Mindele's Journey

for a Jewish boy from Brooklyn to be in the home of a priest with three women in attendance.

Maman Thérèse outdid herself for dinner once again. The table was set for a feast. I was so pleased that she had laid out the antique blue and white porcelain dishes for my homecoming with Alan. I delighted in telling him the story behind these precious dishes and how they had been inherited from a count. I pointed out the photograph of their father, whose face did not look nearly as stern as it had to me when I was a child.

Tante Marthe's freshly picked flowers were set delicately around a greeting card welcoming the newlyweds. M. le Curé had selected some wine bottles from his cellar. When we sat down to eat, Alan acknowledged his appreciation with the few French words he had memorized. It was one of those moments when absolutely everything seemed right in the world, as if it was all meant to be the way that it was. For hadn't the angels guided me to the safety of these loving people? And here I was, holding my husband's hand under the table, feeling unimaginably blessed.

That night we made love between sun-dried linen sheets in the old oak bed by the window, opened wide to a starlit night. The following days were filled from morning to night with visits and excursions. Alan took pictures of M. Evrard, our neighbor, who came to visit every day. M. Evrard was eager to meet the American and tell him how appreciative Belgians were that the Americans came to save them during World War II. M. Evrard had been a soldier during World War I and wore his scars proudly. He sat in a wicker chair placed by the kitchen window so Maman could easily hand him his daily bowl of coffee and bread. He lived with his sister across the road and enjoyed coming to les tantes. He looked frail, but as soon as he sat down to talk with Maman, his eyes glowed with life. He said he was sorry he couldn't speak English with Alan, but that did not take away the pleasure of teaching him how to roll cigarettes, which he had to do with one hand, as the other had been injured in the war. M. Evrard made cigarettes with lightning speed, though he preferred rolling one at a time. He said the tobacco tasted better that way. He showed Alan how to do it, fumbling (on purpose, I think), every time. When Alan finally succeeded in rolling a perfect cigarette, M. Evrard smiled and Alan captured his toothless grin on film. It was the beginning of Alan's appreciation for fine Belgian tobacco and cigarettes.

Because he couldn't speak the language, the camera became Alan's means of communicating with people. He carried it with him wherever we went, mostly taking black and white photos. "It adds drama," he said, "because of the contrasts." Before long, he was taking photographs of everyone who came to visit les tantes. Tante Marthe remarked that since we arrived they had more visitors than ever. The word must have spread about *Les Américains* staying with M. le Curé. The Second World War and the Battle of the Bulge were still topics of conversation, especially with the older people who all had stories of survival to tell. American soldiers had been their saviors, and the presence of any Americans on Belgian soil was still cause for celebration. At least in the little town of Hour.

Mindele's Journey

Alan was fascinated by all these firsthand accounts of the war. Another neighbor, Monsieur Bellevaux, was busy pulling up a row of leeks when he stopped to wave us into his garden. I admired his perfectly laid out vegetables, and when he extended his hand toward Alan, they greeted each other like old friends. I translated as quickly as I could, and within minutes Alan was responding as if he understood French. Monsieur Bellevaux, tall, handsome and rugged, looked like a gladiator holding his hoe against his chest. Alan stared at him intently, hesitating before taking out the camera, but Monsieur Bellevaux didn't mind posing for a picture, especially if it was for an American. After all, he said, he wouldn't be alive if it hadn't been for the Americans. His eyes glazed over as he began recalling the war and the five years he had spent in a German prison camp. He had gone back to work as a railroad mechanic but still thought about the war years every time his old injuries acted up and images of his dying buddies confronted him. I thought that of all the pictures he took, the one of M. Bellevaux was the most profound, as Alan had captured the deep sadness in his eyes.

While the villagers may have been charmed by my husband's boyish good looks and irresistible smile, Tante Marthe didn't seem affected. She had not been impressed by the way he let me carry my heavy suitcase up the stairs when we first arrived. I tried to explain to her that it was my own fault. That Alan had warned me not to take so many things. "I don't need to speak English to understand how critical Alan is of you," she replied, waving her finger at me. "He can't fool an old mountain lady like me!"

221

Mariette Bermowitz

Alan knew she was studying him, especially when we sat down to eat. He tried to make her laugh by pointing his finger at her, but she pointed right back, reminding him that her last name was *Leloup* for wolf. Wolves in the Ardennes had always been known for their cleverness.

Hoping to change Tante Marthe's mind about Alan, I told her how everyone we met on our walks through town had welcomed him. How pleased people seemed to have their photograph taken, like Julia, the baker's beautiful daughter, who posed holding a neighbor's pie before putting it into the oversized brick oven. On major holidays people brought their pies and stews to be baked in the brick oven for a small fee. Most people didn't have an oven in their coal burning stoves. There was nothing comparable to what came out of that incredible bakery, like the taste of the strawberry rhubarb pie Julia sent to les tantes for *les Américains*.

One of my other favorite pictures Alan took that summer was of Madame Renard and her toothless smile. She was eighty years old and still tending the priest's garden. The sun and harsh weather had made her skin into ridges of sunken wrinkles, and her hands were gnarled and twisted from decades of hard work. Yet her smile, in spite of the missing teeth, was very much that of a wise old fox, like her name, *renard*.

Tante Marie impressed Alan with her music. He agreed with me that her impassioned rendition of Grieg on the church organ was as good as that on any of his LPs. Alan seemed genuinely enthralled by Maman Thérèse as well. He raved about her cook-

Mindele's Journey

ing. Every time a new dish appeared on the table his face lit up with appreciation. There was no need to translate his oohs and aahs. Unlike Tante Marthe, who didn't trust good-looking men, Maman Thérèse thought my husband not only a *beau garçon mais surtout très gentil.* She adored him. She framed the photo he had taken of her and her sisters standing together in their neatly starched aprons. It was one of their favorite pictures. She stroked his dark curly hair when he sat next to her. I could tell he found her soft-spoken voice as soothing as I did. One late afternoon we found her sitting alone in her favorite wicker chair in front of the kitchen window, relaxing after having started the preparation for the evening meal. She pointed out the clouds floating into the setting sun, leaving apricot streaks behind, and beckoned us to sit next to her as she started to tell her evening stories. Alan was looking at her as if he understood. She had many stories to tell, but the one Alan loved most was the one about the chicken Maman Thérèse called *Pitite* and wouldn't allow to become a Sunday soup.

Another time she talked about her favorite saints. Her voice quivered when she mentioned Ste. Thérèse de Lisieux, and St. Francis of Assisi. I told Maman that Alan had recently read Kazantzakis' story of St. Francis and it had touched him deeply. I tried to explain to Maman how he had drawn the poor and homeless men on the Bowery. She said, *Tous les pauvres se ressemblent.* Alan had me translate that he admired the humble saint and his compassion for the poor, his devotion to the simple and frail creatures of the Earth. But I couldn't help

Mariette Bermowitz

remembering how he had almost been beaten up by one of those "frail creatures" on the Bowery.

I wondered why Tante Marthe didn't trust Alan. Was it the way he strutted around, or was it his irreverent smirk, his Brooklyn tough guy look? It was appealing to me, but then I was the type who swooned over Sal Mineo and Marlon Brando. I especially wanted Tante Marthe's approval because she had a kind of intuitive awareness that the other sisters lacked. I wish she hadn't said *tout nouveau, tout beau.* When something is new it is always beautiful. It unsettled me. It almost sounded like a warning. But I was reluctant to probe her. Maybe I feared confronting something I already suspected. I knew my husband to be a passionate seeker, a dreamer given to restlessness and moodiness. Yet he was also very deep, which she couldn't have known.

If only Tante Marthe could have seen Alan as I did. But did she even see me anymore? I was no longer the child she had once sheltered. I now lived in another country, spoke another language, and I was married to a Jewish man. I doubt she knew anything about Judaism other than what she gleaned from her prayer book.

In an effort to mesh the past with the present I took Alan to the convent where I was hidden during the war. I wanted him to meet the nuns who had been my childhood protectors. Banneux was quite a distance from Hour but les tantes were as anxious as I was to visit Sister Cécilia. We all set out with M. le Curé in his new Opel. As soon as the top of the building appeared in the distance, I became as excited as

Mindele's Journey

if I were still the child the sisters had known. One by one, the nuns appeared at the door, laughing and talking as if they too were children. They hadn't changed at all. They surrounded Alan with cries of *Oh, Monsieur!* He towered above them, speechless at such a welcome. Sister Cécilia, eager to show my husband the convent, took his hand just as she had taken mine when I was a child, and dragged him off. I felt a deep pleasure watching him skip down the corridor with the tiny nun.

Sister Cécilia insisted I show Alan the site of the apparition. "After all, the Blessed Mother appeared there in 1938 to a young girl named Mariette. The same name as yours—in the year you were born!" Sister Cécilia felt that it was indeed fortuitous that I had been sheltered in Banneux, and she had always felt that I was part of the same miracle. She pointed the way and we set off through the woods to visit the small chapel where Mother Mary had appeared to the schoolgirl Mariette. I was exhilarated by the fresh smell of the pine forest and excited to share this miracle with Alan. Inside the chapel, we came upon the statue of a beautiful woman dressed in a white robe tied with a celestial blue sash. Scattered around the base of *La Vierge des Pauvres*, protector of the poor, were canes, crutches, and grateful mementos for the miracles that had occurred. There were several people praying as we approached the altar. I felt so peaceful listening to the softly spoken prayers. The smell of incense and candles added a feeling of the sacred to the dimly lit space.

Alan had a look of total disbelief. He stared at the crutches hanging down from nails on the wall and turned to me with a smirk on his face. "Bullshit," he muttered.

I was shocked. He had so much compassion for the "poor and downtrodden," why couldn't he be sympathetic to these pilgrims? And what about me? Didn't he understand my connection to the miracle, how I thought of my very survival during the war as a miracle? Sometimes I don't think he saw me at all, or knew what I was about. I didn't say anything, but I felt negated.

We left for Paris. Les tantes came to see us off at the station. They showered us with blessings and good wishes for a safe journey. I watched their white handkerchiefs waving in the distance just like in my childhood. The familiar sadness of departure stayed with me for a while as the train screeched along the tracks.

Alan stared out the window at the landscape scrolling by. He was very quiet. I wondered what he was thinking. He rolled himself a Belgian cigarette and closed his eyes with his head resting on the velvet pillow. I took his hand in mine. Yes, I thought, it will be all right now. I will introduce him to Paris. Paris, where I went with my father before taking the boat to the States. Paris, where Arthur's generosity allowed me the splendor of the Raphael Hotel on the Avenue Kléber, the shops on the Faubourg St. Honoré, the grandeur of the Place de la Concorde. As the train slowed down, Sacré-Coeur appeared in the distance like a wedding cake against the city's contours. I squeezed Alan's hand and cried, "We're here, we're here!"

I wanted my husband to share the love I had for Paris. I remembered the small hotel where my father

Mindele's Journey

and I had stayed, the small room with large flowers running up and down the wallpaper as if it was the inside of a gift box. A silk-lined screen created a private area for a sink and a strange toilet I learned later was called a bidet. Poppa said that if I had to go in the middle of the night I could use it. The window was so high that he had to use a chair to reach the knob to open it. We had a view of the rooftops and chimneys and all of Paris beyond. We went for a walk in the city with a man sent from HIAS, the Jewish organization that made it possible for us to go to the States. I remembered him as kind and generous as he drove us around to some of the fabulous Paris sights. I dreamed about those sights for quite a while after we came to America.

But it soon became evident that Alan didn't care for Paris very much, and it felt like a rejection of me. I even wondered if I hadn't made a big mistake in getting married. But we had one week in Paris and I refused to accept his negativity. He agreed eventually that the Left Bank with its art galleries, art shops, and unexpected visual discoveries were worth the hours of walking. Le Musée d'Art Moderne became a favorite when he recognized the works of some of the artists he admired. On top of Notre Dame he posed as a gargoyle and I snapped his picture. But it wasn't until Alan started taking photographs himself—quaint cobblestoned streets, empty carts, empty chairs in the park, lonely looking windows—that I realized I couldn't show him *my* Paris, he wanted his own imprint of the city. He wanted me to see the city through his eyes. So I followed him, and discovered that what he didn't like was the feminine side of Paris. He needed stones,

Mariette Bermowitz

bigness, architecture, shapes, vistas. We ate sandwiches on park benches, and before long we were as happy as any young couple on their honeymoon. At night we laughed and played poker in the hotel room with the cards spread out over the bed.

Then Mary arrived. We taught at the same high school. In the fall Alan and I were going to take the apartment next to hers on Albemarle Road, which was less expensive than the one we had now. I looked forward to having such a sophisticated woman as our neighbor. Her apartment was filled with objects brought back from her travels, attesting to her refined taste, and especially to her love of all things French. She was a widow, a brilliant conversationalist, and knew all there was to know about my favorite subject, history. We had become good friends ever since I had noticed her reading *Le Monde* and smoking a *Gauloise* in the teachers' lounge. I was immediately drawn to her Old World charm and beauty, and the way she was always impeccably dressed in French couture purchased on her trips to Paris. I soon learned of her left-leaning ideas (we couldn't say communism then), her respect for the working man, her insight into injustices, her understanding of the hypocrisy of governments, and above all, her awareness of man's inhumanity to man. Mary expressed not only my husband's convictions but also my father's paranoia of governments. I was looking forward to seeing her, and accompanying her to the dressmaker where she had her yearly wardrobe made.

Alan didn't want to join me at Mme. Lanval, Mary's dressmaker. "That's your world," he said. The

228

Mindele's Journey

feminine world he seemed to have no use for. Mary left at the end of the week, and he reluctantly accompanied me to the train station when I went to see her off. Afterward, he made a point of telling me that she gave the taxi driver a small tip. "That's a communist for you. She gives lip service to her beliefs then parades like a *grande dame* the rest of the time."

I didn't open my mouth to defend Mary. I wanted to but I held back. I knew Alan would see her differently once she was our neighbor and he could get to know her better. They had so much in common when it came to "man's inhumanity to man."

Yet it turned out to be a mistake living so close to Mary. It had seemed such a good idea at the time. There was more space for Alan's work and I would be near the woman who jokingly declared herself our mother-in-law. I thought of her not only as a good friend and kindred spirit, a confidante, but a surrogate mother. She was someone who understood Europe, the tragic war years, *la condition humaine*, and whose compassion seemed limitless. She never came to visit without a bottle of Remy Martin. We emptied the bottle of cognac while discussing movies and books and politics. Her almost daily presence didn't always please my husband. When Alan started to grumble, I laughed and said, "Perfectly normal feeling to have toward a mother-in-law!" I couldn't do without her. Mary was my connection to all things French, a world from which I could not be separated.

It wasn't just Alan's impatience with Mary that troubled me, but the apartment itself—facing a brick wall—and then what Alan did with it. At least at our old apartment on Ocean Parkway the view

229

Mariette Bermowitz

was pleasant. I had enjoyed the Brooklyn rooftops, the little squares of color and the view of the sky, always changing like a painting in motion. Alan wasn't happy about taking the smaller bedroom, "the closet" he called it, for his studio, but I couldn't imagine us sleeping in such a tiny space. There was a bit of light in the larger bedroom, and if I leaned against the wall, I could see the trees on the street below. With an air-conditioner blocking one window, the living room was dark as well. I didn't want to leave the other window open because the smell of smoke drifted in from the rooftop chimneys. At least the kitchen had room for a table and chairs. After painting the kitchen walls bright yellow it felt warm and cozy. Alan liked it too, and hung a basketball net over the door. I thought it looked funny but I didn't mind. I never imagined that he would use the burners on the stove to melt plastic for his sculptures, or that he would paint a table in psychedelic pink and green.

It was the beginning of his experimentation with color and light. He was working on a project featuring neon lighting combined with plastics. The apartment, now filled with lightbulbs, wiring, an assemblage of clutter selected from various empty train lots, had acquired an unusual smell that I identified as burned-out wires and rancid oil. It oozed out of the electrical garbage scattered all over Alan's "closet." Before long, this noxious odor, combined with the fumes of melted plastic, settled into every corner of the house. I could smell it as soon as I got out of the elevator. It was like the melted tar on Brooklyn streets in the hot summer. I knew it was for

Mindele's Journey

the sake of art, but even with the windows open the smell seeped into the walls, taking over every porous opening.

Thankfully, the space finally became too small for him and he moved his project over to Park Slope where a college friend was renting a studio. I had always wanted to live in Park Slope, but Albemarle Road was in walking distance to the school where I taught French. Meanwhile, we continued with Friday night dinners at Alan's parents. Tillie cooked our favorite pot roast and then we watched TV with Louie, who promptly fell asleep. In spite of the banality of those evenings, I could not have denied Tillie her Friday nights, or myself the pleasure of her warmth.

Our marriage continued through the upheavals of the sixties, which, looking back, seemed like a mad ride on a roller coaster. During our first four years together we tapped into each other, body, mind and soul. I had loved the intensity of his thinking, the talks we had about art, paintings, and music. In spite of our clashes, we laughed more often than not during those early years. We laughed at the birthday cards Alan designed. He saw himself as a fat Louis XIV type and me as a plump handmaiden clutching a blue handbag. He called me Chunky, like the candy bar he loved, and read me passages from *Sexus* and *Nexus*, the Henry Miller novels we smuggled in from our trip to Paris. I thought we'd get caught at customs when his coat fell on the floor, but the agent apparently didn't notice the bulging lining where the books were hidden. Alan drew pictures of me in lovely pastel pink colors even when I had a toothache. Those were the days when he pinched *mon derrière* as I bent over the stove, and used bawdy language, luring me into various corners of the apartment to make love.

By then I had compiled pages of Maman Thérèse's recipes, which I duplicated as best I could in my bright yellow kitchen, which I thankfully had to myself again. Alan delighted in every meal I made. He was unperturbed about the added pounds around his middle, and grinned as he patted his belly. I thought the world almost perfect then. I still took great pleasure in our visits to museums where we spent hours contemplating the brushstrokes of famous artists, the delicate contours of ears and hands, and the styles changing with time. I was mesmerized by Alan's knowledge and I loved the way he wanted to share everything with me. I soaked it in like a sponge. How could I have known that when Bob Dylan came on the scene with *The Times They Are A-Changin'*, the idealistic young artist I had married would become a full-blown rebel?

My husband was consumed by a series of black-and-white drawings he called *Opus Anus*. He was driven by anger and frustration and morbid ideas of destruction and apocalypse he got from the news on TV of the war in Vietnam. They showed everything on TV in those days. Graphic pictures of mutilation and death. I watched him draw his pen and ink figures for hours in silence. He was obsessed with illustrating the worst of America by attacking the hypocrisy of religion and government, the horror of war, the stupidity of rote thinking. His apocalyptic titles were steeped in doom, as nightmarish as *Guernica*. I felt I was losing him, and feared for our marriage.

Mindele's Journey

He had his first show in Park Slope in 1968. I felt overcome when I saw the somber graphics hanging in rows one after the other at the gallery. At home, I had seen them one at a time, but here depictions of Hell 20x30 with titles printed below engulfed me.

Congressional Medal of Honor
Sunday Trench I
Gethsemane
Crap
Opus Anus
Day of Atonement
The Melrah Magicians
Fruits of American Judaism
The Holy Family
Gleichgeschaltet

There was no hope in his drawings. His expert draftsmanship made them all the more difficult to look at. In fact, the whole thing was deeply troubling to me. I had been there. Even though I was only a child, I remembered. During the Battle of the Bulge I was in a cellar when they dragged in a soldier with his arm half ripped off. I smelled the blood. I saw him die. Alan meant his work as a satire on society, but I was reliving the horror of war. I never told Alan how his work upset me. And I didn't tell him that I was the one who had bought two of his drawings. He knew I had invited the parents of a former student to the show. "These people are art collectors," I told him. "They're sure to buy at least a couple of drawings." I had forgotten that one of their sons was mentally retarded.

Mariette Bermowitz

When the mother saw Alan's work she said, "It's quite impressive. But too painful to look at." They were too close to their own tragedy to consider buying something so depressing. I couldn't bear telling Alan that I didn't sell the drawings, so I withdrew some funds from my own account and said the money was from the sale of his work. Then I carefully hid the drawings at the back of my closet.

Meanwhile, I escaped into my French music. American music was all about rhythm, not melody like the French. I retreated into the world I created in the high school classroom where I taught French and introduced my eager students to the melodious lyricism I could no longer listen to at home. Edith Piaf, Yves Montand, Aznavour, and my beloved *landsman,* Jacques Brel, the singing troubadour of Flemish angst. Alan made fun of my taste in music, but I couldn't stand Jimi Hendricks' *Star Spangled Banner,* that atonal screeching that tore at me like an internal lament. I felt trapped in sounds that were unfamiliar, disturbing, annihilating. And even *La Vie En Rose* was beginning to sound like a wrenching sob of hopelessness, and less and less a comfort.

Mary was my salvation. She praised Alan's work, comparing him to the greats she loved like Soutine, Grosz, and especially Pascin. Alan was flattered by the attention and gave her a painting she thought looked like her. He still had a sense of humor because I remembered the painting had been inspired by a homeless person he came across on one of his escapades on the Bowery. I didn't tell this to Mary, because sometimes her admiration of his work was so effusive I suspected she was trying to charm Alan.

Mindele's Journey

She was an older woman, but still attractive, a Greta Garbo look-alike, I thought, and such an intellectual. Alan seemed fascinated by her awareness and knowledge. She claimed that the thirties, when she was a young woman in America, were very much like the times we were living in now. Everything was breaking apart then too. The Great Depression had deadened the hopes of millions of ever finding a way out, while the forces of fascism were rearing their ugly heads in Europe. She thought that communism would rally the downtrodden and give life new hope and meaning. And there were singers like Woody Guthrie, who rekindled people's belief in America, just as Bob Dylan did now. "He will be a great one too," Mary claimed, because, "a great one is one who understands the culture and politics of his times and knows how to rally a people in turmoil."

I listened in rapt attention to Mary's recollection of the thirties, especially when she described how she and her husband fell in love with Paris, and how tragic it was when the fascists took over. She knew young Americans who left to fight with the Lincoln Brigade in Spain and never came back. She talked about Drancy, the town outside of Paris where Jews were held for deportation. The horror of Jewish children taken from their schoolrooms never to return. She shook her head in disbelief when she recalled the anti-Semitism of Voltaire and her favorite writers, Celine and Shakespeare. Occasionally, I interrupted to give her details from my experience of the war. I had my own opinions about the rote thinking that could lead people *en masse* to do unimaginable evil. It was just like Alan's drawing, *Gleichgeschaltet.*

Mary and I spoke French together. Being with her gave me a sense of continuity to my past. She was fascinated to hear about my family in Belgium and I was thrilled to be able to talk about it with someone. I would have liked to have shared more of my past with Alan, but I hesitated to bring it up because he was obsessed with his own work. He never seemed to have time for me anymore. I would have liked to go out for dinner or to the movies once in a while, but Alan hated to leave the apartment except when he went to his studio. He connected to "the splintering of America's soul," but what about my splintering? Alan seemed oblivious to me. For him, pen and ink drawings were enough of a statement about "man's inhumanity to man."

We never talked about having children or buying a home. There was a house in Park Slope with an asking price of $21,000 that reminded me of little row houses in Brussels. There was wood paneling and a winding staircase, even a small backyard. I longed for a home of my own, but Alan wouldn't hear of it. He wouldn't even talk about it. He said, "Owning a house is too bourgeois." I wish I had insisted. But I wasn't strong enough. I couldn't say what I really wanted. I lived in his shadow. Whatever he expressed with his art, I felt he was expressing for me too.

✡ ✡ ✡

In the spring of 1968, I won a scholarship for postgraduate studies in Rennes, France. I was ecstatic. I hadn't been back to Europe in two years. Les tantes kept writing accounts of life in Hour and I missed

Mindele's Journey

them terribly. This gift of two months of study would allow me to return to the place that felt most like home to me.

The lectures in Rennes were by a professor from the Sorbonne who not only looked like Sartre but had known him personally. The student upheavals in Paris that May were over by the time I arrived, but I could still feel the excitement. The graffiti remained, and posters of de Gaulle with his hand over the mouth of a youth with bold print, *Sois Jeune et Tais Toi.* "Just stay young and shut up." I loved being a witness to history. What Alan would feel for Woodstock the following year, I felt for the May Uprising. I had missed it by a month, but I felt exhilarated by the energy of the student movement.

Meanwhile, my own world was changing drastically. It was a terrible blow when my dear friend Mary retired from teaching and went to live in Paris. I felt completely on my own without Mary to drink brandy with and smoke a Gauloise as we talked into the night. The apartment next door was empty, and so was my heart.

It seemed all the neighbors were moving away, as if the neighborhood I had known was being sucked into the void. There was a new population emerging, mostly Haitians and Jamaicans. The school where I had once taught mostly white students, was now a restless battleground between American blacks and the new immigrants from the Caribbean. A malaise had taken over the schools, resulting from the racially and religiously divisive confrontation of Ocean Hill-Brownsville in the fall of 1968. But I never considered requesting a transfer to another school. When

Mariette Bermowitz

my friend Pauline returned to teaching after maternity leave, she filled Mary's place.

I found myself developing a kinship with my Haitian students. I saw the sadness behind their smiles, reminding me of hidden wounds. When I realized they were frightened by the American blacks and steered clear of them, I decided to organize a Haitian club. Many of the students were talented guitar players and songwriters. I hadn't known what an important role poetry and music had in their world. Sometimes their poetry reminded me of the formal French from another century. They were reluctant to answer my questions about Voodoo, but were much more helpful when I asked them to teach me Creole expressions. They giggled at my poor accent, which relieved the tension I felt knowing so little about their culture.

Little Junie-Pierre sealed my decision to persevere in what had become a challenging teaching situation. She was thin and beautiful with deep brown eyes and flawless chocolate-colored skin. Her chemistry teacher raved about her abilities and recommended she come to my class. She was poorly dressed when we met in the Language Office on a cold winter afternoon. As soon as I began talking to her in French she started to cry, and her dreadful story came out. The week before, her mother's boyfriend had raped her and now she was afraid to go home. When she had told her mother, her mother slapped her and accused her of lying. Then the neighbors heard about it, as well as the boys in the neighborhood who teased her. She was so frightened and so cold in her thin winter coat, but said there was

Mindele's Journey

no money for a new one. Suddenly I felt the weight of the world on my shoulders. But at least I found a boy from the Haitian Club to escort her safely home from school every day, and I gave her a wool coat I no longer wore.

Junie-Pierre said, "Would you hug me? I've never been hugged in my life." That simple plea reverberated in my soul. Piaf's song spun around in my head. *Quand il me prend dans ses bras / il me parle tout bas / je vois la vie en rose / il me l'a dit, l'a juré pour la vie.*

From then on, teaching French seemed more purposeful. It consoled me to feel needed, as I often went home to an empty apartment. Alan was into music now and was busy with new projects. When he was at home he holed up with a friend in his room, recording distorted-sounding pieces. Eerie, twisted-sounding pieces I found disturbing. Yet I never complained that it bothered me, nor did he ask what I thought. He was too absorbed in what he was doing to notice me at all. I understood only too well what the title of one of his pieces, *Methadone Mary*, represented, and it added to my feeling of alienation from him.

His new friend Mel was an understudy in *Oh Calcutta* on Broadway, and Mel's girlfriend was a dancer in the show. When they came to visit I felt so dull and plain next to this glamorous theatrical couple Alan was smoking pot with. Also, Alan was letting his hair grow. Iggy Pop had become his new hero. It was like we were living on different planets. I tried to express how I felt with a poem I called *Les Fleurs du Mal Remembered.*

239

Mariette Bermowitz

We met when he was twenty-two
And I a bit behind
He was reading *Les Chants de Maldoror*
And I Beaudelaire

We were, you can imagine, quite a pair
Yet we married, and a year later
Switched from literary bliss
To marital despair

He was an artist, I was a teacher
His muses slept by day and at night began
to play
My work began at eight while inspiration
slowly dripped
Down the kitchen drain

A leaky faucet in need of repair
A clogged-up drain, my mind weeping
In despair, remembering
Les Fleurs du Mal

Les Fleurs, Le Mal, Le Bonheur, Le
Malheur
Time tick-ticking the hours away
Words scratching their way into my
thoughts
Creating ideas, dividing Bon from Mal,
Mal from Heur

Maldoror, this hour, this heure, this hurt
Isidore, Ce mal, Ce bon Comte

Mindele's Journey

De L'autre mon(de) Beaudelaire
Et mon mari aussi

A moi, messieurs, ne vous en plaisent
Je reprends mes fleurs pour embaumer les heurts
Pour parfumer les heures de l'éternité
Inventée par une nouvelle Divinité

And a sigh once more became a kiss
And the imagination soared into bliss.

That November was the tenth anniversary of my father's death. I realized I had never been to the cemetery once, or even lit a candle in his memory. I took a handful of pictures out of the album and spread them out on the kitchen table as if they were a deck of cards. Then I cried. I would never be able to tell my father that I missed him or loved him. I would never be able to confide my pain to the sisters and brother whose smiles I touched on the photographs. I would never be able to look into my mother's eyes again. In the few photographs of her that remained, I could only stare at what the camera had captured. Her soft distant gaze, hands on her pregnant belly. I felt so alone.

As the year drew to a close, I saw even less of Alan. But he was home New Year's Eve. I had prepared dinner and was in the bedroom getting dressed when the phone rang. I picked up the extension and I didn't recognize her voice.

Mariette Bermowitz

She said, "Did you tell her?" Then Alan replied, "Not yet, but I will when I hang up," and the woman said, "Please come over as soon as you can. I need you with me."

I froze. When Alan came in the bedroom I was standing by the bed, still clutching the receiver in my hand. He said, "I know you heard it all. I'm leaving tonight."

I stood there with my mouth open, silently watching him take down a suitcase and hurriedly throw some clothes in his bag. "I'll call you," he said. "I'll explain everything." When I heard the door shut behind him my knees gave way and I sank to the floor, too much in shock to cry.

I needed to get out of the empty apartment. I put on my coat and wandered out to the overpass behind our building, a bridge separating our street from the more affluent neighborhood on the other side. I don't know how long I stood there in the cold, staring down at the tracks and counting the trains as they passed in the dark, but I stood there until a policeman came up and gently pulled me away from the railing.

"Ma'am what are you doing here? A pretty lady like you shouldn't be alone here tonight. You look just like Rita Moreno. Did anybody ever tell you that?" He escorted me back to my building, and asked if he could look in on me the following day. I told him I would be fine. But once inside the dark apartment, I stared at the empty bed. Then I looked at the clock. It was already the next day, January 1, 1970.

The sixties had come to an end and I felt like I had come to an end too. My life didn't make sense

Mindele's Journey

anymore. The days that followed were filled with a harrowing emptiness. I called friends I thought would help me to understand why my husband had left. Nothing they said consoled me. Most of them were busy with their children and their own lives. I had no family to turn to. I wondered if I should call Tillie. I thought she would have called me, but maybe Alan hadn't told her the news. I didn't want to be the one to tell her.

I thought I had been a good wife to him. I thought I had done everything a "good wife" was supposed to do. I went over in my mind the days, the weeks, the months before he left, trying to see if there were any clues or forewarnings that he was planning to leave me. It's true we hadn't been intimate in a long time, but I assumed it was because he was so involved with his art and music. He came home at all hours, but it never occurred to me it was because he was with another woman. I always left dinner out for him. He still loved my cooking. Was my cooking the only thing that had kept us together? I had supported him in every way I knew how, though sometimes I wondered how much longer I would have to be the sole breadwinner.

Our black Labrador Ollie followed me around the empty apartment. Sometimes I sat on the floor beside him and wept into his warm black coat. I couldn't stop reliving the night Alan left. All he took with him was a small suitcase. Was that all there was for him from ten years of marriage? Just what he could fit into a small suitcase?

Somehow, I went back to work. Then I got the news that Nicole, my friend from college, had com-

243

Mariette Bermowitz

mitted suicide. I could neither absorb this additional blow nor face the emptiness of my life. One night I was found wandering the streets of my neighborhood barefoot and skimpily dressed. I remember trying to shelter my head from the buildings I thought were falling on me. Everything was crashing down around me and there was nowhere to hide. I was admitted to the psych ward at a Brooklyn hospital and fed pills. The pills made my head feel like it was being squeezed in a vice. The other patients circled the tables in the dining room like zombies. They reminded me of the zombies in *The Night of the Living Dead*, except that I was in the film with them.

While I was in the hospital Alan's mother died of a heart attack. Alan gave me the news when he came to visit me. Tillie gone? It didn't register. I was too drugged up even to register that Alan had come to see me. My friends told me later that he was very concerned.

After a month of intense therapy and a second hospitalization, I went back to teaching, only to be confronted with a school system spiraling out of control. The deterioration that had been gradual hit me full force. Wooden doors replaced by metal ones. Graffiti scribbled over putrid green walls. I felt like a prisoner inside my classroom. With the school now like a jail, teaching seemed absurd. A mindless journey through an inefficient bureaucracy. I felt incapable of dealing with any of it. The job that had once given me so much pleasure now made me feel inadequate. For a while I continued like Sisyphus, condemned to my burden.

I stuck it out until the day alarming shrieks erupted in the hallway. I was in the dean's office, and

Mindele's Journey

I immediately shut the door. Guards patrolled the hallways; one of them would take care of it. Suddenly the door burst open and a guard was dragging in a student by the collar, smacking the boy's head against the wall until there was blood. A gun fell out of the boy's pocket and landed on the floor with a thud. The bell rang for the next class and I fled. I finished the day by giving my students some busy work, but by the end of the week I'd had enough. I couldn't go back.

I took a sick leave. But it wasn't long before I was back in the hospital suffering from depression. I was *broyer le noir*. In a grinding darkness. The kind of depression that slowly pulverizes you into feeling nothing. I wrote to les tantes and they sent me a ticket to Belgium. My appearance shocked them. I was painfully thin and looked as if I hadn't slept for months. They kept me only a few nights before their doctor recommended taking me to *Le Home*.

Le Home, Belgium

From my table near the window I could see the carefully planned arrangements of flowering shrubs and the path leading to the rose bushes. Such a gracious atmosphere. Everything sparkled when the sun shone through the large bay windows. The glasses, the porcelain dishes set out neatly on white linen cloths, the dainty flowers in small vases so festive looking. My table partner, Liliane, was a retired teacher, and like me, on an extended stay of rest and recuperation after a lengthy bout of depression. She

Mariette Bermowitz

told me the rituals of the dining room, pointing out the tall cabinet with small open cubbyholes. "You'll find your napkin there under your name. It's so much more personal that way."

I went to the cabinet for my napkin. There, above the cubbyhole, was my name in bold letters. Mariette. Neatly tucked inside was the napkin I was to use for the entire week. It took me a moment to register that the napkin was meant for me. That the name was *my* name, and it was my napkin. That it was a linen napkin freshly ironed reminded me of the sun-dried laundry of Maman Thérèse. The memory sent a warm tingle of well-being through me. I closed my eyes and saw her in the garden hanging laundry as I handed her the clothespins. When I opened my eyes and saw my name on the cubbyhole again, I thought what a beautiful name, Mariette. A name with a history. A name connected to a family. For the first time in a long while I felt I had a place in the world.

Monsieur Guillaume was waiting for me in the garden after lunch. We took different paths every day but always ended our walk in the rose garden where we sat on a bench. He listened quietly as I talked and talked. I never went back to my room without a small token of our walks together. Most of the time it was a rose he plucked or an unusual stone he found beside the path. I put the rose petals inside the pages of my journal. From our first session together I knew Monsieur Guillaume was a person I could trust. A gentle man who listened, and when he spoke, his voice was soft and soothing, unlike the doctors in Brooklyn who made me feel more like a burden than

246

Mindele's Journey

a patient. Still, it was a while before I felt safe enough to empty out the sadness of my heart.

After a month in the rest home, Monsieur Guillaume told me that soon I would be able to return to Hour and les tantes. On one of our last walks together he gave me a copy of *The Little Prince*. I had told Monsieur Guillaume that the book was my favorite, and I had used it for many years in my French classes. On the inside cover he wrote, *Comme la rose du Petit Prince, vous êtes une apparition miraculeuse sur la terre*. "Like the Little Prince's rose, you are a miraculous appearance in the world." It was so like him to write that. How I would miss our walks in the rose garden!

The rest of that summer in Hour was calm. I felt peaceful at last. The long years separating me from my beloved aunts began to feel like a vague memory. In the mornings when I looked out my bedroom window I saw the garden, and beyond, a row of almond trees and sheep grazing in the field. Evenings were spent sitting around the old oak table telling stories. When the weather was warm we sat outside under the awning in the back of the house. I was in charge of arranging the wicker chairs. There was an aviary to the side where doves softly cooed. I listened to their plaintive melody while les tantes scurried about on the gravel paths, finishing the day's chores. While Tante Marie put away the last of the dinner plates, Maman checked for weeds among her vegetables and Tante Marthe watered her geraniums with a cigarette dangling from the corner of her mouth. When they finally took their places in

Mariette Bermowitz

the wicker chairs beside me, I felt surrounded by family. By love.

Every evening began with Maman Thérèse making weather predictions for the following day. Tante Marthe would light another cigarette and say, *Tu te rappelles Mariette?* And then the stories were told and recalled with such perfect memory and detail they might have happened only yesterday. These stories from the war years were imbued with a feeling that was almost sacred. Tante Marthe never failed to pick up the corner of her apron to wipe a tear before she lit up again.

One evening it suddenly occurred to me to ask what made them decide to take in a Jewish child during the war. Didn't they know how dangerous it was? How they were putting their own lives at risk? Tante Marie said, "It wasn't a question of choice. It was simply the right thing to do." As the eldest, Tante Marie had made the decision when she went to visit Sister Cécilia that fateful day in 1944 when they first saw me, a five-year-old in danger of extermination. "I couldn't bear to imagine the sisters rounded up and arrested," she continued. "There had been too many rumors and too many betrayals in the area. Besides, aren't charity and love part of God's plan?" Tante Marie leaned back against a pillow on the wicker chair as she spoke about the long and tragic history between Germany and Belgium. When words seemed to fail her, she would sing old folks songs of the region that all the sisters knew. They sang along with her until she felt up to resuming the stories. Her voice became even quieter as she said, "*Notre papa, oui, notre papa.* I haven't thought about him for such

248

Mindele's Journey

a long time, but it marked our childhood." And then she told me what happened in 1917.

Their father, M. Leloup, had refused to give the Germans the names of the young men in the village, most of whom had gone into hiding, and now he was going to be shot. He stood before the firing squad, blindfolded with his hands tied behind his back. Les tantes, who were just little girls at the time, watched their pregnant mother crawl on her knees toward the captain, begging him not to take the life of the father of her four children and a fifth on the way. The soldiers put down their guns. M. Leloup was saved. Their mother lost the baby, but the rest of her family was alive, and she believed that God himself had intervened. As the sun set with waves of color fading on the horizon, Tante Marie said, "The incident was burned in our memory. When adversity came again during the Second World War, we had no choice but to stand up for righteousness." Maman Thérèse nodded as she rose from her chair, reminding us of her weather prediction for a beautiful day tomorrow.

That night when I went in to say good night to Maman, she called me closer and said softly, "You know, not all Germans were bad." I sat on the edge of her bed as she told me that at the beginning of the Second World War the young German soldiers coming through wore Catholic crosses and talked about their families, showed pictures of their children. "I was certain that these young men were being shipped to the front so they would be killed," said Maman. "The real brutes remained behind to spread fear and terror."

Mariette Bermowitz

That was Maman. Her innocent belief that no matter what, goodness and kindness would redeem mankind. I wanted to believe it as much as she did. This dear little *tante*, going to sleep surrounded by books and pictures of saints, her "forces," as she called them. One beautifully illustrated book was about St. Francis of Assisi. Another was a photograph of Ste. Thérèse de Lisieux holding a bouquet of roses. It reminded me of Monsieur Guillaume and the gift of *The Little Prince* with its inscription, *vous êtes une apparition miraculeuse sur la terre*. Perhaps I had "forces" somewhere watching over me too. I remember as a child in the convent being told I had an angel watching over me. I wanted to believe it. I needed to believe it.

I didn't speak about Monsieur Guillaume to les tantes, and they never asked about him. According to Tante Marthe, "You told him what was necessary, and now it is over." What did she mean by over? The marriage was over? Yes, but not the dull ache I couldn't seem to get rid of. Nothing was over, only the hope that it might be someday.

I would never confess to my aunts how I had tried to take my own life in that awful hospital in Brooklyn. I had been in despair over losing Alan, over my childless state, with no interest in teaching, or even in living any longer. Sometimes I would think about my father. Or I would think about the mother I hardly knew. I would see her holding my baby sister in her arms, ten-month-old Frieda, and imagine them gasping for breath in the gas chamber. I didn't know how these wounds would ever heal.

I had never felt more alone or more in danger than during that second hospitalization in Brooklyn.

Mindele's Journey

The patient I shared a room with was always crying. I put my hands to my ears to block out the sound, but really I wanted to block out everything. One day I went into the bathroom and unscrewed a lightbulb. I smashed it against the sink and cut my wrists. Then I watched the blood gush into the sink. I was so deadened inside I didn't even feel any pain. When I woke up later in bed, my wrists covered in bandages, the only remorse I felt was that I was still alive.

I could never tell les tantes. It would break their hearts. Even Monsieur Guillaume looked away when he saw the scars on my wrists, and never asked me about it. I was grateful. It hurt too much to even think about it, let alone put into words the despair I felt.

Before the summer was over we all went to visit Soeur Cécilia in Banneux. I hadn't seen the sisters since Alan and I had come as newlyweds. Nothing had changed. It was like stepping into a dream. The sisters were waiting outside the large welcoming doors looking as small and dainty as porcelain dolls. I barely had a chance to say hello before Sister Cécilia scooped me up and danced me over to the stairs. She paraded me through the halls, greeting the sisters, referring to me as "the little one we had during the war." I was as big as she was now, but to her I would always be *la petite*. We spent the rest of the afternoon talking in the small refectory reserved for family visits. The same room where I first met Tante Marthe and Tante Marie when they came to take me away to Fraiture. To spare my feelings, Sister Cécilia never mentioned Alan or my stay in *Le Home*, for which I was very grateful.

When Soeur Cécilia said, *Tu te rappelles Mariette?* "Do you remember?" it was just like in Hour, out back

251

under the awning watching the sun set as I listened to more stories of the war. Stories of the little girl I once was, and how I was coached into the game of hiding from danger. When the Germans came to the door, Julie, the older student assigned to look after me, called out, "We're playing hide-and-seek!" That was my signal to climb in the wicker basket in the nuns' dormitory and Soeur Cécilia whispered, "Wait until I tell you to come out."

I had all but forgotten those days. I remembered my time at the convent, but the sisters had kept me blissfully unaware of the danger I was in. Now I saw how they had protected me. How they loved me. I laughed and cried and was entranced by the vivid recollections of the sisters. All the same, I couldn't help thinking how little they knew of the war *after* the war. But how could they possibly have known?

When it came time to leave Sister Cécilia whispered, *Je savais que tu reviendrais.* "I knew you'd come back." Yes, I had come back. I had been able to find my way back to the place where I had been saved. I shuddered to think I had almost ended my life. In the years that followed, this would be a recurring dilemma, this "survivor's guilt." Why had I been saved? And for what? What was my purpose? Why was my life spared when so many others were not? I kept feeling I had to justify my existence.

A New Beginning

I was in Belgium when I received a letter from my friend Iris that she was coming to Europe. She

Mindele's Journey

had decided to join me on her sabbatical and invited me to go on a skiing trip to the Austrian mountains. I resisted the invitation, as I had never considered myself a sporty type. The idea of throwing myself down a snowy slope terrified me. But Iris insisted. She wrote back, "Come *on!* We're going skiing—and you're going to have a good time! Two single women roaming the ski slopes of Europe—it's going to be great!"

Like me, Iris was recently divorced, but she was determined to put it behind her. I still felt as if Alan was part of my life. I asked myself all the time, why did he stop loving me? What could I have done differently? And I kept wondering, why didn't we have children? I felt vulnerable and completely lacking in confidence except when I was with les tantes.

Nevertheless, I agreed to meet Iris in Amsterdam. After being abroad for three months, her Brooklyn accent sounded pleasantly familiar. Our first night in Amsterdam my suitcase was stolen and I lost everything. I had left my case in the rental car overnight because it was so large it wouldn't fit up the narrow stairs of the old hotel. The next morning we found the car windows broken and the suitcase gone. When I realized the special bracelet les tantes had given me as a going-away present was in the case, my eyes filled with tears and a feeling of despair swept over me.

"This is a test of your stability," Iris said sternly, tossing her long curly hair. She promised that I could share her clothes, or better still, buy new ones. Iris wore pants all the time. She dressed in leather and suede. We were the same size. As soon as I put on her clothes I started to feel like a different person.

Mariette Bermowitz

Les tantes had always discouraged me from wearing pants, preferring me in skirts and feminine dresses. But now I was like Iris, striding confidently toward the ski slopes.

For the next few months on the slopes I endured the humiliation of falling down hundreds of times. Yet I persevered. Something in me would not give up. No matter how difficult it was learning to ski, how many tumbles and bruises there were, I kept taking hold of that towrope that pulled me back up the mountain again and again, even though I was trembling, shaking with fear as I held on for dear life. One day I reached the top just as the sun was setting on the distant slopes. I was totally alone, surrounded by a vast, throbbing white universe. As I watched the sun's rays glisten on the snow, it seemed as if the mountain had burst into sparks, engulfing me in a vortex of light. Swept up in a feeling of warmth and peace I had never known before, I floated down the mountain on my skis, feeling one with Nature. One with the Universe. It was a moment of true perfection.

Conquering my fear of skiing was just the beginning. I hadn't realized how much I had lost my sense of self. How being married to Alan made me forget who I was. But with skiing, I had refused to give up. I didn't care how many times I failed. I had found something inside me that wouldn't give up. A strength and a will to overcome defeat.

✳ ✳ ✳

But it was hard coming back to the apartment in Brooklyn I had shared with Alan. The lobby was

Mindele's Journey

dismal looking, its once beautiful marble floor now chipped and grimy with dirt. When I opened the apartment door my spirits sank further. The students I sublet to had rearranged the furniture. I could see the outline on the carpet of where the sofa and the coffee table had been. It looked like the outline of my former life. Before I even unpacked I got out the vacuum and erased the marks.

When I looked at myself in the mirror with my stylish new haircut and colorful new sporty clothes, I did not find myself as captivating as all that. I dreaded going back to teaching, resuming my life as a single woman. So as not to fall into the doldrums again, I taped little reminders to myself all over the apartment. The bathroom mirror said, "Smile and the world will smile with you." The refrigerator said, "Pain feeds the soul with possibilities." My favorite was taped to the closet door, "Stumbling blocks are only stepping stones to new beginnings."

I summoned all my courage to go shopping in the neighborhood. The streets were littered with garbage, the bulky apartment buildings were oppressive, devoid of any charm. Gone were the quaint little shops of my early years with Alan. The people I passed in the street, so much taller than Europeans, made me feel even smaller. Cooking, which had once brought me so much joy, was now a haphazard, tasteless affair. Sometimes I'd pick up *The Little Prince* Monsieur Guillaume had given me. Thank God it hadn't been in my suitcase that was stolen in Amsterdam. I would take the book out of its special leather cover given to me by les tantes, and smell the paper. Then I would look at the picture postcards I

Mariette Bermowitz

had placed between the pages with the dried rose petals. Last of all, I would read the inscription, "Like the Little Prince's rose, you are a miraculous appearance in the world." How I wanted to believe it.

I covered the walls of my classroom with quotes from *The Little Prince* and picture postcards of Paris. I also tacked up posters of the beautiful mountains where I had skied. In time I found I was able to ignore the green walls and the dirty floors, and even the dysfunctional school administrators.

Though he had been gone a year already, I still missed Alan, which made me disappointed in myself. And then he came to visit me. As soon as I opened the door and saw his smile, I felt my stomach turn over. His hair was down to his shoulders and he wore the same old baggy pants I remembered. He looked as if he needed sleep and a good meal. I didn't know whether to laugh or cry. Then he sat on the sofa he had always hated, and we chatted away like old friends. But I caught him staring at me the way he used to, as if he was studying me for a portrait. It made me nervous. I crossed and uncrossed my legs, and didn't know what to do with my hands. I wondered what he thought of my new hairstyle and new clothes, but he didn't mention them. I went into the kitchen to make coffee, glad to get away from his piercing eyes.

Over coffee I told him how sorry I was that I destroyed the drawings he had given me after our breakup. I had watched him carefully tape the drawings to the walls, and then after he left I'd ripped them down and torn them up. Sixteen drawings shredded in fury. He looked away from me and said, "I'm sorry I ruined your life." I wanted to cry.

Mindele's Journey

Before he left he said why don't I visit him in the loft downtown? I knew I shouldn't have gone, but my curiosity got the better of me. As soon as I walked in I was hit with the acrid smell of burned plastic. The pile of old wires and junk in the corner almost made me laugh. I wondered how his girlfriend could stand it. Did she complain about it as I had? Red lightbulbs dangled above a table covered with aluminum foil. Garish neon and lightbulb sculptures hung from the walls and were strewn randomly on the floor. I didn't think much of them. They smelled like old abandoned cars and rusted metal. "Where's the kitchen?" I asked.

Alan said, "We never cook. We order hamburgers and pizza from the corner." His girlfriend wasn't home, but there were plenty of photographs hanging on the wall. Sensual, beautiful pictures of a girl ten years younger than me. I remembered when I used to be the object of his lust, when he took pictures like that of me.

Iran

I got on with my life. I cleared out of Albemarle Road and got rid of most of the furniture. Then I settled into a lovely sunny studio in Brooklyn Heights that overlooked a garden. I bought new furniture and filled the room with plants. The portrait of my father that Alan had painted hung against the white brick wall above the fireplace. I had created a place that was just for me, but it was lonely. During the next few years I joined Iris on ski trips to Vermont, wishing it was Europe. I drank too much wine in the après ski gatherings and laughed at everyone's jokes, but I made no new friends. When I came home, I felt lonelier than before. My old friends were busy raising children and I rarely saw them.

Then I met Ed. I almost didn't make it to the party that night. My confidence was low and I wanted to hide. But at the last minute I slipped on a pair of blue bellbottoms and a sexy top and forced myself out of the house. I liked Ed immediately. He was tall and slender with tousled blond hair almost down to his shoulders. His blue eyes matched the dark blue scarf loosely draped around his neck, instantly reminding me of *Le Petit Prince*. I looked into the blue of his eyes that matched his scarf, and was entranced. Though only twenty-six, a full ten years younger than me, Ed seemed so confident, so sure of himself, maybe because he had just graduated from Cornell Medical School.

He spoke of living in a foreign country to do research, but for now he lived in a sixth-floor walkup filled with books. I instantly felt at home in his cozy surroundings. It wasn't long before I was sharing his bed under a ceiling painted with stars, and falling asleep with the contentment of a child. On a ski trip to Vermont, Ed couldn't get over how well I skied. Filled with his praise, I soared down the slopes like a penguin in love. Within six months I abandoned Brooklyn Heights and moved into Ed's apartment on Sixty-Ninth Street in Manhattan. I traipsed off to lectures with him at the Asia Society and delved into his books on Ancient Persia. I became fascinated by the ancient world of the Middle East. One of my favorite volumes was the collection of poems

Mindele's Journey

by Saadi of Shiraz called *The Rose Garden*. Then, out of the blue, Ed announced he was going to Iran for two years. "Do you want to come?" he asked.

It didn't take me long to say yes. The thought of losing someone again was unbearable. I decided to gamble on my "prince." I applied for a leave of absence from teaching, stored my belongings in a friend's garage, and prepared to follow a young man and his dreams to the desert city of Shiraz. The rose garden was my dream too.

Shiraz, the city of wine and roses, nightingales and poets, could not have been more beautiful when we arrived in August, 1975. The sky was an opalescent blue stretching past the rippling Zagros mountain range. The air smelled of flowers. Roses, freesias and countless others speckled across sand colored walls. I quickly got used to leaving my shoes outside, to cooking rice the Persian way, and eating flat bread filled with herbs. It was less easy to adjust to Ed always being addressed first, almost as if I was invisible. Ed did all the talking and made all the preparations for our two-year stay. But I didn't really mind, as it was a relief to have all the details taken care of by someone else for a change.

Pahlavi University was within walking distance of the house. I was looking forward to teaching French in the Foreign Language Department, and Ed was thrilled with his position as lecturer in the Faculty of Medicine. Due to the modernizations under the omnipotent ruler Shah Reza Pahlavi, foreign teachers were welcome in Iran in the seventies. Many of my Iranian students were planning to complete their degrees in America, so they already spoke English.

Mariette Bermowitz

We moved into our house shortly before the fall term began. We had requested to live within the city among the maze of winding alleys and walls dripping with bougainvillea, but the university placement office told us very politely that only Moslems could live there. We were glad in the long run to have our sweet little abode on the outskirts of town. It was clear that while we were tolerated, as foreigners we were not totally accepted.

When I went outside I didn't cover my head with a chador, or at the very least a scarf, like most women did. As a foreigner, I didn't see the need, but I could feel eyes watching me from the windows as I walked the streets. I had been told to step aside to let men pass, which surprised me. I would have thought these sorts of rules would not have applied to foreign women. The only time I ever felt in danger was when a group of teen-age boys cornered me on the sidewalk and wouldn't let me pass. Luckily, I had been taught a curse word in Farsi that made them scatter like leaves in the wind.

Ed bought a Jyane, a facsimile of the French car 4 Chevaux, that looked like a tin box on wheels. But it was inexpensive to run and perfect for the trips we hoped to take. Though small, the house was ample enough with two bedrooms and a modern kitchen. The bathroom took some getting used to. It was just a showerhead in the middle of a small room with a drain on the floor. The toilet was worse. Nothing but a hole in the floor and an *aftabeh,* or water pitcher, used instead of toilet paper for sanitary purposes. We received some basic furniture from the university storage room, but ended up following the Iranian custom of spreading a cloth on the floor and eating our meals

Mindele's Journey

from one common dish. For the bedroom all we had was a mattress lying on a rug. The floors were made of little stones, which kept the house cool. My favorite part of the house was the courtyard with its lovely fountain in the middle. One day I came home to find that Ed had planted rose bushes around the fountain. It was his surprise for me. And I was surprised, as I had never mentioned the Little Prince to him, or told him about Monsieur Guillaume in Belgium. I felt very special having my own little rose garden that I could walk around in or admire from the window. A veil of perfume now permeated the rooms, and I felt as close to paradise, or *behesht* in Farsi, as I'd ever hoped to get.

When Ed and I went to the mausoleum where the fourteenth-century poet Hafez was buried, I brought along a book of his poetry. I had heard that if a young couple brings a copy of his poems and opens the book at random it will foretell their future. I sat close to Ed under the cypress and orange trees on the low stone wall surrounded by roses. Then Ed opened the book of poetry and I read aloud the English translation.

> And in their learned books thou will seek in vain
> The key to Love's locked gateway; Heart grown wise
> In pain and sorrow, ask no remedy!
> But when the time of roses comes again,
> Take what it gives, oh Hafiz, ere it flies,
> And ask not why the hour has brought it thee,
> And wherefore ask no more!

Mariette Bermowitz

My heart beat faster. Ed could not have found a more perfect verse for me. I looked up at him, hoping for a kiss, but he was staring off into the distance. "We'd better be getting back," he said gruffly. "I have to be up early for work."

On my early morning walk down the dirt roads to Abivardi Boulevard, the air was clear and bright and smelled of fresh baked bread. Cypress trees were outlined against the sky. Chants called the faithful to prayer. When I passed by our neighbor Farideh's house, she always said, *Befarmaid.* I thought it meant hello, or have a good day, because she said *befarmaid,* then closed the door. But I learned it meant, "Please come in," and it was just a custom; it didn't mean anything. Ed and I were officially invited in, however, when Farideh's famous cousin, the *Mullah,* came to visit. No one spoke English, yet somehow through sign language and much smiling we got to know each other.

I slowly learned how to speak Farsi. I learned a prayer from one of the janitors at school, and the baker taught me a new word each time I bought the flatbread called *nan.* The vegetable seller at his outdoor stand told me to be very careful to wash the greens as they were often contaminated by dog feces. There were packs of dogs who roamed the fields at night. Moslems considered dogs unclean and shunned them as pets.

After my last class finished at two in the afternoon, I went over to Ed's lab and waved to him from the doorway. If he didn't wave back it meant he would not be getting out early and I faced a long evening alone. I always walked home alone, anyway. As soon as I reached the *kuche,* our street, I took off my shoes.

262

Mindele's Journey

The earth felt so good under my feet, warm and tingling and alive. If Farideh happened to be standing by her window, she'd warn me about the dirt and garbage. She didn't approve of me walking barefoot on the street. She also let me know she didn't think it was a good idea for a woman to stay home alone. "Too much time to think," she'd say—*khub nist*—not good. But in the stillness of my surroundings I felt a fullness of being I had never known, not even in Belgium. Here on the outskirts of Shiraz there was no radio, no TV, or newspapers to divert me from my inner world of books.

Still, I was happier being alone after we adopted Buffy, one of the stray dogs picked up around the city to be used in Ed's research lab. When I came by the lab and saw his soulful eyes I couldn't bear the thought of Ed experimenting on him. I told Ed I wanted him, adding that I would feel safer having Buffy for company on those evenings he worked late. I named him Buffy, because of his dusty beige coat. He could hardly walk on one of his hind paws. But I nursed him, and before long he was cavorting around the patio as if he owned it.

One night before Ed got home there was a loud knock at the gate. Buffy started barking. I called out in Farsi, *Ki-è?* Who is it?

Bebachshid Xanom! "Please, Madam," *Ob darid?* "Do you have water?"

I had heard that the Quasghai nomads, an extraordinary people, were making their annual migration through Shiraz, and unlocked the gate. A man on horseback was holding a chicken. The women with their jet-black hair and green eyes were surrounded

263

Mariette Bermowitz

by goats and sheep. They were stunning to look at in their colorful multilayered skirts that glimmered in the waning light. Unlike most of the women in Shiraz, their faces were uncovered. The rest of the tribe hung back in the distance. For days they had been traveling up from the south on mules and horses with their flock of animals. Shiraz was the first big city they had reached, and our house was the first one they came to. I invited them onto the patio to fill their jugs with water from the pump.

These colorful nomads with their horses and caravans reminded me of the gypsies who came through Fraiture when I was a little girl. For a moment, I almost wished I could take off with them, leave everything behind! Instead, I invited them to have some *chai,* and gave the women roses from the garden. They placed their hands over their hearts in thanks, and with a swish of their long flowing skirts, they were gone.

There were so many other extraordinary events such as my encounter with the Dervish.

I heard about him from the old bookseller on Zand Avenue where I often went to browse through the mystical literature at the back of the store. I met Americans from the University looking for newspapers from home or books in English, and often ran into Professor Amin, who conducted an Iranian poetry club for the American faculty members. When I told him I had gone to the shrine in Shiraz and wanted to read Hafez in the original, he invited me to join as well, saying they studied the poetry of mystics like Hafez and Saadi. I asked Professor Amin if he knew about the Dervish. "Yes," he said, in those

264

Mindele's Journey

rich deep tones he used to recite poetry. "There is indeed a Dervish in Shiraz."

Early one evening when Ed was working late, I put on a chador, the veil Iranian women wore in public places, and went to see the Holy Man, this Dervish who lived in the old caravanserai on the other side of town. I thought I knew enough Farsi to greet him and ask for his blessing, but I memorized a little speech anyway. It was a long walk, and by the time I reached the entrance down a twisted alleyway, I was covered with dust from the streets. An old woman with a face like weathered parchment led me through a large courtyard and up the stairs to a balcony. A little man draped in a blanket was sitting in the corner. All I could see was his face. In my excitement walking toward him, I realized I had forgotten all the Farsi I had so carefully memorized. I sat down on a pillow before him and gathered the *chador* around me, waiting for him to speak. I waited and waited but the Dervish didn't say a word. He didn't look up. He didn't even seem to notice I was there. I closed my eyes and tried to remember my little speech, but I was distracted by the scent of white and yellow freesias growing by the wall. Finally, the old man looked up. He was blind! Perhaps he was mute as well, because he didn't utter a word. I got to my feet making ready to leave, and suddenly his right hand appeared from under the blanket. He placed his hand over his heart in a deliberate gesture, and his face radiated love and kindness. Tears sprang to my eyes and I felt a great warmth spread through my body. I practically floated home. A passage from *The Little Prince*

265

Mariette Bermowitz

came back to me. *L'essentiel est invisible pour les yeux. On ne voit bien qu'avec le cœur.*

When I arrived home, the first thing I saw were rose petals scattered over the patio. I said, "What happened to the garden? Where's Buffy?" because he hadn't come out to greet me. Ed shouted angrily, "I kicked him out. Your damn dog dug up the garden."

The peace and joy I had felt with the Dervish evaporated in an instant. I loved that dog. I had saved him from the lab experiments where he would have died. Buffy knew it too. He seemed to know that I was his protector. He used to sit by my side on the patio looking up with his soulful eyes whenever I patted his head. I had warned him many times not to go into the garden. I knew how much Ed loved his garden, but how he could have turned out the animal I loved was beyond me. Ed had never liked the dog anyway. But how could Buffy resist? It was the only bit of earth in sight. Everything else was cement. The wire fence around the rose bushes was easily breached by a dog who wanted to dig in the earth.

Ed had a short temper and was quick to anger, but I had no idea he could be so cruel. Then I remembered what he did in the lab. What he would have done to Buffy if I hadn't rescued him. I refused to speak to Ed for the rest of the evening, and that night I slept in the other room. I never told him how much he had hurt me. All I did was sulk. I never spoke about my feelings with Alan either. I let Alan make all the decisions and accepted them without arguing. I remembered my father and Mme. Goldman fighting constantly on the Rue Ste. Anne. I never wanted to

Mindele's Journey

be like them. But why was I so passive? Was I afraid Ed would leave me like Alan did?

A few days later a tattered and hungry Buffy reappeared at the gate. I cleaned him up and lectured him in every language I knew. Buffy was allowed to stay. Ed gave way to me on this one. And I ended up forgiving him when I reminded myself that he was ten years younger than me, only twenty-six. Besides, I never would have come to Iran on my own. It was the start of winter, the rainy season was coming and there would be no more gardening, and no more roses to tempt the dog. In the spring, Ed and I would be taking a much longed for road trip across the desert. I couldn't have done that without him either. In the evenings when I heard the rippling echo of the dog pack, I let Buffy out. He never went near the garden again.

The rose garden, I was coming to realize, was an idea as much as a place, and I would never find it with Ed. By now I knew that although Ed and I pretended to be married for the sake of convenience, I could never marry him. He had asked me once, but I put him off, and he didn't bring the subject up again. Instead, he spent more time with colleagues at the university, most of whom spoke English. Ed had boasted how quickly he would learn Farsi, but after a year he still struggled with the language while I was almost fluent.

In fact, a rose garden could just as well be a glittering shrine with high ceilings and thickly woven carpets with exquisite designs. That was how the shrine appeared to me, one of the holiest shrines in Shiraz, Shah-E-Cheragh. Javad, the handsome young

Mariette Bermowitz

taxi driver, drove us there one night. Ed had become quite friendly with Javad, which made me happy, because he hadn't had any Iranian friends until now. When Ed and Javad, deep in conversation, strolled ahead of me into the inner courtyard, I thought I'd take a quick look inside the mosque. The ceiling was covered with glittering mirrors. Thousands of fragments sparkled like glittering jewels, twinkling above like some new heaven. I don't know how long I stood there, mesmerized by the exotic beauty, but when I was finally able to tear my eyes away, I started to wonder where Ed and Javad had gone. They had seen me come inside the mosque—why hadn't they come to look for me? I didn't think it was wise for me to go outside into that maze of courtyards and pillars. It was almost midnight. The place was dimly lit. Beggars lurked in the shadows. I thought it best to stay inside the mosque and wait for them.

A small group of women were making their way toward the shrine in the center. I had heard foreigners weren't welcome in some of the mosques, so I tugged on the chador, pulling it closer, holding the edge between my teeth so no one would suspect I was a foreigner. When they sat on the floor, I sat on the floor too. We faced the silver mesh doors of the shrine, which were flowing with ribbons of wishes. Ribbons instead of candles. When the woman next to me spoke and I made no response, she gave me a nudge. I was afraid if I spoke, she'd know I didn't belong there. But then I remembered the Dervish, and silently pointed to my mouth and ears, then put my hand over my heart just as the Dervish had done. The woman bowed her head toward me and lifted

Mindele's Journey

her hands in prayer. When she started to pray the other women joined in and I was enveloped in their soft murmurings interspersed with choked-up sobs.

I lifted my hands and looked up at the dome filled with thousands of tiny mirrors reflecting the lights and the richly colored Persian carpets below, creating a kaleidoscope of pulsing colors. The longer I gazed up the more I felt swept up into the twinkling colors. My hands began trembling. My eyes filled with tears. Suddenly I understood how I was all those broken pieces of mirror. My life had been broken into so many different pieces. And now, seeing how the bits of mirror made a whole ceiling, something in me connected, and I felt a wholeness inside. I was broken, yet whole. My heart was bursting with love. The feeling was intense. I felt transported to the Divine. Now the women were finishing their prayers, getting up and bowing to me. Did they think I was a saint?

Ed and Javad appeared in the doorway of the mosque. Ed hurried over to me and whispered, "Where have you been? We were looking all over for you! I asked the janitor if he'd seen you, and he said no, all he saw was a deaf and dumb Holy Woman praying at the back of the mosque."

"That was me!" I cried. But Ed just looked at me and laughed. He could laugh. But I know what I saw. I know what I felt. I would never forget the mirrored ceiling of Shah-E-Cheragh. I learned the story of the ceilings filled with mirrors when Ed and I visited Esphehan, known for its architecture and mosques. During the seventeenth century, the ruler of Esphehan, eager to establish alliances with

European powers, sent a delegation to the court of Louis XIV. They were overwhelmed by the magnificence of Versailles, particularly the Hall of Mirrors. A shipment of mirrors was ordered, but by the time it reached Esphehan, the mirrors had shattered. Some ingenious mind suggested they use the broken pieces as architectural backgrounds. The result can still be seen today in many restaurants with their walls decorated with panels of broken mirrors.

Javad invited us to dine at his parents' house, and I was finally able to see inside one of the little houses on the crowded dusty street where we had wanted to live. The houses were set close together and looked as if they were made of mud and straw. Javad's mother served stuffed eggplant, pomegranate soup, and goat cheese with *nan*. Unfortunately I made the mistake of asking if they ate goat meat. Javad's mother looked at me with horror and said, "Only Jews eat goat meat." Goat meat is actually forbidden in the Jewish religion, but I kept quiet. I didn't want to tell her I was Jewish.

The more I fell in love with Iran, the more distant Ed felt to me. Our differences became even more apparent during the trip we made through the desert to visit Kerman, Mahan, and Yazd. We packed the car, our little Iranian *Jyane*, with plenty of water and food and set out from Shiraz before the pastel colors of a new day began streaking the sky. After passing through the imposing Qu'ran Gate with its shimmering blue faience façade, we drove down the

Mindele's Journey

dusty road lined with cypress trees set against a jagged mountain chain. We were headed toward Dasht-i-Lut, the southern Iranian desert. I stuck my head out the window and looked back at the city. The sand-colored walls were fading into the distance. As we passed the last few rows of cypress trees, I thought of the coolness near the river, and how we were leaving that behind.

The road was lonely and bleak. Villages were hidden from view behind mud walls with garlands of spring blossoms hanging outside the dusty enclosures. White flowers of almond trees, lavender heart-shaped flowers of wild pistachio trees, flickering in the breeze of a glorious spring day. The walls reminded me of a green cocoon. In a few short months the flowers and the green would disappear under the relentless sun. But for now it was the beginning of spring, the promise of renewal. I reached into my bag for a book of Hafez poetry. It was the same verse I had read to Ed when we visited the poet's tomb in Shiraz.

> But when the time of roses comes again
> Take what it gives, ere it flies,
> And ask not why the hour has brought it
> thee...
> And wherefore ask no more!

Ed grunted and stared at the road. I read it to him again, emphasizing *the time of roses*. Now he sighed and said, "Why didn't you learn to drive a shift car so I could have a rest?"

I had tried to learn, but Ed was so impatient, snapping at me when I made mistakes, and he finally

Mariette Bermowitz

gave up in frustration. He didn't appreciate how much I wanted to learn. It was like with the plugs on the stereo I could never get right. He belittled me and made me feel inadequate, but mechanical things had always been a struggle for me. I decided not to let Ed dampen my spirits.

After traveling for twelve hours, we arrived in Kerman late that evening and were unable to find a hotel that was open. We sat in the car and devoured the rest of the sandwiches, but did not relish the idea of sleeping in the car, especially Ed with his long legs. He said, "Let's take off for the desert again. We can reach Mahan by morning."

Mahan was forty-two kilometers away, but we knew we'd find an Intourist Inn with a comfortable bed and a hot shower. We looked for signs out of Kerman, but I couldn't read Farsi very well and Ed didn't want to stop and ask directions, so we endlessly circled the labyrinthine medieval streets. Finally Ed backed down and found someone who pointed us to the road out of town. After several kilometers, Ed stopped the car at the side of the road. "Come on," he said, "get out of the car." Were we out of gas? Was Ed too tired to drive anymore? Were we going to sleep on the side of the road out in the open? "Look up," he said, pointing to the sky.

Shooting stars. Millions of shimmering, sparkling, golden eyes. It looked like the entire universe was right there above our heads. Ed squeezed my hand and whispered tenderly, "Kuchuloo." I loved it when he called me Kuchuloo. I wish we could have had that kind of intimacy more often. Kuchuloo the wanderer.

Mindele's Journey

"Kuchuloo," he said, "the stars tell me we're going in the wrong direction. That guy back there didn't want to admit he didn't know the way to Mahan."

He turned the car around and we drove the other way until Mahan appeared out of nowhere. An illusion made of dust and slumbering shadows brought to life in the morning sun. Mud houses with round dome-shaped roofs cascaded into the distance to join the hazy ribbon of mountains beyond. Signs to the inn were in English. Mahan is a place of pilgrimage where the faithful come to pray in the sanctuary of the great Sufi poet and mystic, Shah Nasroddin Nematollah Vali, who died in 1431. The shrine, protected by three hundred miles of desert sands, was empty of tourists. Perhaps that was why the gardener sweeping the entrance was surprised to see us, and doubly surprised to hear me speak Farsi. Raising his broom like a scepter he swung the gate open, and with a broad grin sang out, *befarmaid Khanom.*

"What a wonderful greeting!" I said to Ed. But he made a face. "The guy smelled a big tip when he saw us coming." I looked at the glazed aquamarine tiles shimmering in the morning sun. Framed between the minarets were snowcapped mountains in the distance. The blue and green facades were imbedded with a kufic script that seemed to dance across the arches. Intertwining lines and curves of domes and towers reached up to the blue sky while fragrant cypress and pine trees permeated the air.

We followed the gardener into the shrine. High up in the ceiling the sunlight played through star-shaped openings, creating intricate lace patterns against the walls. I was engulfed by its radiance. As if in a dream of warmth and peace, I followed the twinkling patterns of circling light and was led to the tapestry on the wall with the Dervish symbols of a bowl and two crossed axes. Imitating the woman next to me, I put my hands on the tapestry, then opened my palms as if making an offering. The woman nodded to me and lifted her hands up in prayer. She began to pray, with other women joining in. I was enveloped in the sound of their prayers interspersed with choking sobs, and lifted my hands too. The woman nodded in approval. I followed her to the catafalque in the center of the shrine and stared at the green cloth covering the tomb of the saint. I smelled roses. The scent seemed to come from nowhere. The woman smiled at me, and I smiled back. I felt blessed.

Ed was outside talking to the gardener in sign language, except that he used his whole body as if he was doing Tai Chi. I waved to him and he said, "You look so pale. What happened? Did you see a ghost in there?"

"Oh, no, it was more like stepping into a dream," I said, turning to look at the milky white clouds floating by. How could I explain to Ed, with his rational scientific mind, how the smell of roses had suddenly filled the room? I looked at the gardener. "Isn't this amazing, here we are the three of us, all from different religious backgrounds! I'm Jewish, he's Catholic, and you're a Moslem."

"Ah, yes," said the gardener. "Jewish, Catholic, Moslem, but we are all folds in a piece of cloth, and the same in the eyes of the Beloved."

I felt humbled by his words. When he gave us a tour through the gardens, I told him how difficult

Mindele's Journey

it was learning to read the ancient Persian poetry of Shah Nematollah Vali. "Would you like to see the inner sanctuary where the saint's poetry is painted on the wall?" he asked. The gardener opened a little side door leading to the sanctuary and gave me a candle. Then he shut the door, saying he would be back for me later. I stared in awe at the writing that filled the walls from top to bottom, and held the candle up to try to make out some of what it was saying, but it was in ancient Persian. Then I noticed a huge black sword painted over the verses on one of the walls. I took a deep breath. I felt my heart expand, and closed my eyes for a moment. When I looked at the sword again, it seemed to be moving down the wall. I could have sworn it was sliding down the wall of its own accord! I didn't know if my eyes were playing tricks on me, or if this was like the scent of roses, beyond anything explainable. Suddenly my candle blew out. I was in total darkness, complete and utter blackness. I was frozen in terror, unable to move a muscle. At that moment the door swung open and the room was filled with light again. The gardener smiled at me, but I wasn't ready to smile back at him just yet. I'd had a glimpse of the Void I would not soon forget.

Ed and I got back in the car to drive through the desert to visit another temple. But I would never forget the experience I had in the sanctuary at Mahan, in the little room filled with poetry. Something mysterious happened to me in there. I felt myself expand. I felt something eternal, something of the divine within my own self.

The feeling that I was coming closer to the Divine mysteries grew stronger when we arrived at the city of Yazd, the desert stronghold of the Zoroastrians. We found a small hotel run by an Armenian who proudly spoke some English and invited us to join the Iranian New Year festivities in the dining room, where boisterous patrons were laughing and singing as endless trays of steaming delicacies were brought to their tables. The owner offered us Arak, an anisette liqueur that he said had been made by an old Jewish friend of his. I almost told him I was Jewish, but it might have complicated things. After dinner, there was a concert at the inn. We listened to ancient stringed instruments named tars and cetars, dotars and ouds, and santours. The languorous music pulled at my heart, filling me with a longing I couldn't explain.

The next day we went to the Artesh-Ga, Place of the Fire. The walls of the temple were surrounded by cypress trees and flowers. The temple itself was surprisingly simple, all white with delicate windowsills made from imported wood. There was no furniture except for the chairs along the walls, yet elaborate chandeliers hung from the ceiling in every room. The Holy Fire was sheltered behind a golden gate. I was overcome at the sight of the ancient flame. Two priests dressed in white motioned us to come closer. The older one held a book, and pointed to a passage from the Avestas, the holy book of the Zoroastrians. Ed and I kneeled down on the stone floor and bowed our heads. I was startled when they began to sing, how much it sounded like the prayers in the synagogue in Brussels after the war. My father had taken me there for the High Holy Days. I had to sit in the women's section up in the balcony, but I could

Mindele's Journey

see my father, and I watched his frail body rock back and forth as if he was in a trance. His voice trembled as he sang. Then suddenly he broke into sobs. His prayer had turned to sobs. How I wanted to be with him then, comfort him, but I was in the balcony with the women.

The singing stopped. I looked up at the old priest. His face glowed with kindness. He motioned us to stand, and led us to the golden cage enclosing the sacred fire. The flame was hypnotic. The heat was so strong that even from five feet away I felt it on my forehead, but I couldn't look away. It was as if nothing else existed, only this fire, this eternal fire. I began to feel one with the light. My whole being felt one with the flame. As if the Eternal was now in me.

After Iran

Not long after our return to the States, Ed announced he was gay. Was it his friend Javad, I wondered? The handsome young taxi driver he became friends with? Was he seeing Javad when he told me he was working late in the lab? It didn't matter anymore. Ed was on his way to teach at Howard University in Washington, D.C. I felt a great sadness that our relationship was ending, yet what a blessing I hadn't married him in Iran! When I went down to visit Ed in D.C. he had shaved his beard and was so thin I hardly recognized him. I saw him for the last time a few years later when he was dying of AIDS. I didn't go to the funeral but I cried the entire day. In spite of all our differences, I loved him very much,

Mariette Bermowitz

and I never told him how much. How I admired the way he had taken care of me in Iran, with such concern and devotion. I can still hear him calling me Kuchuloo, the wanderer, as we traveled the parched roads of Iran, and later, Afghanistan and Nepal. He once told me of a dream he'd had, a dream where he rubbed a magic lamp and made a wish to go back twenty-five hundred years into the past. His dream had come true. And he had shared it with me.

Ed had loved the way we lived in Iran, "so unlike in the West," he said. I did too. No furniture, just pillows we bought in the bazaar. "Good donkey bags," the vendor had said. "So easy to move when you leave." After Ed was gone I remembered the way he gathered wood to make a fire, and we sat by the fire watching the sun set over the mountains. Then he pointed things out to me, such as how the turning Earth was creating shadows. He pointed out the newly plowed fields among the trees, the other bonfires in the distance, the lambs and the faint sound of folk singers.

Ed, this is for you. A poem to a friend who left too soon, and a friend I will miss forever.

> Where are you today, my friend
> Blowing your thoughts like a seed
> Into the Universe
> Gathering stardust for those
> Who believe in dreams
> Like you did
> And then you became a star
> A wanderer like me
> In the eternal sphere of possibilities

Mindele's Journey

Never staying too long
To gather what he reaps

✫ ✫ ✫

As for Alan, the man I married, the man I've always thought of as the love of my life, he not only left me, he obliterated me from his life. Over the years, I heard that he was making his mark as a punk rocker under the name of Alan Vega, then "Suicide." I was still drawn to him and his work. Once or twice I went to a performance, or caught a show in a gallery. But I had a shock when I looked him up on the Internet and read his biography. There wasn't a single mention of me. Not one. It was as if our marriage had never taken place. As if I had never existed. As if he had just blotted me out, erased me from his life. Was he ashamed of me? Had I meant nothing to him at all? I didn't understand, and I still don't. Some days I think I still love him. Other days I can't get over his betrayal.

Les Tantes

I spent my forties living in the present, not thinking about the future. I quit teaching for a while and worked for a friend in the flea market. Then I tried catering, but eventually I needed the regular paycheck from teaching again. This time I found a position teaching French in a well-regarded high school in Brooklyn. I immersed myself in what I considered my life's calling—sharing my love for a language that connected me to the past, especially to *Le Petit Prince*. I used St. Exupery's charming story as a classroom text, I always thought of Monsieur Guillaume when I came to the line, *L'essentiel est invisible pour less yeux. On ne voit bien qu'avec le Coeur.* "What is essential cannot be seen by the eyes. One can only see it with the heart." This became the most important message that I shared with my students. It was also the most important lesson that I had learned on my journey so far.

The years passed. I hardly noticed I was getting older. There were some brief relationships with younger men with whom I enjoyed hiking and skiing and other outdoor adventures. I was hoping to meet someone I could share life with on a deeper level, but so far it hadn't happened. I still thought I had all the time in the world.

Every year I returned to Belgium to visit les tantes. Though they were now in their seventies, little about them had changed. They wore the same clothes and hairstyles I'd always known. Time never seemed to move around them. And, though I was now entering middle-age, to them I was still *notre petite Mariette*. Each summer when I packed my bags I knew I was headed for a quiet time, sequestered within those walls of love and protection where nothing would be asked of me and I always felt accepted just the way I was.

Then the eldest, Tante Marie, died in 1989 at the age of eighty-five. It was a great loss not only for her sisters but for me as well. When I went back to visit the following summer, I felt an insurmountable

Mindele's Journey

sadness knowing I would never see her again. I left New York the day school let out in June. This was the last time I would be going back to Hour. Les tantes were leaving their beloved village to live in a senior residence. I couldn't imagine my spirited and independent "little aunts" having to make that choice. But it had been made for them by an old family friend, a priest, who was concerned for their safety. There were rumors that young thieves were preying upon vulnerable elderly people living alone in remote villages. Besides, Maman had difficulty walking and Tante Marthe almost chopped her hand off when she climbed on a window sill to pull down the heavy window guard. An eighty-year-old woman should not have been climbing up on window sills, but she refused to give up her chores. I used to laugh watching her climb a ladder wearing shoes a size too big. It was an impossible task to get her to mend her ways. If anyone tried to correct her she arched her brows like an angry owl and said, *Je suis comme je suis, une Ardennaise têtue jusqu'à la fin!* "I am as I am, a stubborn Ardennes woman to the end!" Everyone in the Ardennes Mountains understood that.

I couldn't stop thinking about the past on that last train ride to Hour. There had been so many wondrous moments that kept me coming back every summer to share a bit more of life with my beloved aunts, and now it was coming to an end. I watched villages and meadows darting past the window as the train picked up speed. To me they were keepsakes of life with les tantes. I knew the familiar landscape of summer so well, the fields bursting with future harvest, the curving outline of the Ardennes Mountains, the rocks, the stones, the sunflowers smiling into the sun, the quaint platforms filled with vacationers. I had made the journey hundreds of times but never had it felt so meaningful. The wheels pounding the tracks sounded like the pounding of my heavy heart. Les tantes were leaving the beloved parish house where they had spent the last forty years. Monsieur le Curé had died, then their beloved sister Marie. In their last letter before I left the States they said they were resigned to live in a home for retired nuns. They described it as a restful place, surrounded by gardens. Tante Marthe added that the halls had lavish antique furniture. And in her usual humorous way, she admitted that it was fitting for the antiques they had become. But reading between the lines I could feel the sacrifices that had to be made. The nuns had rules. Marthe had to give up smoking cigarettes and Maman would no longer be able to tend a small garden or cook her wonderful dishes. I couldn't imagine their being subjected to such discipline. But resignation had always been part of their life. They belonged to another century where obedience, faith, and religion directed and guided their lives.

How I would miss Tante Marie! But at least she wouldn't end up in an old-age home. Yet they had been inseparable, a holy trinity. As the eldest, Tante Marie represented pure love and devotion during all the years I had known her. From the fervor with which she played the organ on Sundays, to the endless hours of choral rehearsal, she taught selflessness and gentle kindness. I will never forget her footsteps clattering against the stone walk as she darted out

Mindele's Journey

to open the front gate, welcoming guests into the house with a lilting, *Bonjour, Bienvenue.*

I remember when she invited her favorite door-to-door salesman into the kitchen. He came every summer with his suitcase brimming with novelties, sewing kits, fragrant soaps nestled in exotic boxes, combs and brushes, pins for the hair, odd-shaped scissors, pen and pencil holders and countless trinkets for the house. He always came in the afternoon, as if he knew that fresh coffee was brewing and Maman Thérèse had just baked a strawberry-rhubarb pie with the fruits picked in her garden. The summer he didn't come round, Tante Marie had prayers said for his safety. *Pauvre homme*, she'd say, shaking her head in acquiescence to the hard life he led. She knew he traveled far and wide to sell his wares. So when he showed up after his long absence, the entire household was there to greet him.

The table was set with a red-checkered cloth, the cups and saucers laid out, the jams lined up on a tray with the butter, the sugar, the cream, and the tantalizing fragrance of pie, coffee, and flowers. We couldn't wait to find out what had happened to him, but he waited to tell us, first opening up his bag to take out a package. Then with great care, he placed the carefully wrapped box with its blue ribbon in front of Tante Marie, explaining that he had gone on a pilgrimage for an entire year. He walked all the way from Belgium to Lourdes near the Pyrenees Mountains. Once there, he prayed for the people who had been so kind to him, especially Mademoiselle Marie. He had brought back a small token of his appreciation. With tears in her eyes, Tante Marie slowly opened the package, making sure not to rip the beautiful blue bow. Inside the box, laid out like precious jewels against a white velvet background were three medals. I think Tante Marie wanted to kiss her *colporteur,* traveling salesman as he called himself. But before she could, he lowered his head, took her hand, and kissed it.

She died peacefully in her sleep that summer. Hundreds of people attended her funeral. People said it was a joyous occasion because Heaven was opening its doors for her. Maman Thérèse and Tante Marthe resigned themselves to the loss, but found it too difficult to continue living in a house that had lost its heart.

When I arrived, Tante Marthe was clearing out Monsieur le Curé's office. His niece and nephew had recently come to remove his antique furniture. The room looked bare without the Flemish credenzas with the stained glass windows, the oak tables and chairs that hosted so many unforgettable receptions, the beautifully ensconced desk by the window. All that remained was a faint odor of furniture polish encrusted in the wooden floorboards. No more pendulum clock chiming the time away in its familiar corner, no more worn velvet chair with its lace doilies on each arm, no more hanging candelabra that gave the room the look of a Flemish painting. It was all gone except for the pieces on the mantel that belonged to les tantes. There was a story for each one that I had heard over and over again during the long winter evenings of the Christmas holidays. That too would be gone, winter hours sitting around the fire, sewing or singing or talking about the past. They loved to

Mindele's Journey

recall their father, who had been mayor and beloved headmaster of the school in Fraiture. Perhaps that was the reason I felt I knew him so well.

Life had not been easy for him. His mother had died when he was a young boy and his father, out of despair, drowned himself in the river. He was sent to live with an uncle who worked as a cook for a count, M. le Comte de Bras. I loved the way my aunts emphasized his name, with all the respect due to a bygone aristocracy. The boy was raised by his uncle, who was most of the time in the chateau's kitchen, and caught the count's attention. Since the count didn't have children of his own, he took special care of his servant's boy, whose intelligence was obvious to everyone who knew him. When he came of age, the count offered him the choice of studying for the priesthood or becoming a schoolmaster. This was how M. Leloup became a revered teacher and scholar. When M. le Comte died, he left him, among other things, a beautiful set of blue and white dinnerware dating back to 1830, which les tantes treasured with the utmost care. These exquisite dishes had survived the war, as we did, and when the table was set it made the meal a true celebration of life.

The house had to be emptied out in preparation for their moving to the senior residence. The day following my arrival, Tante Marthe took me aside and said I should choose some of their treasured items as souvenirs. There were still some of the blue dishes left. I took three plates and two libation cups brought back from one of the count's trips to China. But as I held the pieces in my hands I suddenly felt like crying. There I was, the next in line for souvenirs.

285

Perhaps it was the word "souvenir" that bewildered me, or the fact that I was asked to choose, that made me feel a great emptiness. Suddenly life had been reduced to souvenirs.

Tante Marthe was dusting off a beautiful brass basket with birds adorning the handle when she noticed how quiet I had become. She turned around and said, "We rescued this piece from out of the rubble left of our house after the bombing. It survived as we all did. Take this with you to America. It will always remind you that some things cannot be destroyed."

I knew I would continue to visit Tante Marthe and Maman in the senior residence near Hour, but the people and the place that I called family and home were disappearing. That once vibrant household was being reduced to souvenirs. I broke into tears, as if everything had suddenly been taken from me. I had come to say good-bye to Hour, not realizing that it would leave me feeling so barren and alone, like a story with a sad ending.

But my story hadn't come to an end; it was just beginning.

The time had come to know more about my own family. What had happened to them during the war? Where had I really come from?

Connecting to My Roots

My dear friend Pauline liked to vacation in Israel and asked me many times to come stay with her after my visits to Belgium, but I always said no. I had never wanted to go to Israel. But this year, Pauline was on

Mindele's Journey

sabbatical from teaching and had rented an apartment in Netanya on the Mediterranean. So it happened that in the summer of 1993, I landed in Tel Aviv and put my feet on Israeli soil for the first time. I had finally made it to Israel after so many years of wandering in other places. The hot dry heat and intensity of the light reminded me of Iran. It was a pleasant change after the cool gray damp of the Belgian countryside.

Pauline and I went sunbathing on the beach. The late-afternoon sun raked a blanket of honey-colored tones over the furrows of sand. My thoughts drifted in and out of time. I reminisced to Pauline about life in Brussels after the war. She propped herself up on her elbows and dug them into the sand. "I'm sure your father would have wanted you to come to Israel."

I nodded, remembering how happy I was that Poppa hadn't sent me to a kibbutz at the end of the war, and took me to America instead. I told Pauline about Mme. Goldman and her retarded son, Jean, who lived with us, and her twin daughters, Cécile and Renée, who did not. The girls had to remain in an orphanage because there wasn't enough money or enough room to keep them with us. It would have meant six people living in a two-room tenement. Poppa barely made enough money to keep food on the table and pay rent for our two dark rooms. The only daylight that reached us bounced off the wall of the building opposite. Poppa was sick all the time. I was never quite sure when I would become orphaned. But I wasn't sent to Israel. It was the twins, Renée and Cécile, who went to live on a kibbutz.

Pauline and I talked into the dying sunlight, the sand blanketing our toes as darkness erased the shadows and stars began appearing through the shield of sky above. Then, as we folded up our towels and picked up our beach bags to make the trek back to the houses in the distance, I suddenly remembered the name of the kibbutz, Ein Hanatziv, where Cécile and Renée had gone to live. I told Pauline I had stored their address in a cigar box all those years ago. "How strange to remember it after all this time! Forty-five years." What had happened to Cécile and Renée, I wondered. "Do you think it's possible they could still be at Ein Hanatziv?" I said.

Pauline's face lit up. "We have to try to find them, see if they're still there," she insisted. Even if it was a wild goose chase it was more exciting than spending another day lying on the beach sunning ourselves. We found a bus that would take us north toward Haifa, then we took another bus east toward Jordan. We were dropped off at a deserted outpost in the desert. We watched the bus barreling down the dirt road, disappearing in a cloud of dust, leaving us in the middle of nowhere. The only sound was the drone of flies buzzing around our heads. Pauline, in high heels as usual, balked at having to walk down the narrow side road for God knew how many miles to reach the kibbutz. But the bus was gone, and there was nothing to do but take off our shoes and set off with half-closed eyes against the dust blowing from every direction. Eventually, we came across rows of identical-looking little flat-roofed houses. In the heat and dust of the noonday sun it almost looked like a mirage. There was no one about. We went through

Mindele's Journey

the gate, then knocked at the rickety door at the first house we came to. There was no answer so we went in. A bearded young man was asleep in a beat-up wicker chair. I touched his arm and said softly, "Hello?" He sprang to his feet so fast you'd have thought he heard a gunshot. He shouted in a thick Brooklyn accent, "Oh my God, what happened?"

Pauline and I looked at each other, amazed to find a bit of home way out here in the desert. "Are you from Brooklyn?" I asked.

"I don't want to talk about Brooklyn," he said. "I was born and raised in Brooklyn, and I'm happy to say that I left it to come here."

Yet I managed to find out that we had actually lived quite near one another—the same street, Argyle Road, just two blocks apart. We talked about the neighborhood and even discovered that we knew the same shopkeepers, had the same acquaintances, in fact. Pauline had to nudge me to remind me why we were here. I took a deep breath and said, "We've come to look up some relatives. Do you know a Mrs. Goldman and her daughters, Cécile and Renée?"

He said, "Yes, I do," and I grabbed hold of Pauline's arm to steady myself. "Mrs. Goldman died a few years back, but Renée is still here. The brother too, Jean. Cécile lives with her husband and two sons in a nearby town. I can take you to Renée's bunga-low, but she's probably sleeping now. It's her resting time before she goes back to her job in the nursery."

I could hardly believe it. After so many years, a lifetime of events really, Renée and Jean were still at the kibbutz. Thank God I had remembered the name of the place! Pauline and I followed the young man

Mariette Bermowitz

through a maze of identical little cement houses, all shuttered up against the heat. Then I rang the bell, barely able to contain my excitement. After what seemed an eternity, though was certainly only a few moments, I heard feet shuffling on the other side of the door. It opened very slowly and a small, sleepy-eyed woman, dressed in a mismatched skirt and blouse, stood before us blinking in the light. She looked prematurely aged, but her eyes were the same soft brown eyes I remembered. She started speaking in Hebrew and I interrupted her in French, saying, *Renée, c'est moi, ta petite soeur Mariette!*

The color drained from her cheeks. *Mon Dieu!* Where are you coming from?" We fell into each other's arms and sobbed. Pauline cried too. Even our guide from Brooklyn had to wipe his eyes with his handkerchief.

We spent three days on the kibbutz with Renée. Little by little, Renée's family was told I had come, and before long her cramped little bungalow was bursting at the seams. All of her family lived on the kibbutz, her six grown children and all of her grandchildren. Renée and I shared our stories of the war with them. Then Cécile came. She still had the same curly hair, but there was a weariness, a sadness about her. I learned that her marriage had been unhappy, and then four years later, I heard she died of cancer.

The twins said their mother, that poor grieving woman I had known as Mme. Goldman with her wild hair who rocked herself back and forth singing mournful Polish songs, had found happiness in her later years with a second husband. I was very moved to see Jean again, the retarded boy I used to take to the

290

Mindele's Journey

movies and share treats with. His mass of curly hair was now gray, and though his eyes were still crossed, they were as sensitive as I remembered. I hadn't seen him for almost half a century, and the first thing he said to me was, "How are your aunts?" It made me cry. Jean seemed happy now with his sisters and their families in Israel. When he was sitting beside Renée on the worn sofa, leaning into her, he looked just like the boy I remembered. She put her arm around his shoulder. He looked at me and smiled and I was swept back to my childhood in Brussels.

I remembered his quiet sadness during those six years when we lived together on the Rue Ste. Anne. I was very protective of Jean because Poppa was always yelling at him. Jean couldn't learn the intricate details of tailoring my father attempted to teach him. He either dropped the hot irons or tripped on rotten floorboards, or ripped the patterns by accident, all of which infuriated Poppa. Now, looking at Renée and Jean, I wondered what would have happened to me if I had come to Israel with them. Renée had married a mailman twenty years her senior almost as soon as she arrived. He had died recently, but they had been happy together. She took care of children in the nursery when the mothers on the kibbutz went to work. Renée didn't cook but took us to the cafeteria where I met her friends. The women looked the same in their simple skirts and blouses, no trace of makeup on their faces, their hair hidden under scarves to protect it from the desert dust. Seeing them, I was almost embarrassed by my manicured nails and makeup. The way I matched all my clothes, including my lipstick, I don't think I could

291

Mariette Bermowitz

have adjusted to such a simple life. They didn't seem to lack for anything, but there was no sign of even the smallest luxury either, at least not in Renée's household.

The bookshelves were filled with French titles and photographs of the children and grandchildren beaming in the Israeli sunshine. "Twenty-two grandchildren so far," said Renée proudly. She took out an album where she kept old pictures from Belgium. I had some of the same pictures, like the one of Cécile and Renée in dresses from a donation center standing next to me in one of my beautiful outfits from the seamstress in Fraiture. Even then we led such different lives. They had no choice but to live in the orphanage. I lived with my father, but there were summers with les tantes who showered me with love and attention, and of course custom-made clothes. Yet looking at Renée now, so peaceful, so rooted in her place, secure in knowing that she would be taken care of, I suddenly felt empty and alone. Where were my children or grandchildren? All I had was an ex-husband and ex-lovers. I had spent years traveling, but where had I arrived? Still, I could not see myself ever living on a kibbutz. How different our journeys, Renée's and mine! She had reached her destination, whereas I was still the wanderer. The *kuchuloo*. The *luftmensch*. The one without family, without roots. What had happened to me?

Renée pointed to a picture in the photo album. I felt a rush of adrenaline as I recognized Sarah, Renée's older sister. "She was so beautiful then," said Renée, touching the picture of Sarah as a young girl in Liège. "She lives in Brazil now with Andrée, her

Mindele's Journey

daughter. You remember, don't you, that she married your father's cousin Vladek? They had to leave Belgium because she was still married to her first husband, the collaborator."

I remembered. When I had gone back to Belgium the first time, M. Gianini told me he had met Sarah with her new husband, Vladek. They were moving to Brazil. M. Gianini knew some of the war stories and suspected that she was running away from her first husband, Joseph. He thought Joseph had probably been released from prison by then and might be pursuing Sarah. She and Vladek wanted to get as far away from Belgium as they could. They wanted to take Mme. Goldman with them but she refused because of Jean. She thought that because he was retarded, he would have better opportunities on a kibbutz in Israel.

As I listened to Renée speak of the old days, I felt very Jewish suddenly. Strange, or perhaps not so strange, that it should happen while I was in Israel. Renée said that Andrée was a distant cousin of mine. She didn't quite know how, but certainly Sarah would know. She gave me Sarah's address in Saõ Paulo. "I'll write to Sarah first," she said, "and tell her of your visit and let her know that you're going to be in touch."

When Pauline and I left the kibbutz, I felt like a piece of myself had been given back to me. A piece I had lost and all but forgotten. My mind was filled with questions. Little did I know that I had taken the first step of a journey that would connect me to myself in a new way, and I would finally piece together my story and understand where I belonged.

Brazil

Sarah wrote to me first. Renée had called her from Israel to tell her about my surprise visit, and now here was an envelope with a green border with a stamp from Brazil. I opened it with trepidation, hesitating before I unfolded the thin sheets of lined paper. Then I saw the European style handwriting, neat and flowing, yet quivering in places, almost like a voice about to break. The letter was addressed to "My little sister." Sarah was not my sister but she had known my older sister, Esther. Of course she had known them all. My mother, my sisters, my brother, my whole family.

That first letter was brief. I imagine Sarah was probably stunned to hear from me all these years later. Maybe she wasn't eager to relive the tragedies from the past. But I had to find out what she knew. Sarah had the key to my story. A story that had remained hidden to me, as it was too painful for my father to talk about. A story I had been afraid to uncover because of the burden of guilt it carried.

I knew that I was separated from my family in Brussels in the fall of 1942 when I was not quite four years old. I knew that I had ended up in the Convent of Banneux, sparing me from the fate that awaited my mother and my siblings, but the full story of what happened had been silenced with my father's dying breath. I didn't know how my mother disappeared. It was something we never talked about. I was left to

Mindele's Journey

wonder, often in guilt, why I survived and my sisters and brothers didn't.

I was six when the war ended and my father took me back to live with him in Brussels. We shared the dingy two-room flat on the Rue Ste. Anne with Mme. Goldman. I thought she was a relative of ours, lost, just like us. My father, a tailor, was trying his best to resume the profession that had formerly provided us a living. Then, after five unhappy years, Poppa and I departed for a new life in America. I never knew what really happened to Mme. Goldman and Jean, or Sarah, just that the twins had been sent to a kibbutz. Poppa had liked Sarah. His spirits always picked up when she came to visit her mother, Mme. Goldman, bringing with her fresh fruits and that wonderful milk chocolate for Jean and me. I used to save the wrappings in a drawer, sniffing them from time to time, dreaming about the batch of chocolate that would surely come with Sarah's next visit.

Sarah was in her twenties then. She was very blond with a pinup girl figure and eyes so blue that they reminded me of the forget-me-not flowers I had seen in the fields on one of my school excursions. Sarah had been my older sister Esther's best friend. They were the same height, had the same slender bodies, and wore the same fashionable clothing. The photograph of them laughing together as they walked down a cobbled street in Liège in the spring of 1941 was sealed in my mind. How happy they were then! Sarah was expecting her first child, and Esther was engaged to marry Jean, the brother of Sarah's husband, Joseph.

Mariette Bermowitz

I was overwhelmed at the thought of being in touch with Sarah again. There were so many mysteries of the past I wanted to unravel, yet the years passed without my ever finding out what I wanted to know. We exchanged letters, but she wrote only about her family in Brazil. I learned how proud she was of her son Johnny's children. How she missed Vladek, her deceased husband, the man who took her away from Belgium after the war. How proud she was during the Jewish holidays to be surrounded by her children, grandchildren, and great-grandchildren. She described the Jewish center in São Paulo, a bastion of Jewish culture, but she never answered any of the questions I put to her about what happened during the war. When I persevered, she said that there were certain things best left unanswered.

It seemed the silence and the guilt would go on. When I learned that Sarah was about to turn eighty, I realized that I could no longer wait. She was the last one who had lived through the war with my family. If I did not find the answers to my questions now, the chance would be lost forever. Sarah hinted that I should come to São Paulo to meet the family. I realized it was now or never. When I told Pauline about my decision to finally go to São Paulo, she offered to come with me. Pauline considered herself a "witness to a blessing" that began in Israel when she had invited me to Netanya and we journeyed to the kibbutz. A *blessing*, she called it. I thought it was a blessing too.

When our plane landed in São Paulo, Sarah was not at the airport to meet us. Pauline and I stood with our luggage at the arrivals gate for over an

Mindele's Journey

hour. All the other passengers were long gone. Had I given Sarah the wrong information about our flight? Pauline suggested we change some money and call her, but no one answered. My spirits sank. All the trepidations I'd had about the trip in the first place seemed to be coming true. Was it such a good idea to forage into the past after all? Maybe, as Sarah herself had said in one of her letters, it was better to leave certain things untold. Let sleeping dogs lie. Why go and stir up the shadows of time?

They rose up anyway, regardless of my attempts to escape them. That was what I had done all my life. Run away from confronting a past that did not include les tantes and Fraiture. I blamed the silence on the dead, but it was me really, choosing not to know about my family. I had been afraid to know. Afraid it would be too painful. Yet deep inside I yearned for roots. I yearned for the truth. For what I had come to think of as the essence of my being. It felt like a wound that had never healed. Would the silence never be broken? Would I always feel guilty for having survived the war?

Pauline said we should try calling again. "Perhaps Sarah went out, and now she is home again," Pauline suggested hopefully. She dialed the number, but again there was no answer. We waited another hour. It was starting to get dark. Where *was* she? I couldn't stand it anymore.

"Come on, Pauline," I said. "We're taking a taxi. I'd rather wait in front of her house than here in the airport!" Then, as we were walking to the taxi stand, we passed a frantic-looking old woman with stiff white hair and watery blue eyes hurrying toward the

Mariette Bermowitz

entrance. She was holding up a large sheet of wrinkled paper with my name on it. She stopped when she saw me. I went to her, and without a word we fell into each other's arms. Sarah was patting my shoulder, saying gently, "Mariette, Mariette." I don't know if I was laughing or crying. After a few moments we stepped back from one another and Sarah pointed to a tall dark-haired woman with a horsy face and a toothy grin standing behind her. "Here is your cousin, Andrée."

Andrée gave me a big hug. She was a masculine-looking woman with a strong grip. It was hard to believe she was my cousin. The last time I remembered seeing her was the winter in Brussels when she couldn't have been more than four years old. Sarah had brought her from Liège to visit Mme. Goldman, her grandmother. It must have been my birthday because the table was piled with chocolates and cookies and colorful marzipan animals. Marzipan was always a special birthday treat. Andrée had taken a whole handful without even asking permission and I hit her. How strange to remember that now at this airport in Brazil! But how could this tall, self-assured woman who was bending down and kissing my cheek be my relative? We looked nothing alike. Then it hit me. Andrée must be from my mother's side of the family. I had never met anyone from my mother's side before. I didn't recognize her eyes, or the shape of her face. I hadn't even known that anyone on my mother's side still existed.

When we finally got settled into the car, Sarah explained the family connection. My mother's first cousin, Yankel/Jacques, was Andrée's grandfather.

Mindele's Journey

When Poppa and I escaped from Brussels and took the train to Liège, we hid in Yankel/Jacques' house. I remembered the room on the top floor with all those people sitting quietly on chairs lining the walls. I remembered the baby crying in Sarah's arms. It was Andrée. I stared at the back of her head from my place next to Sarah in the backseat of the car. I caught glimpses of her dark eyes as she nervously glanced in the rearview mirror. She was my cousin several times removed, but she was of my mother's blood. At last I had a relative from my mother's side.

The drive to their house took an hour. Andrée drove very fast. I heard Pauline gasp in the front seat, but Andrée seemed oblivious. She talked nonstop, telling us about how she had become a lawyer ten years ago after her husband died, and now had her own law firm. We heard about her married son with a thriving clothing business, her daughter the medical doctor who had just made her a proud grandmother.

They lived high up in a large apartment complex in the Paraiso district of São Paulo, a middle-class area in the "good" part of the city. I liked the name *Paraiso*. It was just like Rue du *Paradis*, the street where les tantes lived in Hour. But what a difference in the two places called "paradise." Here an ominous-looking fence surrounded the complex. When a security guard unlocked the gate and let us in, I felt like I was entering a prison. It reminded me of American gated communities, those sequestered places I automatically disliked because of how they tried to separate themselves from the rest of the world. Sarah must have seen me frowning. She said, "In Brazil, one has to always be careful. There

Mariette Bermowitz

are so many poor people and so much crime. We never feel safe. You must not walk out alone here," she cautioned.

The apartment was actually Andrée's, and Sarah had come to live with her after her husband, Vladek, died. Andrée unlocked the door with a flourish. "I bought this apartment years ago with my own money," she said with a look of disdain at her mother. I remembered now that Renée mentioned in one of her letters that Andrée and her mother often quarreled.

The apartment was enormous. It was simply furnished, but in a makeshift way, with nothing matching or seeming to go together. Sarah gave Pauline and me a tour before even offering us a drink. I was surprised to see Sarah's room was the smallest one in the house. She invited us in and sat down heavily on the narrow bed. Then her sad blue eyes suddenly brightened as she pointed to a picture on the dresser of her husband, Vladek, in younger days. "You remember that he was a barber in Belgium? He was pretty successful even then and very generous. He was your father's cousin. I met him when I came to visit *Maman* when she was living with you on the Rue Ste. Anne. No, you probably don't remember. You were so young."

"But I do remember! I do!" I said, sitting down on the bed next to her. I remembered how it was such a treat when we had visitors. Such a welcome change from the dark moods of my father and Mme. Goldman. Company always cheered me up. Poppa and Sarah's maman always stopped their quarreling when we had guests. Sarah and her cousin Etka were

Mindele's Journey

young and beautiful then, and Vladek was so handsome. Their talk was full of joy and their love of life.

"Whatever happened to Etka?" I asked. "I'll never forget how she made a new cover for my quilt. Or those wonderful stories of her family that were told during the Passover dinners when I went to Valenciennes."

"Ah, yes. Etka." Sarah said, her voice breaking. "Everybody loved Etka. She was the most beautiful one in the family. Good and kind and loving to her last days."

"Does that mean that she's gone?" I said, suddenly feeling very sad.

"Etka died last year in Valenciennes. But she was not alone. She was surrounded by her children and grandchildren. You know, Etka came to visit us with Maman when we lived in Rio de Janeiro. Well, my mother and Jean had been living with my sisters, Cécile and Renée, on the kibbutz, and Etka insisted that Maman come back to Europe and live with her. Maman wasn't sure about leaving Jean alone with the twins, but she did, and it was a good thing too, because back in Valenciennes with Etka, Maman met her second husband."

Andrée suddenly burst in. "Come with me," she said, hurrying Pauline and me through the door. "I want to show you my territory!" Andrée's bedroom was large with a spacious closet. She immediately began opening dresser drawers, pulling out pieces of frilly lace undergarments to show us. "I have to please my young boyfriend," she said with a giggle. She showed us a photograph of her handsome lover, fifteen years her junior. Over the next

301

Mariette Bermowitz

few days Andrée told me of her affairs with younger men. I wondered at her nervous energy, the way she was always constantly moving. I found out later that she was on medication for a litany of psychological problems.

The maid appeared at the door to announce dinner was ready. As we were about to sit down at the table, Sarah said, "Wait a minute," and pointed to a large framed photograph on the piano. "There's something I want to show you." Pauline and I followed her over to the piano. "See? Here is Maman with her second husband in Valenciennes."

I stared at the black-and-white photograph. This was not the Mme. Goldman I remembered. The pose was almost identical to the one she had taken with my father all those years ago, but the woman in this picture was beautiful. She must have been in her early sixties by then, but her skin was unlined, her expression calm and happy. I looked at her gold earrings, her diamond brooch. She had always loved jewelry. Poppa had given her a gold bracelet and a brooch with diamonds and rubies she wore on special occasions. And then she disappeared, taking all his money. I would never forget that horrible day when Poppa discovered his treasure box was empty and he ended up in the hospital. I had come home from school to find an empty house. I thought I had been abandoned. Left all alone in the world. I shuddered at the memory.

"Here," said Sarah. "I want you to have this. A souvenir of maman." She removed the picture from its frame and held it out to me. "It's for you." she said.

302

Mindele's Journey

But I didn't want it. It was large, an 8x10. What was I going to do with it? I didn't want to be reminded of Mme. Goldman. Then, remembering my manners, I thanked her, and we all sat down to dinner.

The next day, after showing us around the neighborhood and filling her mesh bag with fresh fruit and vegetables at the local market, Sarah sat on the couch and said, *Maintenant on parle.* "Now we'll talk." Pauline and I took a seat on either side of her. Sarah's lips quivered. She looked very tired. I said, "Maybe we should wait till after dinner when you've rested." But Sarah said she would be going straight to bed after dinner and wanted to do it now. I held on to the edge of the sofa and braced myself for the story I had waited so long to hear.

"Your sister Esther was very young, very beautiful when I first met her in Liège. I had just married Joseph and immediately became pregnant with Andrée. Esther was going to marry Joseph's brother Jean. They were made for each other, so in love and so devoted to each other. Jean was in Brussels all the time just to be with her. I hardly ever saw your mother. Zysla had you to take care of, and she was pregnant again. But I did see her once or twice when she came with your father to visit Yankel, my father-in-law. Yankel was your mother's first cousin."

Sarah spoke softly and carefully in a very matter-of-fact tone, and as she spoke the photographs I had found in the wardrobe came to life. In my mind's eye I could almost see my family gathered around me. I had so many questions. Had I been with my mother and Poppa on those visits? What did they eat? What

303

did they drink? Did Poppa hold my mother's hand? Did she talk much? What was her voice like?

But Sarah was now talking about her own disappointing marriage to Joseph. Unlike Jean, who was so kind and loving to my sister Esther, his brother Joseph was a brute. His mother, Mina, was unkind as well, always finding fault with her. Sarah suddenly looked exhausted. I could see how tired she was, how hard this was for her. But Sarah was the last person in the world who had known my family so intimately. When she was gone there would be no one left who knew the story. She was the only person left to confirm that those I had lost had once been alive.

"Please tell me about my mother," I begged. "What did she look like? What happened to her?"

Sarah sighed heavily and closed her eyes. "I don't remember very much. It was such a long time ago." Then, saying she needed a rest before dinner, she retreated to her tiny bedroom down the passage.

The next day after an outing to the Jewish Center, Sarah again sat down with Pauline and me on the sofa. Pauline had enjoyed seeing the Jewish Center, but I had been anxious. I could hardly wait for evening to arrive when Sarah would talk about the past again. I thought it odd, however, that I had been there for two days already and Sarah had not yet asked me a single question about my father or my life in America. She hadn't asked anything about me really. But I realized she was old. The elderly were different, I knew.

The maid brought in tea and Sarah launched into the story of how she and Vladek ran away from Belgium and settled first in Rio de Janeiro where

Mindele's Journey

Vladek became a businessman. "Your father's cousin Vladek was a good man," she said, beaming with pride. "And so is our son Johnny." Then, glancing toward Andrée's room, she added, "Andrée, my daughter by my first husband Joseph, was not an easy child."

I could wait no longer. "Sarah, please tell me, how did I end up at the convent in Banneux?"

Her eyes rolled back for a moment, as if summoning images from the past. She recalled the night in Liége when her mother-in-law Mina, had locked me out of the house.

"I saw Mina drag you outside. As soon as I heard the door slam, I ran out to find you. You were huddled in the corner by the stairs, so small and helpless looking. And so frightened! I had to pull you really hard, and finally carried you back inside. From that moment on, I realized that you and my sisters, Cécile and Renée, had to be hidden someplace that would really be safe, away from Mina. Mina was impossible, always threatening to turn everybody in. That night I went to the nearby church and talked to the priest. He knew what to do, and connected me to an underground organization that arranged for Jewish children to be taken into hiding with families or convents, or out of the country to England. The next day I brought you to the church with Cécile and Renée. You were placed in Mater Dei, the convent in Banneux. Cécile and Renée went to a Catholic family in the same town. I did not see you again until after the war."

So it was Sarah who had saved us children. I hadn't known. I'd had no idea how I had gotten to the convent. Sarah, this fragile old lady with white hair sitting between me and Pauline on a sofa in Brazil. She had been the courageous one. Tears were streaming down my face. Sarah leaned over and kissed my cheek, saying, *Tu es encore si gentille, si gentille.* "You're still so sweet, so sweet." Pauline was crying too. I heard Pauline repeat in French, *Oui, elle est encore toujours gentille.*

Andrée took a few days off from work to take us on a short trip. She said, smiling, "Maman tires more easily these days but it will be good for her to go with us. Of course she doesn't want to admit that she's almost eighty years old. She gave us quite a scare before you came. We thought she was going to die after her last heart attack. But there she is, still getting her hair and nails done, shopping in the market where all the merchants wave to her. She even has a boyfriend in the Jewish Center."

I was surprised to hear Andrée express concern for her mother. Ever since we had arrived I couldn't help noticing the tension between mother and daughter. Yet I felt a kinship with Andrée as soon as she mentioned that her mother refused to discuss either her father or the past in Belgium. Though Andrée had been quiet while Sarah spoke, she was never very far away when her mother talked about "those days."

It was another surprise that Andrée spoke only French with her mother. But Sarah didn't want her to forget it, and French was her grandmother's language. When Mme. Goldman had come to visit them in Brazil, she told Andrée about Belgium. But when Andrée asked about her father, Joseph, her grand-

Mindele's Journey

mother snapped, "That is not something we talk about."

I wondered if I would ever know more about Andrée than her obvious interest in younger men. She was seductive, not pretty, but I could see why younger men appreciated her perfect proportions and strong personality, though they never seemed to stay with her for long. When she admitted to me that all she needed was someone to hold her, someone to love her, she looked very young, very vulnerable. Her eyes had the lost look of an inconsolable child. I felt her sadness when we were having dinner at her brother Johnny's. It was obvious her mother favored him. Andrée smiled and talked nonstop, as if the empty space around her constantly needed to be filled. I sensed the tears behind her smile. Andrée was such a strong-looking woman, not the type I thought of as vulnerable. But I could see how uncomfortable she was in Johnny's apartment with all the luxurious furnishings. I didn't care much for Johnny or his wife. She talked about their visits to Connecticut whenever they came to the States on business, and she never once mentioned getting together with me. Their obvious interest in money reminded me of my cousins in Brooklyn. I found myself wishing I had never met Johnny. I wanted so much to be connected to family, and realizing he was nothing like me was such a disappointment.

Andrée, Sarah, Pauline, and I left Saõ Paulo and headed for the coast. I was glad to leave the city, a gray cement landscape dotted with the red and yellow of the McDonald Empire. There was so little green in a country known for its sunshine. But I kept having to remind myself that August was wintertime in Brazil. Still, the streets seemed devoid of life except for the clothes dangling from makeshift laundry lines along the highway. Farther out we passed the squalor of Saõ Paulo's other world, the slums, where people lived in dwellings of wooden planks that seemed barely held together.

In the town of Santos, Andrée took us to a little restaurant on the beach. A festival was in progress and the promenade was filled with musicians and colorful outdoor markets. "Here we dance," said Andrée, breaking into a naughty little two-step. "It's good to dance. You don't think when you dance." After lunch she took my arm and we swept ahead of her mother and Pauline, who had stopped to look at the array of souvenirs spilling over the stalls.

"You know," she said, "Maman and I have had a difficult time together. I was a rebellious teenager and then a terrible wife. But I married a man much older than me. I'm sorry he died but I'm free now, and I adore the children we had together. I consider myself a better mother to them than my mother ever was to me," she said bitterly. "And what about you, Mariette? Why aren't you married? Why didn't you have any children?"

I was taken aback by her directness. The question unnerved me. I didn't want to think about the choices I might have made had circumstances been different. But I stuffed down my feelings of remorse and said, trying to keep my voice light, "Oh, I preferred my friends and being able to travel. I liked my freedom and having adventures, making new discoveries. Even though I don't have any children, my life

Mindele's Journey

has been a full one." I squeezed her arm. "Meeting you has been one of those wonderful discoveries."

Andrée smiled. "Perhaps you're right, but family is important. It makes the story whole."

"That's why I am here in Brazil," I said. "I want to know *toute l'histoire*."

After the evening meal, it was time to talk about "those days." Sarah and I were sitting quietly on the sofa. I would now gather more pieces of the story, more clues and links to the wholeness of my existence. The shadows of the past were taking shape. The pictures I found in the wardrobe in Brussels were taking on a voice. The faces had a story. I had made sure to bring the photos with me to show to Sarah. She remembered the little blue outfit I wore and my sister Esther's elegant clothes. Esther had loved black, trimmed with red or with fur. I could almost smell Esther's perfume again when Sarah spoke about her. But what had happened to Esther?

Sarah said, "In the summer of 1942, identified by the yellow star they were forced to wear as Jews, your sisters, Esther and Rebecca, and your brother, Zelik, were arrested by the Gestapo. They were sent to the city of Malines where Jews were deported to parts unknown. My brother-in-law Jean, who was engaged to your sister Esther, was in Liège at the time. When he learned about her disappearance, he rushed to Brussels, hoping for information. All he found was the indifference of bureaucrats as he chased from office to office in an attempt to learn the whereabouts of his Esther. He was able to move easily because of his fluent German and his status as a non-Jew. He quickly went to Malines where he knew Jews

Mariette Bermowitz

were being rounded up before being put into cattle cars headed for concentration camps, and learned that Esther was part of Convoy #18. He came back to Liège to tell us the news, then he left again to follow Esther's train into the unknown. The last word we had from him was when he reached Germany."

Sarah got up and went into the kitchen. I heard her telling the maid in Portuguese to make some tea. Then she went down the hall to Andrée's room to make sure Andrée was out. "I want to tell you about Joseph, Andrée's father, but I don't want Andrée to know this.

"My mother-in-law, Mina, felt that Joseph resembled her side of the family more than her other two sons. He was really very handsome. He was twenty-three, tall, and proud with piercing eyes and chiseled features. His German was excellent, and he had recently changed his name from Joseph to Fritz so he could move about more freely in German-occupied Liège. He had also joined Degrelle and his pro-Nazi Belgian government. Mina secretly hoped he did it out of conviction more than as a way to protect me. Though we could easily masquerade as Germans, Mina was still anxious. The Gestapo had so many informants. No one could be trusted. She found herself isolated, bearing a burden she could not confide to anyone. Mina was somewhat reassured when Joseph/Fritz brought home Nazi paraphernalia, including a flag she intended to hang outside the house."

Sarah also remembered Max, Mina's youngest son. "He was secretive and moody, preferring to stay alone most of the time. Sometimes he left the house,

310

Mindele's Journey

not telling anyone where he was going. He never listened to Mina, or answered her questions about his whereabouts. When he turned eighteen, he joined the Belgian Resistance and delivered messages to the members of *L'armée Blanche*, the White Army.

"Mina did not live to see that Max had chosen a different path, or that Joseph/Fritz was arrested as a collaborator after the war. He testified that his only motive had been to protect our family. In their own way, each brother helped the Jews that were hiding in their attic apartment.

But I was afraid of Joseph. I left Belgium before he was released from prison."

Sarah paused to catch her breath. There was a look of anguish in her eyes. She looked away from me and got to her feet. I saw her hands tremble as she grasped the edge of the sofa. Had I summoned up too many ghosts from the past? I was about to go over and take her arm when the maid came in with the silver tea tray. Sarah seemed to revive with the beautiful tea service set before her. She told me to help myself to the cookies she had made that morning. I smiled as I recognized they were the very same round tasteless cookies her mother, Mme. Goldman used to make. I said, "Maybe we should stop for today? Maybe you're too tired?"

"No, no, I must tell you now. I'm eighty years old. I don't want it to be forgotten."

She continued haltingly, *Ton père a beaucoup souffert.* She spoke of the day when my father ran out of cigarettes and decided to leave the attic to go outside. He was warned that it wasn't safe but he went anyway. He was arrested within the hour and taken to join a convoy of Jews being shipped out of the country. We never expected to see him again. But your father was very small and very thin and he managed to pry open a plank from the bottom of the cattle car and slide out onto the tracks. As he ran from the train he was shot in the back. He fell to the ground and didn't move and they thought he was dead. But he was able to crawl, and he came back to the attic where he spent the rest of the war with my mother and my brother Jean.

As Sarah talked, I remembered how Poppa always used to complain about his back, saying that part of a bullet was still there. I didn't believe him. Now I would never be able to tell him how sorry I was. Then Sarah said, "All that mattered to him was that he had at least one of his five children left."

I told Sarah how I remembered that he risked his life again toward the end the war when he found out where I was hidden. I remembered that day so well. "He came to Fraiture with your mother who translated for him. Les tantes were so worried because they knew the Germans were passing through the town again. But my father needed proof that he had one left, *la seule, la seule.* "The only one, the only one," he kept repeating tearfully. And I had refused to go over and kiss him.

On the night before we left Brazil Sarah spoke about Andrée's father again. "He was tough, just like his mother, Mina. They always spoke German so I couldn't understand what they were saying. She was actually Dutch but she came from a town on the German border and felt a kinship with the occupiers. Joseph did too, and used it to further his ambi-

Mindele's Journey

tions by joining the Rexist movement. I threatened to take his child away if he didn't help the family. And that's how I was able to do what I did."

"Is that why you don't want Andrée to know anything about her father? Because he was part of the Nazi movement in Belgium?"

"I told her that her father was dead for me. That's all there is to know. I can tell you that his younger brother Max is probably still alive, living in Belgium. But I've lost all contact with him." Sarah got up abruptly and disappeared into the bathroom. I heard her crying. When she reappeared she had a coat of fresh lipstick and went into the kitchen to tell the maid to make tea. That was all I was going to hear from her regarding Andrée's father, Joseph. But I had been given a sliver of hope. The youngest brother, Max, might still be living in Belgium.

As we were leaving, I took Andrée aside and told her that I would not only write to her as often as I could but that I would find her father. I wasn't quite sure how I was going to do this, but I knew that I had to try. I wished Sarah had been able to tell me more. How begrudging she was about specifics. Yet listening to her helped me remember. A veil had been lifted. Sarah had put me on a trail, and there was no turning back.

The Cynglers

That winter I took my vacation in Belgium. I had made Andrée a promise that I was determined to keep. My first stop was the Department of Records in

Liège. I waited on various long lines for hours with people who pushed and yelled, at the end of it only to be told I was in the wrong place. I returned the following day and found the office where I would be able to locate Andrée's birth certificate. I wanted to shout for joy in that sad office smelling of sweat and despair. My excitement was short lived, when I was denied the certificate because I wasn't a member of her immediate family. I had been hoping it would have given me some information, any information, on her father. Then the most obvious idea came to me. Why not look in the Liège phone book? There might be a listing for Cyngler, my mother's maiden name. Also, Andrée's grandfather Jacques, also known as Yankel, who had been married to Mina. I opened the phonebook, and there I found Max Cyngler. The name seemed to rise from the ashes.

I was staying with some relatives of les tantes in a small town outside of Liège. Around dinnertime I dialed the number. A woman answered. I hadn't rehearsed what I was going to say, and stumbled a bit, pronouncing Cyngler with a Yiddish accent. The woman said harshly, "This is no time to call people. You must have the wrong number. That is not our name." I said I was sorry and hung up. I would try again after dinner. The trouble was, I wasn't sure how to pronounce the name. Cyngler, if pronounced a certain way, meant "crazy" in French. The situation was so ridiculous, I thought surely the angels were laughing at me. Then I thought I should try pronouncing it Cyngl*air*. By now it was getting late and I worried that they might be going to bed. It took all my courage to pick up the phone and dial a second

Mindele's Journey

time, but at least now I had written down what I was going to say.

The same woman answered again, though this time she had less of a bark. I asked for Max Cyngl*air*, and said I was Mariette Cyngl*air*. I heard shuffling in the background, then a tired-sounding old man asked me who I was. I explained that we were related, as his father and my mother Zysla were first cousins. Did he remember she died during the war? He answered slowly, as if turning pages in his mind, "Oh, my God, yes. I remember. You're Mariette, her daughter."

I went to visit Max the following day. It was raining, and he was standing outside under the shelter of the entranceway to his building, waiting for me. I recognized him immediately from his striking resemblance to Andrée, most noticeably the large features. A tall man with a large belly and a full head of black hair though he must have been in his late seventies. He mumbled something when he saw me, but I couldn't make out what he was saying. "Max?" I said, and he mumbled again, something that sounded like "Mindele," as he held out his arms. When I fell into those long arms it was almost as if my mother was welcoming me. He was her family, a cousin, even if twice removed. And he had been listed in the phone book all along.

I followed Max into the apartment he shared with his wife, Judith. Her face was harsh, matching the bark of her voice I heard on the phone. Her smooth skin and red hair interspersed between strands of gray made me realize she must have been a handsome woman at one time, but now she was heavy

315

and sullen looking, and her voice was an unpleasant whine. She directed me where to put my umbrella and where to sit. I apologized for my wet shoes and wiped them on the mat once more. The apartment was immaculate. Nothing was out of place, with doilies on chairs and a white cloth on the massive table that took up most of the dining room. But it had the musty smell of time, as if nothing had changed since their wedding some sixty years ago.

Max got up to make tea. Judith stayed with me in the living room, and called to him not to forget to bring out the cookies, and where to find the cookies. With a cup of warm tea set before me I felt relaxed enough to tell Max why I had come. He sat there silently, not saying a word in reply. His silence now, and the way he mumbled, slurring his words, made me wonder if he'd had a stroke. Judith's expression was severe when she looked at him, brightening only when I complimented the picture on the wall of two handsome boys in communion clothes.

"Those are my grandsons," she said proudly. "They are the most important thing in my life," she added with another severe look in Max's direction.

Max broke into a brief smile when I told him about Andrée, and suddenly came to life, as if her name was the key to open his heart. "I didn't know she was still alive. Her father would have loved to have seen her again. He died only the year before, in Germany, where he had remarried. He named his second daughter Andrée too, for the daughter he lost when Sarah left Belgium."

His words came out slowly, carefully, as if he was searching through the debris of his life. "I was only

Mindele's Journey

fifteen when my older brother married Sarah. But I remember how much in love my brother Jean was with your sister Esther. They were to be married as soon as she finished her studies in the conservatory. Then one day she was arrested with your brother and sisters in Brussels. Jean tried to find her. He spoke German like we all did. He followed every possible trail to have her released. Then he was arrested. We never heard from him again." Max stopped speaking, lost in thought.

I said, "What about Joseph and Sarah? Can you tell me anything about them?" But he was staring at the carpet and didn't seem to hear me. Judith was staring into space with a defiant look. I sighed, realizing I'd never learn about Joseph and Sarah.

Then suddenly, as if waking from a stupor, Max said, "Yes, Maman and Sarah didn't get along. Those were difficult years. People did whatever they could to survive. No one knew that I had joined the Underground as a liaison agent." It had obviously been a time of glory for him. He spoke in a rush, telling me about my father being such a good tailor but addicted to cigarettes. About my sister Esther and how lovely she was. Max didn't know much about my brother or sister Rebecca, but he knew about the newborn, Frieda, saying it was such a tragic time to be born a Jew in Brussels in 1942.

My heart was pounding. I could scarcely breathe. I looked over at Judith. Her lips were quivering, whether from emotion or annoyance, it was impossible to tell. She said, "Mina made it clear that she did not want her children to be brought up Jewish. My father-in-law, Yankel, who had changed his name to

Mariette Bermowitz

Jacques, didn't want to be reminded of his religion, so he didn't mind."

I looked up again at the photographs on the wall of Jacques' great-grandchildren in their communion clothes. They looked so perfect. Max followed my gaze, then got up and went to the bedroom. He came back holding a yellowing envelope and held it out like a gift. Inside were photographs. Finally, a picture of Joseph, Andrée's father. There was one of my sister Esther smiling and her handsome Jean with his arm around her waist. Her face was lit with the inner glow of a woman in love. Her warmth and goodness radiated from the faded black-and-white picture. I remembered everything. The violets and roses of her scent, her lovely hair and gentle voice, her gloved hand and the smile that sealed her beauty forever in that photograph. Her smile was like a caress. She was looking straight into the camera, and I felt as if she was looking at me. And then I remembered the way she used to pick me up, hugging me and kissing my cheek. I used to bury my face in her fur collar. How Esther loved me.

There were no pictures of my mother in the yellowing envelope Max had kept hidden for so many years. My mother was probably too busy with the new baby to pose for pictures. I remember how jealous I was of Frieda, even hiding her milk bottles. Perhaps that was why Esther took charge of me, taking me everywhere she went. Her love was imbedded in me like a precious jewel. I would miss her for the rest of my life.

I was floating on air when I left Max and Judith, and didn't even bother to open my umbrella, absentmindedly letting the rain wash over me. Violets and roses. I was certain I could smell Esther even now. Her special scent hovered in the wardrobe where her clothes had remained in Brussels. When I came across the rose in *Le Petit Prince*, I thought of Esther. Her memory lingered in the rose garden where I walked with M. Guillaume. Then I went to live in Shiraz, fragrant with roses. I fell in love with Saadi and Hafiz, and the poems inscribed on their shrines.

> I'll gather roses from the garden
> But I became intoxicated
> By the scent of the bush.

Meanwhile, in Liège, I headed toward the bus stop humming *La Vie En Rose*.
> *Quand il me prend dans ses bras, il me parle tout bas. Je vois la vie en rose.*
> *Il me dit des mots d'amour, des mots de tous les jours…*
> *Il me l'a dit l'a juré pour la vie…*

During the flight back to New York, I couldn't stop thinking about my promise to Andrée. She was the rebel, the tainted child of the man Sarah wanted to forget. Her life had been such a struggle. I think that was the reason I felt a strong kinship. She had no father, I had no mother. Her past remained locked inside her mother; mine was lost with my father's death. She told me she missed not knowing what her father looked like. When she had asked her mother, Sarah called him *shtick dreck*. That was Tante Rifcha's favorite expression. My cousin Marlene, the only one of my young cousins I actually loved, thought it was her middle name and never got over it. I can only imagine how Andrée must have felt like being called the child of *shtick dreck*. But now I had the picture Max had kept in the envelope. I mailed it with the word "fragile." A picture of her father was the most precious gift I could possibly give her. She was finally going to know what he looked like. Her children would have a grandfather.

After she received the photograph, she made plans to come to Belgium to meet her uncle and the family. She never made it. A scarce six months after our meeting, she died of cancer. Sarah passed away shortly after. I kept Andrée's last letter. It was filled with gratitude and love for me, as well as longing for the father she never knew. I lost Andrée much too soon. We had talked of visiting a ranch in the Amazon, traveling through Brazil, returning to Belgium together. Her grandfather Jacques was my mother's cousin. We were family.

Eventually, I wrote to the Holocaust Museum in Washington D.C. Sixty years after the massacre of millions, evidence had been gathered, processed, analyzed, finalized. The names of my family were among those on the list whose ashes had been scattered to the wind.

Mindele's Journey

Convoy #18

Esther Birencwajg	born May 1, 1923	transport from Belgium Jan. 15, 1943
		Boarding #588
Rebecca Birencwajg	born Sept. 24, 1924	transport from Belgium Jan. 15, 1943
		Boarding #589
Zelik Birencwajg	born June 1, 1926	transport from Belgium Jan. 15, 1943
		Boarding #590
Zysla Cyngler-Birencwajg	born July, 1903	transport from Belgium Jan.15, 1943
		Boarding #807
Frieda Birencwajg	born Feb.10, 1942	departure from Belgium Jan.15, 1943
		Boarding #808

✧ ✧ ✧

I saw a film once, among the many films documenting the transport of Jews to Auschwitz. Among the countless horrifying images I witnessed, none affected me more than the one of a German officer taking a baby from its mother's arms and smashing the child's head against the transport wagon. I couldn't help thinking that it could have been my baby sister, Frieda.

I had been spared from the forces of evil who slaughtered millions during the dark years of World War II. I still didn't know why. But I have always believed in the power of light and love. Les tantes, who radiated goodness, taught me to trust there were forces of good looking after me. I do feel that I have been guided on my journey. Protected by memories that have lingered in my mind and in my heart. And in my soul, the place I call home.

Wilhelm

When Wilhelm and I returned to the States after that fateful party in Germany 2005, I wrote to Annaliesa telling her how it had disturbed me to see a photograph of her as a young girl wearing a swastika on her arm. She replied how difficult it was to make choices in Nazi Germany. Besides, she was only fourteen years old. I let the matter rest. It is not for everyone to be a hero. As a medical doctor, she dedicated her life to causes helping people in need. But I still didn't understand why her son collected Nazi memorabilia.

Wilhelm and I spent another four wonderful years together. I had met him by chance when I had gone to visit a friend in her new apartment on Long Island, and rang the wrong bell. Wilhelm opened the door and smiled. I apologized for ringing the wrong bell, and when he spoke, I detected an accent I thought might be Swedish. He was tall and hand-

Mindele's Journey

some with strong, distinct features I found appealing. I think I hoped he was Swedish. Instead, he was a German who hesitated to visit my very Jewish neighborhood in Brooklyn.

Our second date was on a chilly day in November. We had dinner in Brighton Beach and afterward went for a stroll on the boardwalk. The mist blew in from the sea, and as I pulled the shawl over my shoulders, he cupped his hands around my face and kissed me gently on the forehead, just as my father used to do when he blessed me on Yom Kippur. I didn't know what to think when he told me he was born in Germany in 1939. I didn't ask him what his father had done during the war; it was too painful to imagine. The voice of my own father reverberated in my ears, "I will sit Shiva for you too." And that had only been in response to my wanting to marry a Catholic. God knows what he would have done had he known I was dating a man born in Koblenz under the Nazis. I tried to stifle Poppa's voice in my head.

I had been alone for ten years and had finally met a mature man, someone from the Old World, like me. Why did he have to come from Germany? I was intrigued, but also disturbed by what I might learn. My emotions were stirred up. My guilt was terrible. But Wilhelm had his demons too. He often spoke of his father's shame of wartime Germany. Sometimes it felt we were still being challenged, as if the war within still raged. It took years to process the burden of being a German and a Jew together. At times, it was humorous such as when Wilhelm insisted that *oy vey* was originally a German expression. I found it ironic how similar Yiddish was to German. When we

323

looked at a map, we saw that Belgium and Koblenz were only a finger length apart. We had been born into families on different sides of history, but we were only children then, trying to survive in a world not of our making. That is what I told myself as we held each other in the warmth of Zysla's quilt.

Over the years, my mother's quilt has gone through many transformations. The feathers have been cleaned, exchanged, replaced. The original covering of tattered cloth that came from scraps and remnants of family clothing was dispensed with long ago. Yet the quilt remains intact.

It held my mother's trousseau when she came from Poland as a young bride. It held my books when I came to America with my father. Its warmth is imbued with recollections of ancient customs of love and hope. It was my mother's treasured legacy to me.

And so it was with Wilhelm. I had finally found happiness and peace of mind with a loving partner. I thought that our love for each other had redeemed the shadows of the past. I hoped that we would grow old together. But it wasn't meant to be. Soon after we returned from an idyllic holiday in Canada to celebrate his seventieth birthday, Wilhelm suffered an aneurysm of the brain.

In a nanosecond, the peace and happiness we had known vanished. I was crushed. Some monstrous twist of fate had turned my life upside down once again. I vaguely remember following the ambulance taking him to some distant hospital where I remained for hours not knowing whether he would ever regain consciousness. I felt betrayed, as if God had let go of my hand. My heart kept time with the

Mindele's Journey

beeping machines as I watched the lines zigzag on the screen. I sat there helplessly, watching the nurses float by like amorphous shadows. I was aware the doctor was asking me questions, but I was in shock, inside a glass bowl, in suspended animation. I felt alone, like a child who needed someone to take her in their arms and tell her that she was having a bad dream.

The next day Wilhelm's brother and sister-in-law traveled up from the south. I was staying at the house. My hands were trembling when I opened the door and invited them in. I was expecting some acknowledgment of grief. I thought they would at least hold out their arms or take my outstretched hand, but they simply nodded and silently walked into the kitchen. They barely said a word to me as they put away some groceries they had brought with them. I was surprised that they showed no emotion about what had happened to Wilhelm. Someone later told me, "That's not the way Germans behave."

I didn't sleep that night. The darkness of the room enveloped me like a shroud. Why had love been taken from me? Why had the angels betrayed me? I took out a book I had started to read about the wisdom of no escape. Ironically, I had bought it in Nova Scotia on our holiday when we visited Pema Chodrun's Buddhist monastery. She writes that we need to experience our negative emotions, our pain, in order to transform it. In time, this will help us deal with our pain from a deeper, more spiritual perspective.

But I was not a Buddhist nun, and however wise her teachings, I could not separate myself from the deep grief taking over my soul. Moreover, I needed to share my pain, and if Wilhelm's brother had any emotions, he was not able to share them with me. I kept reminding myself, as if to absolve him in some way, "Germans don't do that."

✠ ✠ ✠

Wilhelm's brother and his wife stayed in the house for a week, and every day of that week felt like an invasion. They settled into the master bedroom, the room that had been our bedroom. The room where we had shared so many loving hours. The room where I had fallen asleep listening to Wilhelm reading passages from his favorite authors, where we laughed and greeted the days and seasons with gratitude. Now, I looked through the door and saw their open suitcases on the floor like blotches on the fading carpet.

The brother took over. When we went to the hospital, I followed behind like a shadow, a person without any rights, since I was not the spouse. If I went to visit Wilhelm by myself, his doctor said he could not give me any information because I was not a family member. The brother applied for guardianship. Wilhelm and I had been together for ten years, sharing each other's lives, but now I was realizing the penalty for not being married. Soon I would have no rights to stay in the house either, the house I had so lovingly decorated with furniture I had bought through the years. Wilhelm had left the decorating up to me. It had taken some time to convince him to update the furnishings. After two divorces, he was quite content with the way things were. He laughed when I told him that his living room looked like a stage set. Amid the faded grandeur, there was a baby grand piano, mismatched pieces of furniture, and an old sofa whose legs had become the cat's scratching board. But he was so proud of the fireplace he built and the large stained glass windows that let the gentlest of light filter in.

Wilhelm's financial matters had to be addressed. The brother was in Wilhelm's office, opening and closing drawers and rifling through his files. He moved slowly, his accountant's fingers, precise and expert, flipped through the pages with a swoosh of a pencil eraser, while on the glass-topped desk, pens and pencils were lined up like so many soldiers. I'm sure the accountant didn't notice the word "love" in different languages etched into the glass. The table was a recent purchase because Wilhelm wanted to look at "love" written in so many different languages. But today his brother had other concerns.

After four months of visiting Wilhelm in the hospital almost every day, hoping for signs of recovery, I came to the realization that he might not recover. I decided it was time to return to my own apartment in Brooklyn. Staying at the house on Long Island had become unpleasant now that I felt the brother was scrutinizing my every move. I tried to resume my old life, but I had forgotten how to be alone. My reality had shifted. How does one approach old age without someone to lean on? I relied on friends to help me bear the grief and anguish of not knowing whether Wilhelm would ever come back to me. I searched through self-help books to find words to sustain me through this new hell. I remembered that a lifetime ago I was able to be reassured by phrases I stuck onto mirrors and the refrigerator door. But now they seemed hollow and trite, and I found them useless.

Les tantes were no longer with me. Maman Thérèse had made it to the twenty-first century. She was so pleased to meet Wilhelm when we came to Belgium to celebrate her ninetieth birthday. He was chivalrous, bowing before her and kissing her hand. She blushed and shyly turned toward me saying *Quel bel homme et quelle gentillesse!* "What a handsome man, and how kind!"

I asked for Divine assistance in leading me forward into this life where there is no escape from pain. But as Pema Chodrun says in *The Wisdom of No Escape*, we're always coming up against new hurdles. She said we have to learn to become warriors.

A month after I returned home, I was summoned to a family meeting in Wilhelm's house. I was hoping to hear about plans for his rehabilitation, but instead I was confronted with accusations claiming that I had misappropriated Wilhelm's money. His brother, a short man with cold blue-gray eyes, was sitting at the head of the table in the dining room where Wilhelm used to sit. Without ceremony, he tossed a folder full of papers across the table and said, "What do you have to say about this?"

At first, I didn't know what he was talking about. Wilhelm and I had a joint bank account where we saved money for our trips. Wilhelm also, in his desire to make some provision for me in case something happened to him, had set aside a money-market

Mindele's Journey

account naming me as the beneficiary. Was his brother suggesting that I was trying to steal money that Wilhelm put aside for me? "What are you talking about?" I said.

He stared back at me without moving a muscle. "You know what you did."

I was stunned. His words hit me with such force I fell back in my seat. Aside from his coldness, the German accent put me in another space. Suddenly, he was no longer Wilhelm's brother, he was the Gestapo I'd seen in the movies, and this was an interrogation. I felt so paralyzed all I could do was mumble incoherently. His eyes roamed around the room. Was he noticing missing pieces? The things that were mine I had taken with me when I moved out. Was he going to accuse me of stealing those too? I got up to go. On my way to the door, I passed the bookcase and grabbed up the framed picture of Wilhelm and me on our holiday in New Mexico. It was the last piece of evidence of my having been in the house, the only picture I had left behind, and I was taking it with me.

I was so shaken that I couldn't drive home. I went to the neighbors, a couple Wilhelm and I had socialized with for the last ten years, and asked if I could spend the night. They told me Wilhelm's brother had been to see them the day before, with bank statements and other papers, asking questions about my character. They had refused to answer. I learned from them that the following day a locksmith was called to change the locks on the doors. I was now officially expelled from the home I had lavished such love and attention on with Wilhelm.

I couldn't believe that he had gone to the neighbors with his accusations, humiliating me before my friends. Then I learned he was compiling a portfolio in his role as executor, to try to retrieve monies he believed I had stolen. Wilhelm's family was not family to me after all, and his brother's cold, insensitive behavior made that obvious. The shocking unfairness and totally biased accusations caused me to wonder if these attacks were because I was Jewish. I thought of the Jews during the war, how helpless they must have felt when they were stripped of their rights and dignity. Now I was the outcast. Perhaps this was my lesson, that I had to stand up for myself. I had to become the warrior and face the dragon, like in Pema Chodrun's book.

Wilhelm is in rehabilitation. He will never be the Wilhelm I knew. But I visit with him. I hold that once strong hand and still feel its warmth. I read him passages from his favorite authors. I remind him of the sunsets we watched together. I talk about the sailboat he once owned so he could sail away from the ordinary world. I bring him a selection of the music he used to play on the piano. I tell him of the time he surprised me not only with breakfast in bed but also *La Vie En Rose* playing in the background. He still has that beautiful smile. Sometimes he surprises me with an astonishing statement such as, "Your presence overloads me with impressions." It makes me want to cry.

I am still angry. I thought I was learning "the wisdom of no escape," but my wounds go too deep. When my life with Wilhelm ended, my past came back to haunt me. Abandonment has been a constant in my life. But I also feel the rekindling of hope. I think about what has given me the strength to heal and restore my faith. I think about Wilhelm and the everyday miracles that seemed part of our lives. I remember my mother's legacy of love and hope. Maybe in time the anger will take on a spiritual perspective so that I can stop resenting that Wilhelm was taken from me, or that his brother treated me so badly. Then I will pick up my broken pieces and assemble them into a new mosaic.

Epilogue

Although I have returned many times to Brussels, the city of my birth, it has taken me half a century to approach the Rue Haute. I come back now because I was never able to before. The memories have become more persistent, almost as if they have a voice of their own. And so I roam, searching to fill the gaps, seeking the family who will not fade from my mind.

How gray Brussels is. The dampness of the early afternoon wraps itself around me like a shroud. The only bit of brightness is the metallic reflection of raindrops filtered through streetlamps. I walk down the Rue Haute, the street where my father worked before the war, looking for the past. I walk the cobbled streets looking for some sign of the family taken from me, some clue to the names without a burial place. This is the neighborhood where Poppa sometimes took me shopping for a gift to bring home. I look for the men's clothing shop where he delivered the custom-made suits he had sewn in the attic workshop above our apartment. But I cannot find any indication of Jewish-owned shops. These are sad houses, plastered with layers of dust and soot from years of neglect. There isn't much traffic. I remember the street as so much wider, filled with people. But it is Sunday afternoon. The shops are closed.

Mariette Bermowitz

The taverns, however, are open. Extravagant names of beers are displayed outside their doors. Inside, the locals are feasting on mussels and *waterzooie*, a classic Belgian dish of chicken simmered in a rich sauce of beaten eggs and cream, with leeks, carrots, celery and onion heaped on top, harmonizing with dustings of nutmeg, cloves, thyme and a scattering of bay leaves. The aromas wafting from a particularly attractive restaurant tempt me to go inside and have a taste. But something more powerful pulls me toward the square at the end of the street.

When I was a child, there was a large flea market on weekends, rain or shine. There was such a maze of stands and merchandise it was almost impossible to cross the street. Adding to the confusion were the hordes of treasure seekers and bargain hunters.

The rain has stopped. I hear a din of voices as I approach the street corner. The flea market is still here on the square just as I remembered it. A Flemish flea market, brimming with color. Suddenly, my father is here again, guiding me through the magical things, the bountiful displays. There are old pewter plates, Blue Delft porcelain coffee grinders with copper handles, bouquets of flowers embroidered on yellowing tablecloths, fiery ceramics, satin garments in shades of faded rose, mounds of glistening items as far as the eye can see. A couple of young girls are mesmerized by the antique jewelry displayed on blue velvet. They begin to giggle when a young vendor in an open shirt approaches them.

At the other end of the square is a café where waiters carry glasses and beer bottles as they dart between tables. Rue du Lavoir begins on this corner

334

Mindele's Journey

where the shoppers are resting, surrounded by the musty smell of spilled beer. I didn't expect to find it so quickly, this street I recalled in my dreams for so many years. I thought I would never see it again. Yet here it is, the hard stones under my feet still glistening from the afternoon rain. It is very quiet, hardly a sound, yet I have come to rattle memories out of these old stones.

Nothing looks familiar. Everything has changed. Arabic graffiti colors the decaying gray walls. Arabic script is painted on storefronts. Women covered in black hurry in and out of shops. Moslem families have replaced the Jews. I am an intruder in this world. The hope I had of touching my past falters at the sight of these newcomers. But I must find the house where we once lived. The houses are forlorn looking. The windows are like sad eyes staring down at me. I look for house numbers imbedded in the crumbling cement. Then I see number 33, still intact above the door. I stop for a moment to catch my breath, and run up the three steps. But there are no names. Is no one living here? I ring the top bell anyway, the one that had been our apartment before the war. There is no answer. I ring again, but all I hear is an echo reverberating down an empty hallway. A veiled woman walks by. I ask her in French whether anyone is living here now. She tells me that the houses on this side are to be torn down soon to make way for low-income housing. So all this will be gone, eradicated, swept into oblivion, like the Jewish family who vanished into the crematoriums. I walk down the street for the last time and say my good-byes.

Monsieur Greenberg, I want you to know that I still love pickles. I want you to know I sometimes feel that gentle stroke you gave my hair when we stopped by your grocery shop, Momma and I. Momma, I see you pushing the stroller where I feel buried under the clean pile of clothes you just washed in the laundry at the end of the street. I carry your fragrance inside of me, Momma, that smell of soap that trailed behind you like a flowing robe. And I see you behind the window of the sixth-floor apartment, holding Frieda in your arms. She was ten months old and you were holding a milk bottle, the one I used to hide because she had taken my place in your affection.

I hear laughter, but all I see in the distance is the outline of elevated train tracks like a dark arm scratching a darkening sky. The cars are rumbling along to some place unknown. Down the street, two shadows run toward the moving trains. It is Poppa and me. We race for the stairs. Soon we will board the train that will take us to Liège. And we will never return to 33 Rue du Lavoir.

Acknowledgments

I have lived a lifetime with the memory of the family I lost during the war. It is time for me to release the emotional wounds I have been carrying. For this, I owe special thanks to my writing coach and editor, Nancy Wait. Her indefatigable insistence, challenging my recollections, has resulted in a memoir of which I am deeply proud. This work has been in progress for many years and its completion is the culmination of an unfailing belief that it would come to light and redeem the shadows of the past. I owe her profound thanks for everything she taught me, as well as for her indomitable energy and faith in me.

I also want to thank my longtime friend, Harriet Lyons, for her invaluable comments and the hours of devotion she spent bringing clarity to my thoughts. Her empathy, encouragement, and belief in me, have been of profound assistance. Her unfailing friendship has been a beacon in my life. I likewise want to thank my friend, Pauline Yousha, for a lifetime of friendship and love. She has accompanied me on my journey and has always believed in my ability to complete the enormous task of bringing my story to light.

Mariette Bermowitz

I am fortunate to have many wonderful friends who gave me courage to continue during the difficult times when I struggled with my writing. They have been guides for me throughout. With gratitude I thank them all: Dr. Carl and Fran Rosenzweig, Chandrika Behymer, Dr. Daniel Allan, Elaine and Jeffrey Levin, Deborah Maier, Myrna Greenfield, Laurie Gunst, Margia Kramer, Eric Appel, my cousin Marlene, Dr. Rita Clark, AnnMarie and Ray Peterson, Phyllis Murray, and Leon Tomash.

Special thanks to Amy Edminster and Dr. Marge Blaine for the long hours of listening to me and their invaluable advice.

I owe immense gratitude to my European friends whom I consider family, Susan Dorlen, Didine and Jules Voz and their sons Michel and Tanguy, Louise and Jean Calbert, Monique and Dominique Renard, Françoise Gassies, MaryJo and Guy Jaumotte, Ginette Furet, the Pellegroms and Franckinioulle families. I would also like to thank Eddy Monfort for his help in clarifying the facts of the war in the Ardennes.

Special thanks to Melle. Dorien Styven, Assistant Archivist for the Jewish Museum in Malines, Belgium. Her indefatigable devotion to her work and research has helped so many survivors bring closure to their burden of pain.

I am finally at peace.

Mindele's Journey

Mariette Bermowitz, (Mindele Birencwajg) was born in Brussels in 1938. During World War II her mother and four siblings perished in the camps. Mindele escaped with her father, and was hidden with a family in the Belgian countryside. Her father survived the war and in 1951 they emigrated to the States. She taught French in New York City, and was married to Alan Bermowitz, later known as Alan Vega Suicide, artist and musician. In the mid-Seventies she lived in Iran and taught French and English, traveling extensively in the Near East. She currently lives in Brooklyn, New York.

Made in the USA
Lexington, KY
25 May 2012